BRITAIN'S
EUROPEAN QUESTION

THE ISSUES FOR IRELAND

Edited by

Paul Gillespie

Project Chairman Garret FitzGerald

INSTITUTE OF EUROPEAN AFFAIRS

Published by the
Institute of European Affairs
Europe House
8 North Great George's Street
Dublin 1
Ireland
Telephone: (01) 874 6756
Fax: (01) 878 6880

© Institute of European Affairs 1996

ISSN 0791-588

ISBN 1-874109-22-2

Cover design and typography
Butler Claffey Design

Originated and printed by
Brunswick Press Limited,
Dublin, Ireland

CONTENTS

▨ TABLES

CONTRIBUTORS

Ronan Fanning
Ronan Fanning is Professor of Modern History at University College Dublin. He was joint editor of the premier Irish history journal, *Irish Historical Studies* from 1976 to 1987. In 1989 he was elected a member of the Royal Irish Academy. His main research interests are in twentieth century Irish and British history and in international relations. His major publications include *The Irish Department of Finance 1922-58* (1978) and *Independent Ireland* (1983). Ronan Fanning is a regular political columnist for the *Sunday Independent*.

Garret FitzGerald
Dr FitzGerald was Taoiseach (Prime Minister) from June 1981 to March 1982 and from December 1982 to March 1987. He was a co-signatory of the Anglo-Irish Agreement in 1985. He was a member of Seanad Éireann 1965-69 and Dáil Éireann 1969-92, Minister for Foreign Affairs 1973-77 and Leader of Fine Gael 1977-87.

Stephen George
Stephen George is Jean Monnet Professor of Politics at the University of Sheffield, where he has lectured since 1973. His publications include *The United Kingdom and EC Membership Evaluated* (1992), *Britain and the European Community* (editor, 1992), *An Awkward Partner: Britain in the European Community* (1990, revised 2nd edition 1994), *Politics and Policies in the European Union* (1996).

Paul Gillespie
Paul Gillespie is Foreign Editor and a duty editor of *The Irish Times* with overall responsibility for international policy and foreign news coverage. He has travelled and reported extensively in Europe, the Middle East, North America and Japan. He is leader of the Institute of European Affairs's project on Britain. He was one of the principal authors of the IEA's study *Maastricht: Crisis of Confidence* (1993) and *Constitution-building in the European Union* edited by Brigid Laffan (1996) and was co-author (with Rodney Rice) of *Political Union* (1991).

Brendan Halligan

Brendan Halligan was General Secretary of the Labour Party 1967-80, a Member of Seanad Éireann 1973-77, Dáil Éireann 1976-77 and the European Parliament 1983-84. He was a founder member of the Institute of European Affairs and has been Chairperson of the Institute since its foundation in 1991.

Patrick Keatinge

Patrick Keatinge is a Professor of Political Science at Trinity College, Dublin. He was Senior Research Fellow of the Institute of European Affairs 1994-96. His publications include: *Maastricht and Ireland: What the Treaty Means* (1992), *Political Union* (1991), *European Security: Ireland's Choices* (1996 forthcoming).

Gerard O'Neill

Gerard O'Neill is Managing Director of the Henley Centre in Ireland, which he founded in 1989 after working as a senior consultant at the Henley Centre's head office in London. The Centre specialises in futures research, ranging from forecasts of economic and technological trends to the development of business strategies. He has recently been appointed as a special advisor to the Irish Government's Information Society Initiative and as a member of the Government's Task Force on Enterprise and the Environment. His publications include, *The Future of Offices* (1992), *Ireland 2000* (1994) and *The Coming Boom in Direct Marketing* (1996).

Lochlann Quinn

Lochlann Quinn is the Deputy Chairman of Glen Dimplex, a privately owned Irish company with an annual turnover of £400 million. Prior to joining Glen Dimplex he was a partner with Arthur Andersen and Co. He will become non-executive Chairman of Allied Irish Banks in 1997.

# PREFACE
PAUL GILLESPIE

This project was conceived in the aftermath of the 1992-93 currency crisis, following the 10 per cent devaluation of the Irish pound within the Exchange Rate Mechanism on January 20th, 1993. The outgoing Fianna Fáil/Progressive Democrat Government resisted such a decision, in the belief that Ireland would secure support from its European partners and that a unilateral devaluation against sterling would reinforce an incorrect international and market assessment of the Irish economy as being dependent on Britain. Such a perception would, the Government felt, jeopardise Ireland's ambitions to join a single European currency, as agreed in the Maastricht Treaty on European Union, even if Britain exercised its opt-out. The election in November 1992 and the negotiations that followed, which culminated in the formation of a Fianna Fáil/Labour coalition, delayed devaluation longer than would otherwise have been the case, once it became clear that there would not be support from Brussels or the Bundesbank to sustain the existing parity.

But debate continued intensively as to whether the policy pursued had been valid or not. It became clear that the issues at stake were much more broadly political than might have been suspected by the narrow concentration on trade relations, market share and employment prospects in different sectors, critical though these admittedly are. The currency question came to symbolise a wider set of issues concerning Ireland's relations with Britain in the European Union, most notably the question of Britain's own position with respect to the European Union after the end of the Cold War.

Would Britain remain semi-detached or seek to exert its influence at the heart of the Union? Would it even be tempted to leave the EU altogether rather than pool its sovereignty in order to build a more powerful Europe in conjunction with its war-time antagonists and allies? In which direction would its economic, political and strategic interests drive it? After the undoubtedly traumatic experience of Black Wednesday on September 20th 1992, in the middle of its EU presidency, would its government pursue a competivive devaluation, low cost economic strategy intended to attract international investment? What would be the competitive implications of such an economic model in Ireland's largest trading partner — notably for an Ireland entering into an intensive period of negotiations with Britain in order to find a settlement in Northern Ireland and explicitly designed to bring Northern Ireland and the Republic, Britain and Ireland, closer together politically and economically? How should one understand Britain's own intensive debate about its constitutional and institutional future, the renewed concern about its national identity? What difference would a change of government make, given that so many of Mr Major's political difficulties were presumed to originate in his small and dwindling parliamentary majority? Within the EU how long would the British support for a wider, shallower and more variable Europe be expected to last? How would it line up with other larger states within the 1996 Inter-Governmental Conference? Is it likely to continue to support Atlanticist positions within NATO and the WEU? How would Britain's own pursuit of interests and allies within the EU affect Irish interests?

These were the kinds of question that in the summer of 1993 animated the setting up of a project entitled, ponderously, 'Britain's Prospects and Policies within the European Union: The Implications for Ireland', with Dr Garret FitzGerald as chairman and myself as project leader. It has not been possible, alas, to answer all the questions we posed; but as an intellectual exercise this has been a fascinating and challenging project, given the extraordinary pace of events in the neighbouring island in the intervening period, right up to the BSE crisis this year, which so sharpened the tone of the British and European debates.

Ireland has a privileged knowledge of Britain arising from long historical association, contemporary political engagement and close economic, social and cultural interdependence, which may be of value to other EU member-states less familiar with the terms of the British debate on Europe.

We were fortunate to have the advice of a distinguished steering committee, of which the authors of the chapters in this volume were the most assiduous members. They have acted as rapporteurs and commentators on the project as it proceeded with four seminars involving specialist authors and some hundreds of participants and deserve special thanks for their commitment and enthusiasm. In December 1993 the first seminar heard papers on the economic dimensions of the subject from a distinguished group of Irish and British authors. In March 1994 political and security perspectives were examined. In September 1994, in association with the Institute of European Studies in Queen's University, Belfast, a seminar examined the Northern Ireland aspects of our subject. Contributions to these three seminars were rewritten for inclusion in the separate volume of Seminar Papers published with this book. A contents list is included as an appendix on pages 201-202.

The format of this book evolved in line with a growing realisation of the complexity and the pace of events in Ireland, Britain and Europe. Political, historical and economic perspectives are combined in Part I, which presents a model of identity change and dependence/independence/interdependence as a means of explaining contemporary Anglo-Irish or, more properly given these issues of identity, British-Irish relations, within the European setting. This part is intended to reflect this complexity and to offer perspectives and scenarios on how the policy issues involved might best be handled in coming years. In Part II the authors comment on different dimensions of the project in the light of the seminar discussions and papers. Chapter 11, 'Britain and the IGC', by Stephen George, one of the foremost students of Britain's role in the EU, was delivered as a paper at the Institute in March 1995, in association with the Irish Committee for Contemporary European Studies. It gives a valuable insight into the British approach, especially relevant during the Irish EU Presidency. The Summing-up and Conclusions draw these strands together and reflect the combined views of the seven authors involved (not including Professor George).

In addition to the authors the following people should be thanked for advice and support as members of the steering committee and sympathetic observers. From the business world Seamus O'Carroll of Cement-Roadstone and Tony Richie of Smurfits gave us valuable insights into the patterns of British-Irish trade. Dermot McAleese of TCD advised on currency matters and British-Irish economic relations. Mary Holland and Frank Millar kept a watching eye from a media perspective. Colin Stutt and Michael Smith provided advice and help on the Northern Ireland dimension. Eamonn Gallagher drew on his long experience of Anglo-Irish relations within the EC/EU context to advise us from Brussels. We are grateful to successive British ambassadors David Blatherwick and Veronica Sutherland, who were especially helpful in providing funding, facilities and access to official thinking, ably assisted by Ian Whitting, Simon Buckle and Ted Hallett. Senior officials of the Department of Foreign Affairs encouraged the project, in which a number of their colleagues participated. Lochlann Quinn and Glen Dimplex hosted a lunch for participants in the second seminar, including the then Foreign Secretary, Douglas Hurd and the Minister for Foreign Affairs, Dick Spring. Successive drafts of these chapters were circulated widely among members of the IEA and we have benefitted enormously from their responses, both in written form and as delivered at a fourth seminar held in April 1995.

Over three years the Institute of European Affairs has supported our work to the fullest possible extent. Brian Farrell and Terry Stewart as directors general, and Brendan Halligan as chairman as well as an author have helped us to keep it on track. Jim Dooge spotted several faux pas in the final draft.

Odran Reid and his staff, including Jean Barker, Mary-Lou McDonald and Pete Glennon, bore the heavy burden of seminar organisation, steering committee and authors' meetings and successive drafts cheerfully and efficiently. Iain MacAulay and his editorial colleagues have been scrupulous and patient advisers. My editorial colleagues in *The Irish Times,* and in particular the Editor, Conor Brady, have given encouragement and much appreciated time-off to complete the tasks of editing and writing. Finally to my wife, Deirdre, and children Fintan and Tom, must go thanks for their forbearance and understanding of the time required to bring this project to a conclusion.

INTRODUCTION
GARRET FITZGERALD, PROJECT CHAIRMAN

Britain's attitude to, and relationship with, the European Union, has become even more problematic in recent years than in earlier decades, and is posing serious problems for its European partners. For its Irish partner these problems are particularly acute, both because of the close economic and social relationship between these two states and because of their joint involvement in a search for a resolution of the Northern Ireland crisis.

This Irish aspect of Britain's European stance is the subject of the present book and of the accompanying volume of papers delivered by a wide range of speakers at seminars of the Institute of European Affairs in Dublin and Belfast between late 1993 and early 1995. This volume comprises four Commentaries on matters raised in these papers and in the discussions that followed them; a paper by Stephen George of the University of Sheffield on Britain and the Intergovernmental conference; but also, by way of introduction, an extended essay reviewing the complex web of inter-related issues that have emerged from this exercise.

Running through all that has been said and written here is an underlying theme: the complications introduced into both the Anglo/Irish and Britain/Europe relationships by a range of problems of role and identity — quite different in the case of each geographic area — which in recent times have emerged in Britain, in Northern Ireland and in the Irish state.

Thus Britain, following the loss of empire, has quite recently had to face the post-Cold War unravelling of the 'special relationship' that it believed itself to have developed with the United States during and after the Second World War. In its relationship with Europe, where for centuries its wealth and its 'balance of power' strategy had enabled it to be a 'change-maker', it has been faced with becoming instead a 'change-taker'.

Moreover, within Britain itself the over-arching British identity that came into existence in the eighteenth century has recently been challenged by the emergence of a form of English nationalism that is notably xenophobic, especially in relation to the continent of Europe. Far from being shared in the 'Celtic fringes' of the island, this challenge has tended to exacerbate centrifugal pressures in Scotland and, to a lesser extent, Wales. The unitary political structure of Britain is thus threatened by the disappearance of the ambiguity — a constructive ambiguity from the English point of view — that used to exist between the sense of being 'English' and being 'British'.

The double pressure upon the formerly insular and centralised British polity which is now emanating from Europe on the one hand and from Scotland and Wales on the other, and perhaps even from parts of the north of England itself, is challenging the previously objectively confused but subjectively untroubled English sense of a fused English/British identity.

In Ireland, too, previously comfortable identities north and south are being challenged. In the north the unionist sense of a British identity has traditionally been challenged by the nationalist sense of an all-Ireland Irish identity. However, that challenge reinforced rather than weakened the British identity of the unionist community in the north and indeed served to erode the pre-independence dual Irish/British identity of Protestants in Ireland. But since 1969 unionists have had to face a radical change in British attitudes towards Northern Ireland in general and towards unionists in particular: for many of them the people of Britain and many British politicians appear no longer to see them, or indeed Northern Ireland itself, as British. This is a much more disturbing challenge to the sense of being British than anything nationalists could ever mount.

Finally, the majority in the Irish state itself have had to re-think fundamentally their former sense of a Catholic, post-Gaelic identity that excluded both Northern unionists and the remaining elements of the Anglo-Irish community in the south. A new pluralist Irish identity that recognises the equal validity of the different traditions in the island of Ireland has, with increasing success, albeit not without some trauma, been challenging the older exclusive nationalism. And in parallel with this phenomenon, isolationist elements in post-revolutionary Irish nationalism have been giving place to an acceptance of the advantage of sovereignty-sharing with neighbours in the European Union.

At the same time as these identity issues have had to be faced in the different parts of these islands, a huge expansion of Irish exports to continental EU countries has greatly weakened, even if it has yet to eliminate, the debilitating Irish economic, (and therefore to some degree political), dependence on Britain. The whole British-Irish relationship has evolved into one of greater equality, reflecting the interdependence of the two countries both in the European context and in their joint search for a peaceful settlement in Northern Ireland.

The advantage that the Irish state has secured by being able within the European Union to pursue its own interests, often quite divergent from those of Britain, raises a question about Northern Ireland. On issues where Northern Ireland's European interests diverge from those of Britain and are similar to those of the Irish state, some in the north feel that it could be advantageous for it, in the context of an agreed settlement, to be able to deal with Brussels on these matters jointly with Dublin: the choice of whether and when to do so would be a matter for the North of Ireland administration that emerged from such a settlement.

However, Britain's troubled relationship with its EU partners poses particular problems for the Irish state. Between 1979 and 1990 Britain's self-exclusion from the EMS, of which Ireland was a member from the outset, led to wide fluctuations between their currencies, and Britain's precipitate departure in 1992 from the System it had belatedly joined just two years earlier eventually forced a devaluation of what had as a result become a too-strong Irish pound. British non-participation in the single currency, which Ireland is likely to be both qualified and willing to join, is thus an unwelcome prospect, especially as it could coincide with and complicate the emergence of a new, closer and more constructive north-south relationship within the island of Ireland.

Irish interests are thus closely tied to the adoption by Britain of a more positive approach towards the European Union. And to the extent that this may depend upon a resolution in the first instance of Britain's domestic identity problems, Ireland has a particular interest in the evolution of events within that country.

Pending a resolution of Britain's domestic and European problems, however, Ireland may face something of a dilemma in seeking to reconcile its conflicting European, British, and Northern Ireland interests. In retrospect it can be seen that a policy dilemma of this kind was in some sense implicit in the Anglo-Irish settlement of 1920-22, when a truncated Irish state emerged from the struggle for Irish self-rule.

For, in a manner that probably no one in the island appreciated at the time — or indeed for a long time afterwards — the link then preserved between a part of Ireland and Britain had the power to complicate the exercise by the Irish state of its sovereign right to pursue its interests in the international forum. But it is only with the recent emergence of the first real prospect of a constructive north/south relationship that this potential constraint has emerged as a factor to be taken into account in the formulation of Irish foreign policy.

What is ultimately far more significant than the possibility of such a constraint, however, is the manner in which political independence has enabled the Irish state to secure and advance its interests within the European Union context. During the first half-century of Irish political independence, continuing economic dependence on the United Kingdom imposed some practical limitations on the exercise of the new state's sovereignty. But the diversification of Ireland's trade within the multilateral European Community structure has greatly weakened this constraint.

Ireland has thus been free within the European Union to pursue its own economic and political interests, even where these diverge from those of Britain. And because of such factors as its greater peripherality, earlier stage of economic development, larger agricultural sector, and much smaller size, Ireland's interests frequently tend to diverge from those of Britain.

Yet owing to the fact that within this Union the British-Irish relationship has been multilateralised, disagreements between the two states on EU issues rarely carry any emotional charge. Indeed, despite the much wider range of issues on which the two states now find themselves ranged against each other within the EU context, and despite the parallel disagreements that have often marked the two countries' handling of the Northern Ireland issue during the same period, the British-Irish political relationship has paradoxically become more relaxed than at any time in the past. A factor in this development has been the fact that the Community framework has provided opportunities that never previously existed for personal contacts between politicians of the two states.

The British-Irish relationship was always a complex and subtle one, with far more positive features than any stereotype ever allowed, but also with hidden tensions deriving not just from history — and from a geography involving two islands unequal in size, population, and resources — but also from striking differences in national temperaments. Given the character of the issues that now involve them jointly, it is, perhaps, as well that despite inevitable differences of approach to the Northern Ireland problem their relationship has developed along broadly constructive lines during the past quarter of a century.

Part 1

Britain's European Question:

the Issues for Ireland

Garret FitzGerald, Paul Gillespie, Ronan Fanning

■ CHAPTER 1
BRITAIN: A CRISIS OF IDENTITY

Britain and Ireland joined the Community together because of a sense of our place in history. For the British it was about finding a new place in the world after two centuries of imperial experience. It was returning to roots in Europe. For most of us [it was] a difficult transition and today there are still some who wish it did not have to be made. But it was the right transition. For the Irish membership in 1972 was about Ireland's place in history, confirming Ireland's position in Europe as a modern state ... and its decisive shift away from the embrace of Britain.

Douglas Hurd, address to IEA, Dublin, 21 March, 1994.

Great Britain has lost an empire but has not yet found a role.

Dean Acheson, 1962

INTRODUCTION

Britain faces a crisis of identity concerning its position in the world, in Europe, and in relation to its internal political arrangements after the end of the Cold War. The evidence is multi-faceted and daily apparent in its political rhetoric and argument. The implications for Ireland of how these issues are resolved are fundamentally important, but insufficiently analysed or understood on this island. Because of the history and political structure of British-Irish relations it is clear that if Britain faces a crisis of identity it will affect Ireland as well. Britain's place in Europe is but a part of a larger conundrum: how to manage a decline in political prestige and economic power. In brief, how is Britain to be re-invented? It is a paradox, tragic for both Britain and Europe, that in the post-war period re-invention has proven easier for the vanquished than for the victorious. Adaptation to the role of an intermediate, but respected, world power pursuing its destiny within Europe would be painful even if British society were internally cohesive and, at least, at ease with itself in domestic affairs; but this is far from being the case, which accentuates the problems of Britain accommodating to radical change

7

in its external relations. The common point at issue is sovereignty. At European level it centres on the extent to which sovereignty is to be shared externally with other nation states. At national level it revolves around the question as to how it is to be shared internally within the nation state. Looked at from the vantage of the British state as currently constituted, there is a dual concern. Sovereignty could be simultaneously drained from the centre in two opposite directions: outward towards Europe and inwards towards the regions. Britain has a double constitutional problem.

The dilemma is obvious, and requires sympathetic understanding. To yield sovereignty in one direction could create the preconditions for conceding it in the other. Consequently, a determination to maintain the United Kingdom as a unitary state is consistent with continued resistance towards a United Europe. It also explains why Britain is so insistent on subsidiarity at European level and so averse to it at home. The key to the double constitutional problem lies in the debate about Britain, rather than the debate about Europe. The solution to the first is the precondition for the solution to the second.

This book seeks to examine Britain's role in Europe and its policies within the European Union from an Irish perspective — sympathetically but critically, availing of the privilege accorded the world over to smaller neighbours of larger powers. The Irish are better informed about Britain and its affairs than the British are about Ireland, just as the Canadians are about the United States, the Danes and Austrians about Germany, the Finns about Sweden, the Portuguese about Spain or the Koreans about Japan.

In the case of Britain and Ireland a long history of political engagement, occupation, colonial rule, and partition, together with a dialectic of political and economic dependence, independence and interdependence, have endlessly complicated the facts of geographical propinquity. But these factors are overlaid on another, equally important, set of realities: the extremely close social, familial, cultural, and artistic links between the people of these islands, both historical and contemporary. There are an estimated 550,000 people born in the Republic living in Britain; were those born in Northern Ireland to be added the figure might reach 800,000. Republic-born migrants make up about one-quarter of non-nationals working in Britain. The number of Irish citizens there is two million. Some 10-12 per cent of the British population, perhaps 6 million people, are of Irish ethnic background. A lively cross-disciplinary literature testifies to the vitality of these links. They are reinforced by a common language, cross-cutting media and consumption patterns, and, of course, by a common labour market and a right of free movement.

The UK is Ireland's largest market, still taking almost 26 per cent of Irish exports. The Republic ranks seventh in the list of British export destinations. And if exports to Northern Ireland from Britain were separately identified and added to the figure for the Republic, Ireland would certainly rate as fourth or fifth. The Republic is by far the most important recipient of British exports on a per capita basis. The economic relationship is of the first importance for both islands, as must be the development of the Northern Ireland economy, e.g. through a more dynamic north-south relationship. The priority that ought to be accorded to this, and the potential tension between the Irish government's Northern and European policies if Britain takes a different path in Europe to Ireland, are central features of this book.

In Northern Ireland we have a veritable cauldron of the identity questions evident on both islands — unionists are having to face the fact that the Britain to which they have devoted their loyalty is itself changing in ways that could undermine their identity. Britain's Protestantism, its constitutional monarchy, its post-imperial identity, its world role and its industrial prowess have all come under question in the most challenging manner, not from external enemies or Irish nationalism but from disillusion and dissent within Britain's main political forces and parties. The very unity of the United Kingdom is put into question, according to the prime minister, Mr John Major, by the Labour Party's proposals for devolved assemblies in Scotland and Wales. Labour responds, on the contrary, that the most effective means of preserving the Union is to renovate it by decentralisation in order to avoid separation.

The idea that constitutional change in Northern Ireland, including devolution, a power-sharing assembly, proportional representation and a bill of rights, should be ring-fenced off from that in Britain is increasingly and radically disputed by a range of British influential opinion-makers and analysts, who feel that what is sauce for the Northern Ireland goose should be sauce for the British gander as well, and some of whom point to Ireland's historical role as a laboratory for British political innovation.

In the Republic of Ireland the past 25 years have seen a redefinition of political identity vis-à-vis Northern Ireland and Britain, within the increasingly significant framework of membership of the European Community, now Union. Ireland had little option but to pursue membership along with Britain in 1961 and again in 1969-72, in confirmation of its post-colonial economic dependence. But as Mr Douglas Hurd, the then British Foreign Secretary, told one of the seminars organised by this project in Dublin in the passage quoted in the epigraph, Ireland's decision to join was about 'confirming its position in Europe as a modern state ... and its decisive shift away from the embrace of Britain'. The point was well taken by his audience. It underlines the very different approach towards sharing or pooling sovereignty taken in the two countries. Ireland, to adapt Acheson's cutting remark, never had an empire and has found a role — within a wider community of nation-states in which it has regained economic and political self-confidence and self-respect and lost much of its former debilitating Anglocentricity.

Whereas Britain, with its absolutist conception of sovereignty exercised by the Crown-in-Parliament, has been constantly reluctant to cede it, in Ireland the multilateralisation of economic and political decision-making has been something of a liberation, amounting even to substantive completion of the formal political independence won from Britain in 1921 and affirmed by its — cooperative — neutrality in the Second World War. This has confirmed Ireland's own international experience that a small state has more to gain than lose by sharing sovereignty with larger ones.

However reluctant the British attitude may be, the facts of EU interdependence have had to be accepted pragmatically, so that Mr Hurd could say in 1992 that it is 'right to think of the Treaties as part of the Constitution'. Now that the conditions of membership of a greatly enlarged EU are becoming more explicitly political, it remains to be seen whether Ireland will be as comfortable with pooling political sovereignty if it involves modifying military neutrality or the disproportionately favourable access to and representation on EC/EU institutions, factors upon which membership has so far been predicated. In that case we might see some convergence of attitudes on certain crucial aspects of sovereignty-sharing between Dublin and London through the 1996 inter-governmental conference and beyond, despite many differences of approach towards that agenda.

As William Wallace has pointed out, 'nations define themselves partly in opposition to their neighbours — Irish against English, English against French, thus providing a basic orientation to their foreign policy in terms of assumed friends and allies.' He goes on to say that when threats and alliances change, definitions of national identity must adapt. So it has been historically — and there is no more ahistorical a phenomenon than traditions that have been invented to justify nationalisms as they adapt to changed circumstances. The changing British identity after the loss of empire and the end of the Cold War has produced a plethora of revisionist historical writing, on the left and the right, to demonstrate that much of the justification for imperial and nationalist policies, or of institutions such as the monarchy, is of recent not ancient origin, and to point the way to new circumstances requiring new identities. Their very appearance and the passionate responses such revisionism invokes are themselves important indicators of a crisis of national identity.

The term crisis implies a moment of crucial decision in the face of acute difficulty or danger. It has a pathological connotation, which one needs to be careful about over-generalising, but the term usefully denotes not only a political condition of great psychological uncertainty, but of changing historical conjunctures requiring innovation and resolution as well. As for national identity, it includes territorial boundedness, shared myths of origin, a common culture and common legal rights and duties.

A CRISIS IN FOUR DIMENSIONS

It is useful to organise an analysis of Britain's crisis of identity in four dimensions, all of which intersect with one another:

- Changing global and transatlantic relations

- Changing relations between Britain and Europe

- Proposals for changes in Britain's constitutional and institutional structures

- Changing relations between Britain and Ireland.

These can be seen as a composite, reflecting Britain's historical experience of nation-building, conflict and war with its neighbours, industrial revolution, global trading and financial reach, imperial grandeur and decline. The full consequences of these changes were temporarily masked from its leaders and citizens by the settlement after the Second World War, from which Britain emerged victorious but incapable of maintaining a dominant or even an influential position without becoming subordinate to the new United States hegemony. This arrangement lasted through to the end of the Cold War in 1989. Since then the elements of Britain's international and national identity have rapidly unravelled. As the historian Linda Colley has put it in an influential formulation:

'Whereas the Germans and the French, who are more confident about their unique identity, see a Europe without frontiers in terms of opportunity, the British are far more inclined to see it as a threat. This is partly because they have fought against Continental European states so often in the past; but their growing insularity is to be explained also by their growing doubts about who they are in the present. Consciously or unconsciously, they fear assuming a new identity in case it obliterates entirely the already insecure identity they currently possess' (Colley 1993, p. 375).

Will it be possible for the British to construct a new identity, either out of the elements of their existing political regime or by rearranging it and constructing another one? Needless to say, this is highly contested ground within Britain's political, policy-making, academic and media culture, into which outsiders should step only with care and sensitivity. The issue is certain to be, at least implicitly, a central ingredient in its forthcoming general election campaign. But precisely because it affects them so intimately this cannot be an excuse for non-engagement by neighbours in a discussion and decision-making process which requires sympathetic understanding. The political writer and analyst, David Marquand, poses the question even more sharply:

> 'Imperial Britain *was* Britain. The iconography, the myths, the rituals in which Britishness was embodied were, of necessity, imperial, oceanic, extra-European: they could not be anything else. Empire was not an optional extra for the British; it was their reason for being British as opposed to English or Scots or Welsh [or Irish, one might add]. Deprived of empire and plunged into Europe, "Britain" had no meaning', (Marquand, 1995, p. 22).

What is noteworthy is that the nature and structure of the British state is now a highly contentious matter among its citizens and political parties and in its media and academic journals. This is a real departure from the position that obtained in its politics roughly from the Treaty settlement in 1921 to the 1980s' experiment with Thatcherism, when the state itself was taken for granted, even as argument about what it should do, and how the resources it could command should be distributed, dominated British politics. Much of the dissatisfaction with Britain's political structures arises from disappointment, frustration or disgust with what was achieved or not achieved in the 1980s; it is a touchstone for both left and right. In the words of another close observer of the British scene, Tom Nairn, a long-standing Scottish socialist and nationalist:

> 'The "Thatcher revolution" ... set out to restore British grandeur. What it actually did was to break the back of British identity' (Nairn, 1994, p. xxiii).

We may have to anticipate a most turbulent period in British politics, in which that country is likely to be an awkward, unpredictable, even a volatile partner for Ireland and other EU member states, because of the need to resolve its crisis of identity. It would therefore be a mistake to expect rapid or categorical decisions on some of the most important issues facing its political leadership, such as whether Britain should be among the first group of EU states to join a monetary union.

CHANGING GLOBAL AND TRANSATLANTIC RELATIONS

Britain's effective transfer of global power to the US during and after the Second World War was traumatic and decisive, the most important hegemonic shift to have been seen in the modern period. The extent of British dependency on Washington was privately acknowledged by those responsible for administering it, but is only now coming fully into public discourse. Initially Britain's leaders genuinely hoped to preserve the Empire, transforming it into a functioning Commonwealth, but it became apparent that this was neither politically feasible nor economically sustainable. They opted instead for an important niche position in the administration of the liberal internationalist system, as a trusted lieutenant of the US, with a senior role in NATO, the UN and the Bretton Woods institutions. Britain has been one of the few post-imperial states capable of power-projection, maintaining a relatively high military-security capacity and a continuing world-class global financial, if not industrial, presence. So long as the Cold War continued Britain had an important if subordinate role in the western system, which enabled it to keep much of its political structure intact.

But when the Cold War came to an end in 1989 the political structure that had sustained the Anglo-American special relationship unravelled. German unification, which Mrs Thatcher did her best to persuade the Americans to prevent, went ahead with US blessing. Under President Bush, Washington's central focus in Europe shifted from London to Bonn, despite Britain's indispensable role in the Gulf War. The US has expressed renewed interest in the construction of a more coherent European Union, which could take on more of a partnership role in a post-communist Europe. Britain is now of interest to Washington to the extent that it moves genuinely to the heart of Europe, in particular to engage the newly powerful Germany. If, on the other hand, Britain prefers rather to revert to a nineteenth-century balance of power model of relations with Europe, despite its reduced circumstances and lack of allies, not least by throwing her weight against the strongest political force, i.e. Germany, or, more radically, to cut loose from the integration project in pursuit of global interests, then Washington would be much less inclined to accommodate British aberrance and exceptionalism. This became clear when London found it no longer had the influence to prevent President Clinton granting a visa to Mr Gerry Adams, or to discourage the administration from becoming fully engaged in the Northern Ireland peace process in response to the new political power of the Irish-American diaspora – much to London's irritation, at least initially. The falling away of these Atlantic certitudes has been quite traumatic for Britain in the past few years, provoking much discussion about the need to construct a new international identity. There is still a strong emphasis on Britain's global, as distinct from its European, interests; indeed the sharpest edge of its political debate concerns whether the global interests are best protected by a full engagement in the EU rather than by a policy of semi-detachment.

CHANGING RELATIONS BETWEEN BRITAIN AND EUROPE

There is in fact a disturbing continuity between Britain's classical posture in relation to Europe and that of today. The nineteenth-century British foreign policy model sought to create a stable balance among the continental powers, the better to allow Britain to pursue its genuine global interests, hindered as little as possible by continental entanglements. However, the collapse of the balance of power system into two world wars, after it evolved into a pattern of unstable alliances, convinced both France and Germany, which were conquered and occupied — unlike Britain, victorious thanks to US support — that a new model of international relations in Europe must be sought. The resulting psychological and political casts of mind have had a profound influence on subsequent developments to this day, affecting the readiness of different states and peoples to accept political innovation and renewal of their own political institutions, as well as those of the emerging European polity.

As Stephen George points out in his contribution to this volume, British 'pragmatism' must be understood in contrast to the 'teleological federalism' implicit in much continental rhetoric about the EC/EU. This is, however, a matter not only of national intellectual tradition, but also of quite different historical experiences. Instead of defeat, Britain experienced relative decline; its leaders were very slow to come to terms with these new realities in an integrating Europe. In that respect Britain must be said to be a victim of history, a systematic late and reluctant joiner of European projects.

Britain's debate on its role in Europe has been very uneven. At parliamentary level and in the popular media it has all too seldom gone beyond a somewhat lop-sided exchange of slogans and prejudices, during which those in favour of British involvement with the EC/EU have been notably ineffective in challenging the simplistic and increasingly xenophobic, populism of their opponents. In this sense the British public has been ill-prepared for the latest phase of integration, which has a much more political cast than previously. But at the same time the very intensity of the developing debate about Britain's identity, across the various dimensions we have suggested, has deepened political and popular understanding and has raised the level of discussion in policy and academic circles and in the more serious media. Britain may well benefit in due course from the fact that it has had such a political opportunity to clarify its interests and objectives; but in order to do so it will have to be prepared to make choices.

There has been a consistency as between the Thatcher and Major administrations on certain fundamental approaches to integration. These include a belief in a Europe of nation-states, an insistence on competitiveness and on a Europe open to the world, on the commitment to NATO, and on financial probity in the conduct of EC/EU affairs. The White Paper on the IGC published by the Foreign and Commonwealth Office in March 1996 expressed this clearly, despite its tactical minimalism. As many commentators have pointed out, in this key policy area there may be much more continuity than discontinuity between a possible Labour government after the next election and the long period of Conservative rule; the parties' European policies overlap significantly, despite differences on, for example, the Social Chapter, neo-Keynesian interventionism at the EU level and a notable difference of tone. This may mean that the variable model of integration suggested by the Major government could command continuing support from a Labour successor — not to mention the possibility, which should certainly not be ruled out of the reckoning, that the Conservatives could be re-elected.

PROPOSALS FOR CHANGE IN BRITAIN'S CONSTITUTIONAL AND INSTITUTIONAL STRUCTURES

The British political debate is increasingly concerned with demands for more or less drastic change in its constitutional and institutional structures. This is a key feature of the long electoral campaign that effectively began in spring 1996. The issue of devolution in Scotland and Wales has become a matter of controversy — and what the British government proposes for Northern Ireland could set precedents for changes elsewhere in the United Kingdom.

Thus, for example, Vernon Bogdanor, an influential academic, is concerned that the options proposed for Northern Ireland should be available to the rest of the UK as well. He remarks that the Framework Document 'provides a whole raft of constitutional devices — proportional representation, devolution, referendums, power-sharing and a charter of rights — which

John Major has ruled out for any other part of the United Kingdom as destructive of the constitution'. The government, he adds, would hardly dare say that they have no selfish or strategic interest in any other part of the UK. And yet Northern Ireland's acknowledged exceptionalism in that document, viz. that there is a 'fundamental absence of consensus' on constitutional issues between majority and minority, could also be applied to Scotland in relation to devolution, although Scotland's majority is not prepared to use violence to achieve this objective.

The British constitution, Bogdanor adds, is unfair not only to minorities but to majorities: through the first-past-the-post electoral system the Conservatives have quite happily governed in the face of the nearly three-fifths of voters who rejected them and who voted in 1992 for parties proposing constitutional change of the kind that Britain is willing to bestow on Northern Ireland — and previously on colonies before they were given independence, and on the new Federal German state after the war. 'Is it not time', Bogdanor asks, 'that we began to consider whether we might not at last bestow these same benefits upon ourselves?' (Bogdanor, 1996 a).

It is a telling critique, and one that has been taken up politically, at least in part, by the Labour and Liberal Democrat parties. Mr Paddy Ashdown's offer of an electoral pact based on an understanding about electoral reform has been received gingerly by the Labour leader. Many commentators wonder whether Tony Blair would, if elected, pursue constitutional change wholeheartedly, although he is publicly committed to a referendum and legislation for Scottish devolution within the first year and also to a referendum on electoral reform. In a keynote speech on constitutional reform on 7 February, 1996, he said that Labour would also reform the House of Lords, create a new London Authority, incorporate into British law the European Convention on Human Rights, and introduce a Freedom of Information Act.

It may well be that he would need Liberal Democrat support to sustain a small majority, or to fend off left-wing or Eurosceptic Labour MPs. There would be winners and losers in his party were he to go for either option; with relentless Conservative opposition to such changes, combined with such potential splits, this could be a very volatile parliamentary period, which might absorb most of the legislative timetable for the first two or three years of a Labour government. But over that horizon there is the alluring prospect for Labour, as a cabinet minister was reported in the *Daily Mail* to have said, that if the voting system was changed, 'there would not be another Conservative government for 25 years'.

Institutional change is also a highly contested area. Over-centralisation of government, the proliferation of quangos and in the words of Philip

Stephens of the *Financial Times*, the replacement of 'parliamentary sovereignty by executive despotism' are matters of public controversy. In Scotland and Wales national identity and the demand for devolution have been associated with a new awareness of European identity that would ease the burden of rule from London. The Labour Party in Scotland and Wales is increasingly enthusiastic about devolution.

It would be wise to end this summary on a cautionary note. There is nothing inevitable about such changes or about victory for the political parties that undertake to bring them about, no matter how convincing the arguments made for them. Two items from *The Irish Times* on the day it reported Mr Blair's keynote statement explain why this should be so. In a fiery speech extolling the virtues of the existing Constitution, the chairman of the Conservative Party, Mr Brian Mawhinney, who is from Northern Ireland, said Labour's reforms would 'rip apart' Britain, causing 'chaos and division'. 'There is no appetite across the nation for Labour's constitutional agenda. Radical change to Britain's constitution may be all the rage at Islington dinner parties, but it is not the subject of debate in shopping queues or during half-time at any football match in the country.' And the newspaper's London Editor, Frank Millar, warned in a column on educational choice that 'we should not confuse disillusion with the performance of this government with wholesale rejection of the ideas which have underpinned the party's four electoral triumphs.'

CHANGING RELATIONS BETWEEN BRITAIN AND IRELAND

Subsequent chapters deal with this subject in detail; here it is only necessary to point out that just as 'British strategic interests in Ireland were thrown into sharpest relief at times of international crisis' during the French revolutionary wars, the Great War of 1914-18 and the Second World War, so it has been during the crisis that has followed the end of the Cold War. This is the setting for the current efforts to find a Northern Ireland settlement. As we have seen it coincides with a period of great uncertainty about Britain's relations with Europe. The European institutions' involvement in the Northern Ireland peace process has been significant in providing the cross-border fund but qualitatively less political than that of the US government.

Nonetheless the Framework Document pledges 'to develop on a continuing basis an agreed process for the whole of Ireland in response to challenges and opportunities of the European Union'. How joint interests could be represented in Brussels presents a fascinating and constitutionally innovative aspect of potential future governance. It is one that worries unionist opinion, especially if it is seen in the context of an 'ever closer union'; but this is a closer union of peoples, not states, as expressed in the preamble to the Treaty of European Union. Free movement of people, a Single Market, common European citizenship and identity, have a potential to transcend Northern Ireland polarities.

In his contribution to the accompanying volume of seminar papers, the head of the Northern Ireland Civil Service, Sir David Fell, speaks of the possibility of creating an 'ingenious variable geometry' to coordinate both Irish approaches to Brussels. This potential was starkly underlined during the BSE scare about beef. Functional rather than territorial integration, in which various identities are preserved, offers the most fruitful way forward. But as Paul Teague argues in his paper in the accompanying volume there is an important distinction between a functionalism which specifies institutions for cooperation in concrete terms and a neo-functionalism, defined more dynamically, which would allow for 'spillover' into other areas of north-south cooperation. The theory of EU integration may have a good deal to offer in understanding these processes better.

THE INEVITABILITY OF VARIABILITY?

A central feature of Britain's attitude to the future of the European Union will be its emphasis on a flexible model of integration; in Douglas Hurd's words, a 'multi-track, multi-speed, even multi-layered approach, which will increasingly be the way of the future'. The model, spelt out successively by its political leaders — with undoubted consistency, as George argues in his contribution to this volume on the 1996 IGC agenda — stresses diversity, the preservation of the nation-state, subsidiarity, inter-governmentalism, as well as free trade and a global orientation in competition with the US and Asia.

Because of its slender parliamentary majority and dependence on Europhobe right-wing Conservative MPs, the British government approached the 1996 IGC with an ultra-minimalist agenda. This is not inconsistent with its longer-term policy, encompassing enlargement and the necessity to rationalise the Union's own resources by cutting back on the Common Agricultural Policy and diverting those funds to the central and eastern European states rather than creating additional redistributive mechanisms to ease their transition towards membership. An abiding feature of British government and official attitudes towards monetary union is a fear that the absence of real economic convergence and fiscal mechanisms in the existing design will make it necessary at a later date to impose new financial burdens upon the net contributor states, involving an economic union to complete the monetary one, as well as a more integrated political structure for the Union as a whole.

It is precisely the geopolitical necessity of a political union to complete the monetary one that impresses itself upon the German government and most of that country's policy-making elite. Without it they will not be able, they believe, to convince the German public to give up the deutschmark for the euro. Dr Kohl has warned the British in the bluntest possible terms that the alternative to a more integrated Union is a reversion to the anarchic balance-of-power Europe and its nationalisms that produced two world wars this century. 'The policy of European integration is in reality a question of war and peace in the twenty-first century,' he declared at the University of Louvain on 1 February, 1996. He fears that a hegemonic Germany, not bound by common European rules, would provoke antagonistic nationalisms in its neighbours. Far better to have EU borders than German ones. A supplementary fear is that Germany alone could not bear the burden of supporting the reserve currency role that is transferring to Europe because of the dollar's decline.

Despite public hostility in Germany, and a Social Democratic opposition tempted to oppose plans for EMU, Dr Kohl is determined to see it through. He has given general support to plans by close associates for a form of differentiated integration which would allow states that are willing to go ahead faster than the slowest to do so, not towards a superstate, which he says nobody wants, but towards a political structure that can contain the German and continental demons he fears. The British are inclined to see this as special pleading. They dispute the history and are worried about being bullied into choices they do not want to make. They already have their opt-outs from monetary union and the Social Chapter. And they propose a different, looser, model than the German one, in which security and defence matters could be handled more flexibly, basically within the existing Maastricht pillar structure, with which they are well satisfied.

Whatever way one looks at it, this Anglo-German polarity pits one proposal for a variable Europe against another. It seems likely, therefore, that the negotiations will tend to crystallise around the two poles of the argument. The Germans are in a much better position to muster allies than the British, since they are not undergoing the same kind of identity crisis and internal political uncertainty, despite the need to absorb unification. The British could have attracted support from those states that are willing but not yet able to join a monetary union and are otherwise keen to preserve the integuments of national sovereignty; but it is generally believed after their policy of non-cooperation in the BSE crisis that they have sacrificed this opportunity to make allies, at least in the short to medium term. Britain must decide on whether it should be regarded as an 'out' or a 'not-yet-in', but economic and political events could yet move towards the kind of model they espouse. A possible outcome of the negotiations, therefore, is a model which would combine multi-speeds and might develop into a tiered variable geometry.

On the 1996 IGC issues Britain and Ireland will often be at different points in the argument. Britain takes a conventional large-state approach to Commission representation and the EU presidency and is determined to insist on a solid representation of population weighting in qualified majority voting. British attitudes towards the European Parliament are decidedly minimalist; they may coincide with Ireland's traditionally sceptical position. Britain's Atlanticism on defence will keep it firmly in the inter-governmental camp — which coincides with the Irish Government's approach; but there are stirrings which could tip the balance and convince the British to take a more open approach to WEU. Messrs Hurd and Rifkind have argued strongly in favour of CFSP remaining inter-governmental. On eastern enlargement Britain will be to the fore in insisting that CAP and the structural funds should be recast. It will resist suggestions that the EU budget should be increased. On EMU and the Social Chapter much depends on the outcome of the next election. Any shift by the Tories on these issues before that event can be ruled out. This may not make much difference in practice — many multinationals find they have to implement the social regulations anyway. All told, there is little enough scope for Anglo-Irish alliances in these negotiations, although there are significant convergences, voluntary on matters of defence, involuntary on EMU and Schengen, where Ireland is more constrained by a relationship with Britain.

Since Ireland is deeply affected by economic interdependence with Britain, and engaged furthermore in a fundamental negotiation over Northern Ireland designed to normalise relations, it is much more exposed than other member-states to British exceptionalism. It therefore faces a very difficult series of choices over which direction to take in its European policy in coming years, whether with a core group, a 'not-yet-in' grouping or an alliance with a Britain that might decide to go its own way. The next two sections, on Britain's economic prospects and its dilemma over EMU, are intended to assist the evaluation of the economic choices facing Ireland.

HAS BRITAIN'S ECONOMIC DECLINE ENDED?

If one compares British economic growth in the period since 1979 with that of the rest of the EU, it appears on the face of it that Britain is no longer lagging significantly behind its EU partners. Between 1979 and 1995 its GNP rose by 33 per cent as against 37 per cent for the Union as a whole. A closer examination of these figures shows, however, that this relatively better British performance was confined to two sub-periods comprising barely half of these sixteen years — viz. 1981-87 and 1992-95. At other times, 1979-81 and 1987-92, Britain continued to lag behind its continental partners. It is, however, possible that these sub-periods of slow growth were themselves reflections respectively of two specific factors: of an initial adjustment to the policies of the new Thatcher government and of that government's 1987/8 fiscal policy blunders.

The significance of Britain's 1979-1995 economic performance is discussed in detail in the papers by FitzGerald, Crafts, Minford and Huhne in the accompanying volume of seminar papers, in which stress is laid on the effects of the curbing of trade union power during the 1980s. Crafts argues that during the 1980s there was a very general narrowing of Britain's manufacturing productivity gap vis-à-vis Germany.

It has been suggested that three-quarters of the German/British productivity gap of 1979 had been closed by 1995, although Crafts believes that eliminating the remaining one-quarter would be slow and difficult because the process was slowing down in the early 1990s. Minford suggests that this catching up process may have involved an element of existing British firms copying methods introduced by new firms investing in Britain.

However, although Crafts sees some significant improvements in Britain's education system, he nevertheless quotes a study suggesting that illiteracy and innumeracy among young adults remains 'alarmingly high' and no better in 1992 than in 1981, while Huhne comments on the belated character of Britain's education reforms. The fact is that even in 1992 the proportion of British 18-and 19-year-olds in full-time education was little more than half the country mean for the OECD and was well below that of any other developed country except Turkey. British training is also seen as still lagging well behind that of its continental partners especially in relation to intermediate skills, and according to Huhne most analysts see this as a brake on Britain's long-term performance. Finally, although Crafts reports an improvement in the quality of British investment he adds that the volume of investment in manufacturing has stagnated.

As factors which may continue to exercise a negative impact on British economic growth, FitzGerald mentions the persistence of a more rigid class structure than elsewhere, accompanied by deepening social divisions — which may be particularly relevant to Britain's unique education deficit. He also raises the question of whether Britain's political system may not have an adverse impact on economic growth through the reversals of policies that tend to follow changes of government in a polarised two-party system, contrasting this with the less traumatic shifts in policy that are more common in multi-party systems with coalition governments.

Another possible negative factor may be the absence of an independent Central Bank, which has tempted British governments to disrupt economic growth by short-term monetary and fiscal measures designed to yield temporary electoral advantage at the expense of longer-term stop-go effects. In this connection it is worth noting that the Labour Party in Britain has recently indicated that it does not propose to make the Bank of England independent of government, a decision which, if adhered to by a Labour government, would rule out British participation in EMU and a single currency, for which an independent bank in each country is a pre-condition.

Other features of Britain with possible negative effects which FitzGerald cites include the effects of Anglo-American finance-oriented short-term-motivated capitalism — contrasting with the more industry-oriented long-term capitalism of the continent, which may, however, be under pressure from the Anglo-American model; a neglected and under-invested infrastructure (e.g. railways and water supplies); and the adverse effects of excessive credit expansion due to lack of control of capital markets.

This perception of the persistence of factors that may be constraining the growth of the British economy has until now continued to influence Irish policy-makers against tying their economy too closely to that of Britain. And this attitude has been reinforced by consciousness of the dramatically favourable impact of Ireland's post-1972 trade diversification upon its growth rate, relative to Britain and the rest of the EU.

As will be seen from Table 1 below, between 1972 and 1995 the share of Irish exports to continental EU countries increased two-and-a-half times, while the proportion going to the UK more than halved. And Table 2 shows that, while the Irish growth rate was temporarily reduced during that part of the 1980s when severe action had to be take to correct a huge fiscal imbalance, Irish growth has in recent years been at a higher level even than in the 1960s and 1970s. By contrast the British growth rate has been lower by one-third, and in the rest of the EU by over one-half, than in the period before the first oil crisis.

It may well be, however, that Irish concerns about future British growth, based on unhappy memories of the period up to the end of the 1970s, are exaggerated or misplaced. At the very least it seems likely that to the extent that, pending further reforms, British growth continues to lag behind that of its major continental partners in the period ahead, such a growth differential is likely to be much smaller than in the past, and thus should not, perhaps, of itself be such a significant determinant of Irish external economic policy. There is much room for dispute about how to interpret the figures concerning Britain's relative position; the OECD reports in August 1995 and June 1996 were convinced that it has turned the corner.

TABLE 1: PATTERNS OF IRISH TRADE 1972 AND 1995

	Exports		Imports	
	1972	1995	1972	1995
UK	61.5%	26%	51.5%	37%
Rest of EU*	18%	48%	23%	22%
Rest of World	20.5%	26%	25.5%	41%

*Present 15-member EU
Source: Irish Trade Statistics

TABLE 2: ANNUAL GNP GROWTH RATES, UK & REST OF EU, 1960-95

	1960-72	1972-79	1979-87	1987-95
Ireland	4.2	4.2	1.7	4.7
UK	2.8	2.0	2.0	1.6
Rest of EU	5.0	3.2	1.7	2.2

Source: OECD National Accounts 1991, updated from 1991 to 1995 by data from *Irish Central Bank Bulletin*

BRITAIN'S EMU DILEMMA

Debate on the issue of British EMU membership has been inhibited by the belief that EMU may never happen, thus sparing Britain the agony of choice. This remains, of course, a possibility, and for more than one reason.

First, the necessary conditions of economic convergence may not be achieved between the original six member states of the EU which, Italy perhaps apart, represent the minimum participation needed to get a genuine European Monetary Union, including France, off the ground. Without France, an EMU established by the automatic procedures provided for in the Maastricht Treaty (Art.109j, Par.4) would clearly be little more than an enlarged DM zone, as it would comprise only Germany and some of its smaller and economically-dependent neighbours. And while France's economic performance has been very much better in recent times than in the first quarter of a century of its EC membership, its *franc fort* policy — widely seen as necessary to its participation in EMU — has undoubtedly shown severe signs of strain at the level of management and has come under great social pressure because of the impact of the budgetary cuts necessary if France is to qualify for the convergence criteria. Under President Chirac, France's commitment to European integration as a means of 'containing' Germany is less strong than in the past, although the indications are that he is determined to stick by it.

Second, even if the necessary economic conditions are fulfilled in time for France to participate in the automatic establishment of a monetary union, and if President Chirac maintains France's European commitment, there remains the possibility that despite the automaticity of the Maastricht Treaty provisions, Germany might be unable to proceed with a union which is unpopular with German opinion and which, the German Constitutional Court has ruled, requires German parliamentary approval.

On the other hand those in Britain who hope that for one or other of these reasons EMU will not happen probably, as so often in the past, under-estimate the inherent dynamism of the European project. Frankenberger points out in the accompanying volume of seminar papers that, whatever the faults of the Maastricht Treaty, it represents a Franco-German insurance policy for the future which both countries will be loath to abandon because it reflects both the French interest in 'anchoring' the now much larger united Germany and the German will to assure her partners that there will be no 'Sonderweg' — that Germany will not succumb to new temptations and potential dangers following its post-Cold War return to its traditional position at the heart of Europe.

Attitudes to EMU among the public and interest groups in Britain are less negative than might be presumed from its political rhetoric. A 1994 survey of Confederation of British Industry member-companies, for example, has shown that 25 per cent believe EMU is a necessary adjunct of the single market and a further 56 per cent that it is desirable. Only a small minority was opposed in principle. In 1995 41 per cent of companies said EMU would improve their business prospects, 43 per cent that it would have no impact. The CBI has taken a cautious line on the subject, waiting for its membership to reach conclusions and for more analysis to be conducted.

The CBI's approach is compatible with the line taken by the government and the Bank of England, but markedly more sympathetic and more characteristic of the classic pragmatist tradition in Britain. The Irish chairman of the CBI's Europe Committee, Niall FitzGerald, expressed fears about the Government's policy of non-co-operation over the beef crisis, indicating that it might lose Britain's influence in the EU. Most observers are convinced that Britain will have to balance the temptations of a competitive devaluation model against the anti-inflationary commitment that has become a hallmark of policy-makers. To some extent the 'Hong Kong', offshore, low-cost labour model proposed for British capitalism overlaps with the idea that Britain is consolidating its non-European trading interests. Others point out that the comparative lack of investment reinforces this model's attractions; but not, it is widely felt, to the point of a perpetual opt-out from EMU.

Attitudes in Britain range from the committed and enthusiastic proponents, including those who accept the political and constitutional consequences of EMU for British sovereignty; through those who believe Britain will have little option but to follow a hard-core initiative; through the sceptics properly so-called, who are not convinced that EMU is in Britain's or Europe's interest but retain an open mind on the subject; through finally to the Europhobes, who oppose the whole project. Insiders say the city of London is split down the middle, reflecting these differences of attitude. In addition, there is division on what would happen if the project succeeds, with some analysts arguing that money would flow to Frankfurt and Paris, others saying that if the European Central Bank imposes reserve requirements, money would flow to London. Much will depend on the precise rules adopted.

These issues, like so many others about EMU, are still being decided. The British government and financial establishment have become much more aware that, in or out, there will be inescapable consequences for them. Mr Major made much of these issues at the Madrid European Council in December 1995. He commanded an attentive audience from the other heads of state and government when he posed the following questions:

- How would decision-making be affected by having some in and some out of a single currency? Would those 'in' vote as a bloc, and if so how would the 'outs' and/or the 'not-yet-ins' protect their interests?

- What if some of the less competitive regions within a single currency demand further aid for the loss of jobs they may suffer? What if weaker countries outside seek ever higher payouts from the Union to help to develop their economies to join a single currency?

- What if those inside speed up the arrangement, creating a greater distance between the ins and outs?

- What does all this mean for the single European market?

Several supplementary questions may be posed about how a 'cohabitation' arrangement would work, including how to control the possibility of competitive devaluations by means of an exchange rate mechanism. Mr Major says Britain would not join one if it decides not to join EMU (Major, *D Tel,* 18.12.1995); the indications are that a Labour government would do so. And what of shocks within the system — who would pay for them?

Mr Major is not the first leader to raise these questions. They have been exercising Irish ministers since the currency crisis of 1992-93 and were taken up sharply by President Chirac at the Cannes Council in June 1995 and thereafter. The universalising of the issue and the agreement to coordinate policy reached in Verona in April 1996 is welcome to Irish policy-makers. Clearly it is the stability of the pound-sterling relationship that is crucial from the Irish point of view, whether guaranteed by EMU membership for both currencies, or by a responsible and well-defined relationship between a pound within EMU and a sterling in a relatively fixed position outside it. Clearly, too, it must be a major priority for the Irish government to ensure that the cohabitation problem continues to be addressed squarely.

From Ireland's point of view there has, of course, been a double uncertainty both about the emergence of the EMU and about Britain's participation in it, whether from the outset or at some later point. The potential Irish dilemma will become a real one if EMU proceeds according to the Maastricht timetable and if the United Kingdom decides not to join at that point. The implications of such a scenario for Ireland are developed further in subsequent chapters. They argue that Britain's decision on whether to join an EMU is inextricably bound up with the crisis of identify spelled out in this chapter. This is the wider context of politics and political economy, in which economic decisions will be made. It is also clear, as is argued in Chapter 2 and 3, that Britain's crisis of identity has profound implications for its relations with Ireland.

CHAPTER 2
IRELAND: REDEFINING IDENTITY

IRELAND AND BRITAIN: THE ASSERTION OF INDEPENDENCE

Geography, rather than history, first tied together the destinies of Ireland and Britain. It was Ireland's misfortune that the neighbouring island was larger and wealthier, more populous and more powerful, and that it pursued expansionist policies over a period of 700 years. Conversely, it was Britain's good fortune that the neighbouring island offered easy opportunities for partial conquest, plantation and the expropriation of natural resources; its occupation also provided a strategic bulwark on the Atlantic approaches which for over 300 years British statesmen deemed essential for their security and defence.

Hence the massive historical significance of the disclaimer in the Downing Street Declaration, signed by John Major and Albert Reynolds on 15 December 1993, that Britain has 'no selfish strategic or economic interest in Northern Ireland'. That Britain *had* selfish, strategic and economic interests in Ireland which she was determined to defend was for centuries the essence of Britain's relationship with Ireland.

In the centuries before independence, Irish leaders resisting British dominion traditionally sought to redress this unequal balance of power by seeking support from Britain's most powerful continental enemy: Philip II's Spain in the case of the Gaelic leaders at war with Elizabeth I; Napoleon's France for Wolfe Tone's United Irishmen; Kaiser Wilhelm's Germany for the republican revolutionaries of 1916. All formed part of the tradition of resistance epitomised by the nineteenth-century slogan 'England's difficulty is Ireland's opportunity' and all sought to maximise nationalist opportunity by exacerbating British difficulty.

The British, unsurprisingly, responded in kind. Ireland, in the words of Lord Salisbury in 1892, 'must be kept, like India, at all hazards: by persuasion, if possible; if not, by force'. Nothing served more swiftly to dispel the miasma of apathy and indifference which commonly characterised the British view of Ireland than the prospect of a Spanish or a French fleet or a German U-boat in Bantry Bay.

British strategic interests in Ireland were thrown into sharpest relief at times of international crisis; or, in other words, Anglo-Irish crises often originated in and were subsumed by greater international crises in which British governments inevitably subordinated concern for harmony in Anglo-Irish relations to calculations of where their larger national interest lay.

Three such international crises are specially significant: the French revolutionary wars at the end of the eighteenth century and the two world wars. The first gave birth to the United Kingdom of Great Britain and Ireland established under the terms of the Act of Union of 1800. William Pitt, the chief architect of the Union, was preoccupied not with Ireland but with the war with France which had begun some seven years before the Union was introduced and which did not end until fifteen years later. The 1798 rebellion, the alliance between the United Irishmen and the French and, above all, the abortive French invasions of Ireland made the Act of Union and the consequential abolition of a separate Irish parliament imperative in British eyes.

The second, the Great War of 1914-18, temporarily swept aside the forces of constitutional nationalism which had traditionally dominated Irish parliamentary representation and set in motion forces which in 1919-22 led to the establishment of the Irish Free State and to the deconstruction of the United Kingdom and its reconstruction as the United Kingdom of Great Britain and Northern Ireland. In both cases Ireland became a mere fragment in the global mosaic as Britain's Irish policy was bent to the exigencies of grand strategy.

It is no coincidence that just as one great European war played a decisive part in forging the Act of Union, the next great European war played a decisive part in breaking it. Another striking similarity is that both wars persuaded the British to embrace policies that would enable them to devote less rather than more of their energies to Ireland.

In the eyes of its advocates the Act of Union was more an end than a beginning: an end to apprehension about an Irish-French *entente* and to a chapter in Anglo-Irish relations which supporters of the British connection viewed only with abhorrence. The Anglo-Irish settlements of 1920-22, more even than the settlement of 1800, sought to exorcise the Irish incubus which had haunted British parliamentary politics so relentlessly for thirty-five years before the Great War, and to end the international outrage (especially damaging in the United States) caused by the anti-guerrilla war conducted by British forces in Ireland in 1920-21.

The outcome was partition. The partition of the Government of Ireland Act of 1920 (which established what was essentially a separate home rule parliament and government for the six north-eastern counties of Northern Ireland in June 1921) was compounded, moreover, when the Articles of Agreement (commonly known as the Treaty) signed on 6 December 1921 led a year later to the establishment of the twenty-six county Irish Free State with the status of a self-governing dominion within the British commonwealth.

But Britain's continued strategic interest in Ireland was spelt out in the defence articles of that treaty and in an annex which provided for its retention of three ports and associated aviation facilities in the twenty-six counties; article 7 also provided that, 'in time of war or of strained relations with a foreign power', the Irish Free State government would moreover provide such harbour or other defence facilities as the British government might require.

The continuing centrality of the British connection as the pivot of political debate in Ireland north and south has clouded the significance of the changed British perspective on what for them was the Irish connection. The architects of the Government of Ireland Act 1920 had sought British disentanglement from all spheres of Irish domestic government in Ireland as their primary objective. The much larger disengagement from the twenty-six counties embodied in the Treaty of 1921 was still more welcome, notwithstanding Britain's continued strategic interests in Ireland.

Put simply, the Anglo-Irish settlements of 1920-22 were a remarkable success from a British perspective because they allowed the British massively to dilute the importance of the Irish connection without sacrificing their strategic interests. Hence the unanimity of five successive British governments and four prime ministers (Lloyd George, Bonar Law, Baldwin and Ramsay MacDonald) between 1922 and 1924 that nothing must imperil the Treaty settlement. Hence the insistence that the domestic affairs of Northern Ireland fell outside the jurisdiction of the Westminster parliament. Disengagement was the objective and for the better part of half a century, from 1922 to 1969, disengagement was achieved to an extent that would have seemed inconceivable before the Great War.

Partition meant that British-Irish relations were conducted on two axes after 1922: the Dublin-London axis and the Belfast-London axis. What little movement centred on the Belfast-London axis before the collapse of the Northern Irish system of government in 1969-72 tightened rather than loosened the bonds of the diminished and diluted union of the United Kingdom of Great Britain and Northern Ireland; notably the tripartite agreement of December 1925 which consolidated the boundary of Northern Ireland, and the Ireland Act of 1949 which incorporated the most comprehensive British reaffirmation of Northern Ireland's constitutional status and territorial integrity since 1920. Both were reaffirmations of Northern Ireland's dependence on Britain for its legitimacy and protection.

In the south, the civil war of 1922-23 ensured that the Treaty represented in the politics of independent Ireland what the Act of Union had represented in the politics of Ireland in the United Kingdom and what it remained in the politics of Northern Ireland: the touchstone of political allegiance. Although pro-treaty versus anti-treaty replaced nationalist versus unionist as the fundamental political divide, within the Irish state the British connection, albeit in a diluted form, remained the great divisive issue.

The respect of the first Irish Free State government for a treaty on behalf of which they had fought and won a civil war meant that there was little initial movement on the Dublin-London axis apart from that arising from the application for membership of the League of Nations (the Irish Free State was admitted in September 1923), the registration of the Treaty as an international agreement with the League in 1924 and the decision, also in 1924, to become the first dominion to be diplomatically accredited in its own right to the United States. Such decisions, all taken in the face of British objections, showed the Irish government's determination to take foreign policy decisions independently of Britain; but it was only after Fianna Fáil came to power under Éamon de Valera in 1932, on a platform of dismantling the Treaty and breaking the British connection, that movement on the Dublin-London axis accelerated dramatically.

'The ultimate test of independence', declared Pandit Nehru speaking in his capacity as prime minister of another dominion just come to independence, 'consists fundamentally and basically of foreign relations' (Fanning, 1983, p. 120). Irish independence was not tested until the Second World War and, until then, the exercise of Irish independence never ran counter to vital British interests. True, the British resented de Valera's action in dismantling the Treaty and expanding the limits of Irish independence; but resentment never turned into resistance. The abolition of the oath of allegiance, the External Relations Act of 1936, the 1937 Constitution (which made Ireland a republic in all but name and as independent of Britain and the Commonwealth as de Valera wanted) — all alike were the results of unilateral decisions taken by Irish governments which British governments chose to ignore rather than resist.

The Anglo-Irish agreements of 1938 — the defence agreement handed over the Treaty ports to Irish control and enabled Ireland to remain neutral in the Second World War — were the exception to this pattern of unilateral Irish action. Why did de Valera abandon unilateralism and enter into negotiations with Neville Chamberlain and — at first sight a much more puzzling question — why did Chamberlain suddenly abandon the British stance of remaining independently aloof from de Valera and instead reward him by surrendering the ports on the eve of war with Hitler's Germany? The answer is that the Second World War — the third of our great international crises and the only such crisis since Ireland became independent — was the crucible in which Irish and British assumptions about dependence, independence and interdependence were forged and, sometimes, reforged in quite different shapes.

Irish neutrality, the preferred foreign policy option of all Irish governments since 1922, has been defined as 'the ultimate expression of independence' (Lyons, 1973, p. 554); but it was also the outer limit of Irish independence, for none realised earlier than de Valera that the traditional revolutionary readiness to enter into alliances with Britain's enemies made no sense once Ireland had achieved in fact the independence to which republicans had long laid claim in theory. Indeed, de Valera had publicly recognised as early as 1920 that, in the event of another major European war, an independent Ireland's fate would be interdependent with Britain's:

'An independent Ireland would see its own independence in jeopardy the moment it saw the independence of Britain seriously threatened. Mutual self-interest would make the peoples of these two islands, if both independent, the closest possible allies in a moment of real national danger to either.' (Moynihan, 1980, p. 34)

By 1938 de Valera had achieved his independent Ireland and, with war clouds looming over Europe, was ready to act in accordance with this formulation of Anglo-Irish interdependence.

Interdependence was also the spur for Chamberlain. For as long as there were neither wars nor rumours of wars in Europe, the continuance of the Anglo-Irish economic war (in which Britain was the net beneficiary) and the fact that Britain was generally on such bad terms with the Irish government mattered not a whit. But by 1938 Chamberlain was troubled by the spectre that had haunted William Pitt in 1798: what if, in the event of war, his

European enemy were to form some sort of alliance with or, worse still, successfully invade an unfriendly Ireland? The advice of his chiefs of staff was unequivocal: better to return the ports in the hope that it would at least ensure a benevolent Irish neutrality than run any risk of a hostile Ireland on Britain's western flank.

De Valera's practice of Irish neutrality throughout the Second World War at once embodied both his concept of independence and his concept of interdependence. Publicly, de Valera's gestures of neutrality — his highly publicised visit to the German legation to pay his condolences on the news of Hitler's death, for example — were indeed the ultimate expression of independence. Privately, the secret but highly significant transmission of information to both the British and American military and intelligence authorities — the Irish government 'have been willing to accord us *any* facilities which would not be regarded as *overtly* prejudicing their attitude to neutrality' (authors' italics), acknowledged the British Dominions Secretary to his Cabinet colleagues in February 1945, before appending a remarkable fourteen-point list of the facilities in question (Fanning, 1983, pp. 124-5) — was at once the ultimate expression and the outer limit of de Valera's commitment to interdependence.

But for the British, and for Churchill in particular, interdependence demanded abandoning neutrality and joining the Allies. Ireland as a dominion, insisted Churchill (who had been a Treaty signatory in 1921 and who had argued in 1932 that the Statute of Westminster was not applicable to Ireland), was not entitled to be neutral: her true status was 'not at war but skulking'.

The virulence of British denunciations of Irish neutrality both during and after the war is partially explicable in terms of the 'affinity paradox': Machiavelli's dictum that neutrals will get little thanks from those who see them as potential allies but will win the gratitude of those who perceive them as potential enemies. But the enduring resentment about Irish neutrality and its later recrudescence, for example, during the Falklands war — 'that absurd and self-wounding gesture' (Gilmour, 1992, p. 261) — also owes much to the British inability to come to terms with the reality of Irish independence when put into practice in time of war.

De Valera also tried to apply the concept of interdependence to the problem of partition, which in 1938 began to assume the status of the one outstanding grievance of Irish nationalists with the British government. But here he argued in vain, because conciliating Dublin on partition made no sense to Chamberlain's government if the price were the alienation of the Northern

Irish government, with all that might imply for British access to Northern Irish bases and industrial resources in the war that lay ahead.

Although, under the stress of the darkest days of the war, Churchill, in 1940 and less seriously in 1941, flirted briefly with an interdependent approach to the partition issue when he held out the prospect of a united Ireland to de Valera in return for his abandoning neutrality, nothing came of this; from de Valera's perspective, that form of interdependence was unacceptable because it would involve the sacrifice of independence. Ireland's sovereign right to determine its relations with other countries was embodied in the first article of his 1937 constitution and, in February 1939, de Valera went on record that he would not sacrifice that right for a united Ireland.

But extending the boundaries of independent Irish action also deepened the divide separating it from Northern Ireland. The Second World War drove the lesson home. Northern Ireland's contribution to the war effort transformed its relations with Britain. It proved the strategic value of British interdependence with Northern Ireland and at the same time eroded the strategic significance of Britain's inability to depend on independent Ireland.

The point was highlighted again in 1949 when the Irish government's rejection of the invitation to join the North Atlantic alliance was framed in terms of the interdependence of the partition issue; Seán MacBride's *aide-memoire*, wrote one of his officials in the Department of External Affairs, 'left no room for any doubt that, but for partition, the Irish government would be prepared to participate in the [North Atlantic] pact' (Fanning, 1983, p. 177). Again, the British (and American) perspective was utterly different: Ireland's participation in NATO was not essential to NATO's success because Northern Ireland (as part of the UK) was also part of NATO.

It was at just this time that the Republic of Ireland Act — another unilateral act on the part of an Irish government and one which severed all remaining vestigial diplomatic ties between Ireland and the Commonwealth — widened the North/South divide still further. But on this occasion the British responded: Clement Attlee's Labour government, conscious of the debt of gratitude owed Northern Ireland for their role in the war, passed the Ireland Act of 1949 which incorporated the most comprehensive British reaffirmation of the constitutional status and territorial integrity since 1920.

Seán MacBride complained in vain about the consolidation of partition. Members of the British government, responded Foreign Secretary Ernest Bevin, were in broad sympathy with the ideal of a united Ireland. 'But we could not ignore the history of the last forty years. Northern Ireland had stood in with us when the South was neutral. ... Until the majority of Northerners were persuaded, therefore, that it was in their interests to join the South, the British people would oblige us to give them guarantees that they would not be coerced' (Fanning, 1981-2).

The strategic imperative here enunciated by Bevin underpinned the British perspective on Northern Ireland for another forty years, until the fall of the Berlin Wall in November 1989 signalled the end of the Cold War. A year later, on 9 November 1990, Peter Brooke, the secretary of state for Northern Ireland, made his seminal speech declaring that Britain had no strategic or economic interest in Northern Ireland and would accept the unification of Ireland if the people of Northern Ireland so consented.

No British government had entertained the concept of interdependence with the Irish government in respect of Northern Ireland for as long as Northern Ireland remained stable. But the collapse of the Northern Irish system of government in 1972 had prompted the first genuflection in the direction of interdependence at the tripartite conference at Sunningdale in December 1973. Interdependence was institutionalised in the shape of the system of inter-governmental conferences embodied in the Anglo-Irish agreement of November 1985 and it later found further expression in the Downing Street Joint Declaration in December 1993.

TOWARDS THE POLITICS OF ECONOMICS

The ultimate assertion of Irish sovereignty embodied in the Republic of Ireland Act of 1948 ended the phase when foreign policy was determined by the politics of independence, and paved the way for a foreign policy founded on the politics of economics. By the 1960s the primary motivation of Irish foreign policy had become economic rather than political, and positive rather than negative: a desire to maximise economic advantage through integration with the more dynamic economies of continental Europe.

Not merely has the motivation of Irish policy vis-à-vis Britain changed radically: the impetus for these two stages in the evolution of Ireland's British policy has also come from two quite different sources. At the earlier, purely political, stage the impetus came from political leaders whose inspiration derived from the struggle for independence in the second decade of the century and whose vision was one of an economically self-sufficient and culturally isolationist Ireland — a vision that found its purest expression in de Valera's famous 1943 St Patrick's Day broadcast.

This revolution was led by people who, while rejecting the narrow and sterile political anglophobia of the past, had a vision that was not bounded by any reactive anglophilia. They felt no temptation to seek a closer economic relationship with Britain.* Rather did they look towards continental Europe: not at first because of any perception of a differential between continental and British growth rates — that came somewhat later — but because the happy coincidence of the establishment of the European Economic Community in 1957 provided a new focus for Irish hopes.

At first these hopes were directed principally towards the economic opportunities that might be offered by membership of the European Community, which were substantial. Not alone would access to the six-member European Community of that period virtually quadruple overnight the markets to which Ireland had free access: it would also liberate the Irish farm sector from a debilitating dependence upon a UK market in which prices had for long been depressed by Britain's cheap food policy.

Geographically close to Britain but lacking the possibilities of extensive farming that were open to overseas producers in the Commonwealth and the United States, Ireland had been the principal victim of that policy. Since the immediate post-war period this century-old British policy had been considerably intensified by the introduction of deficiency payments to British farmers — a practice that removed any inhibitions about encouraging the dumping of world food surpluses on the UK market. This intensified cheap food policy had been a major factor contributing to the stagnation of the Irish economy during the 1950s — a decade which elsewhere in Europe had been one of exceptionally rapid economic growth.

Some time was to elapse before the deeper significance of the fundamental change that EC membership would bring about in Ireland's external economic relations came to be understood and appreciated. Eventually, however, it became clear that this new relationship with its continental neighbours had the capacity to transform Ireland's relationship with Britain — which, to an extent that Irish people had been unwilling to admit even to themselves, had since 1922 involved a degree of continuing economic dependence that had effectively constrained the free exercise of the political independence gained in 1922.

*Despite all appearances to the contrary, on the Irish side at least the negotiation of an Anglo-Irish Free Trade Association Agreement in 1965 was not designed to reinforce economic links between the two countries but was rather intended to impose pressure for rationalisation on the Irish manufacturing sector with a view to what was seen as an imminent EC membership that would *reduce* Ireland's long-term dependence on the UK. (See FitzGerald, *The Irish Times*, 28/12/1965 — 3/1/1966).

In Ireland's case, indeed, European economic and political integration had a positively liberating effect, for it soon began to be seen as involving not so much a diminution of Irish sovereignty (which in practice had not been exercisable in the economic sphere), but rather as a welcome constraint on *Britain's* all-too-evident ability to exercise *its* sovereignty to Ireland's economic disadvantage and thus as the effective completion of the process of securing its independence vis-à-vis its larger neighbour.

This was a dramatic illustration of the fact that in practice sovereignty — the internationally recognised unfettered right of a country to pursue its interests by peaceful means vis-à-vis, and even at the expense of, other states — has a quite different meaning for small and large states. In the real world large states can — and do — use this power vis-à-vis smaller ones without fear of retaliation — whereas by contrast small states have to be very careful about how they deploy their theoretical sovereignty vis-à-vis large ones.

Thus in the British-Irish relationship that had existed during the first half-century of Irish political independence, Britain had been free to exercise its sovereignty to the disadvantage of Irish agriculture through its cheap food policy, and continental states had used their sovereignty to exclude Irish exports from their markets. But much smaller Ireland had no comparable economic leverage that it could deploy against any of these countries through the exercise of *its* political sovereignty; the exercise of its right to protect its industries had done little damage in absolute terms to its trading partners — but arguably had done quite a lot of damage to Irish industrial development, at any rate from 1950 onwards.

Membership of a Community within which Ireland and its trading partners — including Britain — are legally precluded from exploiting each other by discriminatory trading measures was thus, on balance, enormously beneficial for Ireland. For the positive effects of other countries giving up their sovereign right to discriminate against Ireland have far exceeded any possible benefit Ireland could ever have secured by exercising its sovereign right to discriminate against other member states in trading matters.

The belated realisation of this truth eventually had profound effects upon the shape and expression of Irish nationalism.

Everything in the history of the Irish state during its first fifty years of existence might have suggested that within a common market it would be reluctant to share with other states any more of its newly-acquired and greatly valued national sovereignty than was absolutely necessary — and that it would, therefore, adopt a minimalist approach to economic and political integration. But economic realism rapidly led to a recognition that within the EC Ireland's interests lay in pursuing from the outset a strongly integrationist stance. Only in relation to defence did inhibitions remain — arising from the fact that in 1948-49 the Irish government of the day had sought without avail to use its possible participation in the North Atlantic Alliance as a bargaining counter to secure political reunification. Ireland's consequent self-exclusion from the Alliance, coming so soon after its wartime neutrality, gave rise to a popular commitment to a neutrality ethos.

Ireland's commitment to an integrationist policy within the EC was clearly established, within months of accession to the Community, in a Dáil statement on foreign policy made in May 1973 on behalf of a Fine Gael/Labour coalition government which had taken office ten weeks after Ireland had joined the Community at the beginning of that year. This statement identified Ireland's long-term interest as lying in an evolution of the Community towards a more democratic structure that would involve a greater supranational element in the form of a strengthened European Parliament and possibly a move from unanimity to qualified majority voting.

Thus it was that in the sphere of external policy a rational conclusion was reached that Irish interests would be better served by maximising the limitations on the all-too-real sovereignty of its near neighbours than by seeking to retain as much as possible of its own less effective sovereignty. And thus it was that Irish and British policies towards the EC were from the time of accession set on opposite courses.

THE BENEFITS OF EU MEMBERSHIP

The economic benefits of Irish membership of the Community, aspired to since 1961 and achieved in 1973, have hitherto included significant current and capital transfers through the European budget. For much of the period since Ireland became a member of the EC, transfers from the Community have added some 5-7 per cent to each year's national disposable income; this flow of resources seems to have helped to boost the underlying Irish growth rate by about 0.5% from just under 4 per cent a year to just over that figure and in any event the scale of those transfers has since declined to about 4.5 percent of GNP. Most of the growth remained endogenous rather than created by the EU transfers.

The long-term significance of these transfers should, therefore, not be exaggerated — especially as the country's high rate of economic growth is rapidly bringing Irish *per capita* output and incomes so much closer to the EU average that its entitlement to Structural Funds in the early years of the next century will be greatly reduced.*

* Thus whereas in 1972 Ireland's Net National Disposable Income per head was 39 per cent below the EC average, by 1995 this gap had been reduced to 17.5 per cent, and on current trends is likely to fall to around 10 per cent by the year 2000.

The Community's contribution to Ireland's high growth rate has lain rather in three other areas: First, in the ending of its almost exclusive dependence on what until at least the 1980s had been a slow-growing British economy operating a cheap food policy that had debilitated the important Irish agricultural sector. Second, in the country's ability to exploit the access it thus gained to the wider continental market, in particular by attracting employment-generating industrial investment from outside the EU. Third, in the discipline it helped — albeit belatedly — to impose on the country's fiscal policies.

Moreover, although an undue emphasis on the flow of funds through the EU Budget has fostered something of a 'begging-bowl' mentality towards the Community amongst sectors of the Irish public, there have also been important countervailing psychological benefits from membership.

The first and perhaps most obvious has been that it has assisted a society, which in the post-revolutionary half-century had become inward-looking, to turn outwards and take its place confidently in the world. But it has also helped to modify in a constructive direction attitudes towards Britain: the replacement of the former polarised bilateral relationship between the two countries by a multilateral and less unequal one within an EU context has reduced tensions and has significantly modified the inferiority/superiority complex factor in that former relationship.

It has moreover contributed, through the frequency of ministerial contact at EU level, to greatly intensified inter-governmental relations. During the past two decades the latter development has made a most important contribution to the ability of the two governments to handle together constructively the long-running and potentially explosive crisis in Northern Ireland.

That said, it remains true that when Ireland was seeking membership of the Community in the 1960s the benefits then envisaged were primarily economic — and mainly in respect of agriculture, a sector that now accounts for only 9 per cent of domestic output and 12 per cent of employment, but one for which in 1961 the equivalent figures were both three times greater than today. Indeed up to the end of the 1950s Irish agricultural output had continued to exceed that of industry.

Although the Community's Common Agricultural Policy did not take its full shape until the mid-1960s, by the start of that decade it was already clear that membership would offer a prospect of stimulating the whole Irish economy by liberating the agricultural sector from the debilitating effects of Britain's cheap food policy. The adverse impact of that policy upon the prices of agricultural imports to Britain had been aggravated a decade earlier when the introduction of deficiency payments to British farmers had removed a domestic constraint upon the intensification of this policy.

By the later 1960s, however, Irish policy-makers had become conscious of another more general economic factor favouring accession to the Community: the gradual emergence of clear evidence that the disparity between the rates of growth of Britain and her continental neighbours that had emerged since the end of the nineteenth century had become even more marked since the end of the immediate post-war period. It became clear that this had been imposing, and might continue indefinitely to impose, a severe constraint on Irish economic growth so long as the country's exports of industrial as well as agricultural goods were excluded from free entry to more dynamic continental markets.

The success of Ireland's belated end-1950s shift from a protectionist to an outward-looking export-oriented policy depended upon the achievement of access to these markets, not so much because of new opportunities this would provide for existing Irish industries* as because this access would be vital to the attraction of the external industrial investment that would be needed in the first instance to replace jobs in existing protected industries which would disappear with free trade, and subsequently to assure rapid and sustained growth of the Irish economy.

On the other hand, the positive impact of EC membership upon Irish domestic fiscal policy was much-delayed. In the earlier years of membership there may, indeed, have been a perverse negative effect on fiscal prudence, especially in the late 1970s after the economy had recovered its equilibrium following the shock of the first oil crisis. For the destabilisation of the economy as a result of the 50 per cent increase in the volume of public spending between 1977 and 1982 certainly owed something to the mood created by what proved to be a temporary leap of 45 per cent in the real incomes of farmers during the farm price adjustment period 1974-78.

Even membership of the EMS in 1979 had no immediate effect on Irish fiscal policy, the painful adjustment of which did not begin until 1981. However, during the present decade the indefinite continuance of the strict fiscal policies of the 1980s has been substantially assured as a result of the Maastricht EMU decision and the introduction of the associated macro-economic criteria. The model performance of the Irish economy in the

---

* A survey carried out by the Federation of Irish Industries in 1965 showed that domestic industry's expectations from EEC membership were then minimal — a total increase of 5-6 per cent in manufactured exports — although in the event exports by domestic firms to the original EEC Six have increased by much more than this — almost certainly by well over 50 per cent.

current decade in terms of inflation, fiscal balance and the rapid reduction of the public debt/GDP ratio, as well as economic growth, certainly reflects the impact of Maastricht upon Irish government policy.

The almost uniformly favourable impact of EU membership on the Irish economy, running well beyond anything foreseen at the time of accession, has given widespread popular backing to an integrationist European policy stance that initially had been founded on a fairly narrowly-based intellectual commitment at the level of policy-makers. The clear balance of advantage to be derived from a sharing of sovereignty in the case of a small country such as Ireland is now widely accepted — earlier fears of a loss of identity through this process having largely disappeared. Moreover, an extension of Community competences to the third pillar — Justice and Home Affairs — does not arouse in Ireland the kind of fears that clearly exist not alone in Britain but also, for example, in France.

In Ireland today there is in fact only one policy area where a sharing of sovereignty appears threatening: defence and foreign policy. And in this area Irish reticence may owe more to the character of neutrality in the post-war period than to a failure to re-think Irish nationalism.

FROM INDEPENDENCE TO INTERDEPENDENCE: TOWARDS A POLITICS OF PLURALISM

The fundamental rethinking of Irish nationalism in relation to foreign policy that was induced by the prospect of EC membership in the early 1970s coincided with the outbreak of violence in Northern Ireland — which itself forced a reconsideration of the stance of Irish nationalism in relation to the political division of the island that had accompanied the achievement of Irish political independence half-a-century earlier.

The collapse in 1925 of the Boundary Commission, upon the outcome of whose work Irish hopes of an early ending of the division of the island had centred, had effectively removed this issue from the practical agenda of subsequent Irish governments — although not from their rhetorical agenda. A combination of factors — a sense of guilt and frustration at this outcome, as well as competition in domestic politics for the high ground of emotional nationalism — contributed thereafter to recurrent outbursts of irredentism encapsulated in such phrases as: 'The North has no right to opt out' or 'Give us back our lost Six Counties'.

Privately, few believed in the practical possibility of any early move towards re-unification of the island. And the negative impact of this irredentism on Northern unionist attitudes could be and was widely ignored; so also were its potentially inflammatory effects on elements in the Northern nationalist community and even within the Irish state itself.

Although from the late 1950s onwards the utility and wisdom of this kind of rhetoric had begun to be questioned by some people outside politics, and also by a minority of thoughtful Northern nationalists, it was not until the actual outbreak of violence in Northern Ireland in 1969 that this element in the political psyche of the Irish state was seriously challenged within its political system.

Thereafter, however, a radical re-thinking of this traditional irredentism began within the political establishment in the Republic. This was precipitated by the Northern violence and was given fresh momentum by such related events in the south as the arms crisis that rocked the Fianna Fáil government in 1970, and the demonstration that culminated in the burning of the British Embassy following the killing of thirteen people by the paratroop regiment in Derry in January 1972.

By 1973 this process of rethinking attitudes towards Northern Ireland had reached the point where an Agreement such as that concluded at Sunningdale in December of that year proved widely acceptable to members of all parties in the Republic, despite the fact that it involved acceptance of Northern Ireland remaining in the United Kingdom — only very loosely linked to the Republic by a Council of Ireland within which unionists were to retain a veto over the development of any practical links with the south.

It is true that the irredentist thesis retained some hold over sections of opinion in the Irish state, but developments such as the New Ireland Forum of 1983-84 and the Anglo-Irish Agreement of 1985 contributed to its gradual erosion. This process culminated in the unambiguous commitment to the principle of the consent of a Northern majority as a precondition of re-unification, contained in the Downing Street Declaration negotiated by Albert Reynolds as Fianna Fáil Taoiseach in 1993, and in the February 1996 report of the Forum for Peace and Reconciliation, at which only Sinn Féin demurred.

Underlying this abandonment of irredentism lay a fundamental rethinking of the whole basis of Irish nationalism which had been under way throughout this period. In theory Irish nationalism had since the late eighteenth century been inclusive and non-sectarian, seeking to unite the Catholic, Anglican and Presbyterian traditions of the island. In practice, however, it had come

41

to reflect the ethos of the Roman Catholic indigenous population vis-à-vis the descendants of the post-Reformation settlers who had acquired the great bulk of the land of Ireland by conquest in the seventeenth century, either as landlords in the south or predominantly as peasant farmers in the north.

It was in the image of this narrower nationalism that the Irish state had in practice been constructed. The Irish language, the rich cultural heritage of the indigenous population, was given primacy in education and the public service; the possibility of divorce was first removed from the parliamentary arena and later excluded by a constitutional provision; contraceptives were banned; and censorship of publications was introduced. Thus, while the Protestant minority was given extensive transitional representation in the Senate and while their continuing disproportionate representation in business and the professions was not challenged, they were effectively discouraged from participation in the public administration and were culturally marginalised.

Two factors eventually led to a rethinking of the new state's mono-cultural nationalism: a growing unhappiness amongst its own people at the narrowness and at times illiberal character of this cultural mould and — an important reinforcing factor since the 1970s — a burgeoning recognition of its negative impact in relation to Northern Ireland.

As to the latter, the violence in Northern Ireland alerted public opinion in the Republic to the extent to which this irredentism had served to perpetuate the unionist fears that underlay discrimination against the nationalist community, while at the same time helping directly to keep alive the alienation of that community by fostering unreal hopes of a reunification of the island against the wishes of the unionist majority.

Breaking out of the mindset responsible for this irredentism required the development — or, thinking back to Tone and Davis, perhaps one should say the rediscovery — of a wider pluralist sense of Irishness that would concede parity of esteem to the unionist tradition. And in the 1980s a conscious effort was made within the Irish state to re-formulate nationalism on just such a pluralist base — a process aided by the parallel domestic process of reformulating the domestic ethos of the Irish state itself along broader and more liberal lines.

Thus from the early 1970s onwards the Irish nationalist ethos and identity, which in the immediate post-revolutionary period had shaped the political culture of the new Irish state not only domestically but also in relation to Northern Ireland and to Britain and the wider world, was consciously reshaped in a more fundamental way than has happened in any other

European country except Germany in the post-war period. Certainly neither of Ireland's nearest neighbours — Britain and France — have attempted a similar exercise: during this period France's readjustment to a new relationship with Germany within the European Community context has involved a much less fundamental reshaping of its identity and Britain — perhaps one should say England — has experienced an actual narrowing and intensification of its nationalism.

BRITAIN AND IRELAND IN EUROPE

'Britain and Ireland joined the Community together because of a sense of our place in history', argued Douglas Hurd (IEA speech, 21 March 1994). 'For the British it was about finding a new place in the world after the two centuries of imperial experience.' For the Irish, it was about 'confirming Ireland's position as a modern state in Europe ... and its decisive shift away from the embrace of Britain'.

That assessment epitomises the basic imbalance between British and Irish perspectives on Europe. The British perspective is not merely Atlanticist but global and, in that sense, extra-European.

British attitudes towards her engagement in Europe have little or nothing to do with British attitudes towards Ireland. From a British perspective, Ireland is no more than one of an ever-increasing number of pawns — and the more pawns the merrier — on the edge of the European chessboard. In the present as in the past Britain has inevitably loomed far larger in the Irish consciousness than Ireland has in the British, and Britain's present obsession with Europe, like all her European obsessions of past centuries, flows from her alarm about what is happening at the heart of Europe, not from any apprehension about the position of Ireland and other peripheral states.

That said, the fundamental conflict between the British and Irish perspectives on Europe — in the broadest political sense — must also be recognised. For Ireland, participation in Europe has been an essentially emancipating experience. In 1963, long after the Republic of Ireland Act of 1949 had severed all political ties with Britain, Anglo-Irish economic interdependence — and the dependence of Irish producers on the British market in particular — was still so great that when the French vetoed the British application to join the EEC, the theoretically independent Irish application also fell without a whimper. Engagement in Europe since 1973, notably in 1978 the decision to join the ERM when Britain remained outside (notwithstanding the fact that some 47 per cent of Irish exports were then still being sold on the British market), has symbolised Irish liberation from that economic dependence.

Liberation psychology is especially important from a political perspective. Membership first of the EC and now of the EU has afforded Irish leaders a more prominent and prouder place among the statesmen of Europe than at any time in Irish history. One symbol will suffice: Margaret Thatcher renegotiated British terms of membership of the EC in Dublin Castle, long the seat of British rule but now the Irish venue for meetings of the European Council.

The British perspective could scarcely be more different: Europe is perceived as standing not for liberation or emancipation but for restriction, even for alleged national humiliation arising from infringements of their sovereignty.

But however great this gulf in perspective, pragmatism dictates that neither Irish nor British diplomats choose to dwell upon it. Official pragmatism similarly demands that the likelihood of any significant diplomatic linkage occurring between Irish and British differences on Europe, on the one hand, and the inter-governmental partnership on Northern Ireland on the other, be dismissed as remote. Indeed Foreign Office officials and Department of Foreign Affairs officials alike are adamant that such linkage never occurs.

But to recognise that the linkage between Europe and Northern Ireland seems unlikely to prove a problem *in* Anglo-Irish diplomacy does not mean that it may not ultimately prove a problem *for* Irish diplomacy. Papers or submissions which have formed part of this project have identified as highly significant the potential tension between Ireland's European and Northern Irish aspirations. The root of the tension is that Ireland's European aspirations (as distinct from her interests) are essentially economic, while her Northern Irish aspirations are essentially political.

Paul Teague put the point in a nutshell: 'The situation may arise where European integration hinders deep forms of political and economic collaboration emerging between the north and the south which many regard as central to any sustainable agreement.' He highlights, in particular, the outcome of a two-tier Europe, with Ireland in the core and the United Kingdom in the periphery, where 'the economic and political orientation of the Republic would be inextricably tied to Germany as the dominant power in the new first-division Europe', while Northern Ireland, like the rest of the UK, remained tied to the political and economic priorities of outer Europe. Thus the central dilemma for Irish foreign policy at the beginning of the new millennium may be that its 'moves towards deeper integration in Europe, through adopting a single currency, may put a brake on the very same processes inside Ireland'. The alternative is to give priority to rebuilding closer economic ties between Dublin and London as 'a clear and unequivocal signal to the unionist community that the Republic is truly committed to a historic compromise between the traditions on the island' (Teague, *Seminar Papers,* pp. 51-52).

Gerard O'Neill has posed the dilemma in the following terms: Should the Republic wait for the UK 'to "see the light" in the early twenty-first century', or 'take the pain of dis-engaging from the UK economy more abruptly than planned — with inevitable consequences in cross-border trade and the whole north-south relationship?' (this volume, p.140). He also reminds us of the dangers of assuming that such questions may be answered by mere economic analysis without reference to the power of emotional energy — that 'spiritual or moral or emotional dimension' that, so Vaclav Havel argued in his 1994 speech to the European Parliament, was missing from the Maastricht Treaty. If the historical perspective on the dynamics of dependence, independence and interdependence in the Anglo-Irish relationship teaches us nothing else, it should remind us of the power of emotion.

Members of the Irish business community who have participated in this project are divided between pessimists and optimists, although some might prefer the description realists and idealists. Lochlann Quinn personifies the realist school when he challenges the assumption that if we were to follow the UK in opting out of an inner-core Europe, we would be isolated — if, for example, Greece, Spain, Italy, Sweden, Finland, Portugal, Poland, the Czech Republic, Hungary, Slovakia, Slovenia were also outside the core about the year 2000. In an observation on an early draft paper, he said: 'There is a legitimate pride in Ireland being a member of the inner-core but we must ensure that this is not substituted by the pride of politicians — of all parties — who want to be members of an exclusive club and are willing to "put the entrance ticket down on expenses". The outer core could be a very acceptable — and maybe much more profitable — location.' Quinn also argues that: 'If we join, with the UK and other EU members (including potential members) joining over time the results will, almost certainly, be beneficial. However, if we join and the single currency remains essentially a Franco/German currency zone the outlook must be different. If the UK, most Nordic states and Eastern and Mediterranean Europe remain outside for the long term, then this is a risky strategy' (Quinn, this volume, p. 133). His call for a comprehensive study of the employment effects was indisputable. Such a study has since been completed by the Economic and Social Research Institute on behalf of the Minister for Finance, and has broadly favoured EMU membership (*ESRI,* 1996).

The argument that, in Britain generally and in the Conservative Party in particular, post-Maastricht Europe 'is no longer a take it or leave it proposition' but has instead become a question of 'how much Europe do you want' (Howard Davis, 9 Feb. 1995) has made little headway in Ireland and it is worthwhile considering why.

One suspects that the attitude of many in the Irish business community is epitomised by the respondent to an earlier draft of one of this project's papers, who argues that 'trade must find its own level and exporters/traders should determine that level and those markets without political interference, except in circumstances or for reasons of major adverse humanitarian proportions. *Ireland should pursue a course of accommodation in the EU which would permit and facilitate Britain's full participation in further European integration'* (authors' italics).

Such optimism is difficult to reconcile with the argument of another prominent businessman based in Dublin, first, that 'we should be much more cautious in expressing the view that the Treaty of Maastricht will lead on to monetary or political union', in which case the Irish position vis-à-vis Britain 'may be alleviated'; and, second, that 'the implications of the peace process necessitate that we change our thinking and seek greater convergence rather than allow continued divergence with Britain' — especially with its implications for stronger sterling links.

In the last analysis, however, as Maurice O'Connell, Governor of the Central Bank, was also at pains to point out in a newspaper interview, 'you are talking about a political decision and that is a matter for the politicians. If the politicians decide yes, then it will happen ' (Taylor, 1995). That is why it is not unreasonable to demand in the national interest, that all the *political,* as well as the economic, criteria be put before the politicians in advance of their taking a decision which, one way or another, will have such momentous consequences for the national interest.

This chapter has argued that these political criteria must be understood in terms of a complex pattern of dependence, independence and inter-dependence in the relations between Britain and Ireland, which provides the essential context for the relationship between their respective identities. Membership of the European Community helped to loosen the economic bonds that had previously been imposed by Ireland's historical and geographical relationship with Britain, consolidating independence. The next chapters explore how the new British-Irish interdependence is expressed in, and mediated through, Northern Ireland.

CHAPTER 3
NORTHERN IRELAND: CONTESTED IDENTITY

NORTHERN IRELAND AND BRITAIN

The relationship between Northern Irish attitudes towards Britain and the problem of contested identity is inextricably linked with the circumstances in which the Northern Irish parliament and government were established by the Government of Ireland Act of 1920.

Ulster unionists and nationalists alike opposed the Act. Nationalist opposition was irreconcilable: the Act partitioned Ireland, denied them their rights as part of the large nationalist majority on the island and instead turned them into a permanent and, for the next fifty years, an oppressed minority in Northern Ireland. Nationalist opposition was compounded by what they have always denounced as the gerrymandered foundations of a Northern Ireland which was composed not of all nine counties of Ulster but only of the six north-eastern counties where a two-to-one majority of the inhabitants were unionists and Protestants; the three Ulster counties where nationalists and Catholics enjoyed a decisive majority became part of independent Ireland.

The great majority of Ulster's nationalists detested their status as citizens of the new United Kingdom of Great Britain and Northern Ireland and instead identified with independent Ireland. Their children went to segregated Catholic schools where they learned Irish history and the Irish language, sang Irish songs and played Gaelic games. Nationalists preferred newspapers and radio and, later, television broadcasts emanating from Dublin; their sense of identity was not British but anti-British; their national flag was not the Union Jack but the Irish tricolour. Hence the fate of Patricia Mulholland from Belfast who 'lost her outstanding credentials as an Irish-dancing teacher ... because she took a troupe to perform abroad as part of a British team — which meant that at some point they danced under a British flag and stood for *God Save the Queen* '.

Nationalist attitudes to Northern Ireland's British identity, which they saw as having been imposed upon them against their will, ranged from grudging resentment to revolutionary resistance. Although only a small minority joined the IRA, very many shared the IRA's aspirations for a united Ireland: what divided them was the means, not the end. Or, put another way, although the great majority of Ulster's nationalists obeyed the laws of Northern Ireland, they denied its legitimacy and refused it allegiance.

Initial unionist distaste for the Government of Ireland Act of 1920, on the other hand, was rooted in their sense of British identity. They did not want a separate parliament for Northern Ireland because neither Scotland nor Wales nor England had such a parliament; and, to that extent, the powers devolved to Northern Ireland under the Act diminished their sense of British identity.

But although none of the Ulster Unionist MPs voted for the 1920 Act, they grudgingly accepted it because, while it diluted their British identity by denying them that full integration in the United Kingdom they had enjoyed since 1801, it enabled them to escape what they perceived as the greatest threat to that identity: subjection to the jurisdiction of a parliament in Dublin.

In spite, or perhaps because of, that 1920 dilution of identity, Northern Ireland's unionists prided themselves on being more British than the British; once Northern Ireland was established as a separate entity the apparatus of government was swiftly invested with all the visible signs of British identity. Union Jacks were more in evidence on public and quasi-public buildings than in any other part of the United Kingdom, and Irish history was taught in Northern Irish state schools only where it had influenced the course of British history.

After 1932, as the Irish state became more and more independent of Britain, the exclusively unionist regime in Northern Ireland responded by emphasising their Britishness ever more heavily. The Second World War, when Northern Ireland made a not insignificant contribution to the defence of Britain while independent Ireland remained neutral, was a defining moment in this process. So strong was unionist aversion to the marks of Irish identity that when independent Ireland took the name of the Republic of Ireland and severed all links with the Commonwealth in 1948-49, Northern Irish ministers tried unsuccessfully to persuade the British government that Northern Ireland should be renamed 'Ulster' — notwithstanding the 1920 exclusion of three of the Ulster counties from their jurisdiction.

Unionist self-confidence about their identity reached its high point in 1965 when Terence O'Neill's talks with Seán Lemass were seen as 'the beginning of an attempt to rationalise their relationship with the Irish Republic. It was perhaps the beginning of an acknowledgement that to be Protestant in a Protestant part of Ireland, even under a British system, was nevertheless to be Irish. The phase did not last. The civil rights marches and their aftermath revived all the old fears and insecurities' (Ferguson, 1990, p. 44) — although that year also witnessed Northern Irish nationalists, while not renouncing their nationalist aspirations, simultaneously asserting their civil rights as *British* citizens.

The rapid destabilisation of the devolved government of Northern Ireland following the eruption of violence in 1968-69 was much the most serious threat to the unionists' sense of their Britishness in the history of their state. For as long as British troops, first committed to Northern Ireland in August 1969, could be broadly represented as acting in support of the unionist government, a precarious façade could be maintained; that façade crumbled rapidly when the dramatic escalation of violence, following the introduction of internment without trial in August 1971, destroyed such residual confidence as the British government had reposed in the advice of unionist ministers.

The crunch came in 1972-73 when the British government first suspended and then abolished the Northern Irish system of devolved government which had served as the apparatus for unionist celebration of British identity. The contest of identities was neatly captured in an *Irish Times* cartoon published before the Ireland-England rugby match during the fateful talks between the Northern Irish and British prime ministers, Brian Faulkner and Ted Heath, that culminated in the introduction of direct rule from Westminster. 'I say, Prime Minister', Faulkner was depicted saying to Heath, 'is it all right if I cheer for Ireland?'

The concept of power-sharing which was at the core of the Sunningdale agreement of December 1973 involved the admission of nationalists (in the shape of the SDLP) to political power for the first time in the history of Northern Ireland. The proposal to establish a Council of Ireland (made up of a joint north-south ministerial council and consultative assembly), though it came to nothing because of the collapse of the Sunningdale initiative in May 1974 following the Ulster Workers Strike, sought to legitimise the nationalist sense of Irish identity. The Anglo-Irish Agreement of November 1985 moved much further in the same direction, notably by establishing an Anglo-Irish intergovernmental conference, jointly chaired by British and Irish ministers and staffed by a secretariat at Maryfield, near Stormont, which gave Irish civil servants a permanent presence as nationalist intermediaries in Northern Ireland.

Until 1972 British perceptions of Northern Ireland's best interests, if only because of the British government's 'benign neglect', had broadly coincided with unionist perceptions. The broad thrust of developments since 1972, however, has bolstered the nationalists' sense of Irish identity and so eroded the unionists' sense of British identity. Or, to put it another way, Northern Ireland's unionists are still experiencing the massive identity crisis about their Britishness that was triggered by the introduction of direct rule in 1972. A classic recent example was the outraged reaction of Belfast's Queen's University's unionist graduates when the university decided to abandon the practice, unknown at most British universities, of playing *God Save the Queen* at graduation ceremonies.

Yet in another sense, among many unionists the deaths and destruction sustained by their community in the violence of 1970-94 (with the British army and the Royal Ulster Constabulary fighting side by side against the Provisional IRA) reforged a sense of British identity, encapsulated by the republican slogan 'Brits Out'. Other unionists, however, were driven by what they saw as British betrayal to express a preference for some sort of Northern Irish independence.

The events of the last quarter of a century may have reshaped, but they have not resolved, the contest of identities. A 1993 survey showed that 69 per cent of Protestants described themselves as British, 15 per cent as Ulster, 11 per cent as Northern Irish and only 2 per cent as Irish. Catholic responses predictably presented a mirror image: 1 per cent described themselves as Ulster, 12 per cent as British, 24 per cent as Northern Irish and 61 per cent as Irish. In 1968, by contrast, 39 per cent of Protestants saw themselves as British and 20 per cent as Irish.

Fionnuala O'Connor's study of Catholics in Northern Ireland is entitled *In Search of a State*. What divides the history of Northern Ireland before 1972 from all that has followed is that, since then, while unionists may have little else in common with their nationalist neighbours, they too are in search of a state with which they can identify.

NORTHERN IRELAND AND THE IRISH STATE

In the Republic the members of each new generation of Protestants have tended to identify themselves more and more as Irish and, while notably less anglophobic and more sympathetic to Britain than many of their compatriots, have largely lost a sense of being British as well as Irish. The contrast with Northern Ireland is striking, especially since the IRA campaign of violence: fewer and fewer members of the majority community there consider themselves as being Irish as well as British and, as the above statistics show, a proportion have developed a separate 'Ulster' identity, in most cases as a supplement to their sense of being British. A previously more relaxed sense of a two-level British/Irish identity among some Northern unionists has crumbled.

This confusion of identity has been aggravated by a growing consciousness that, both culturally and politically, the Britain of today has changed in fundamental and — to many Northern unionists — disturbing ways. For Britain today is no longer infused with the Protestant ethos of earlier generations with which Northern unionists felt at home and which made politicians and people in the other island more instinctively sympathetic with the unionist majority in Northern Ireland than with the Catholic and nationalist minority.

Northern unionist perceptions of the Irish state are shaped by the fact that they still instinctively think of themselves as an embattled minority in the island of Ireland who have been under violent attack by terrorists for the past quarter of a century. This is why they perceive the concern of successive British governments during this period, to hold the balance between the two Northern communities and to devise a settlement acceptable to both, as smacking not just of compromise but of betrayal. Manifest British impatience with what appears to politicians and public opinion in the larger island as unionist intransigence has undermined the sense of security which in the past Northern unionists derived from the British connection. Evident lack of international sympathy with unionists has intensified their sense of insecurity and isolation.

Although Northern nationalists are not faced with the same kind of identity pressures, they, too, are conscious of the fact that there has been a quite radical rethinking of Irish nationalism in the Republic which has important and, for many who have historically expected the Irish state to identify exclusively with their interests and concerns, disturbing implications.

Northern nationalists do not have the same incentive as their Southern counterparts to identify with a reformulated and more pluralist nationalism. In so far as they themselves have to some degree begun to find a new focus of interest in the European Union, this has not, as in the south, entailed a difficult decision in favour of sharing national sovereignty but has been rather a way of escaping, to a marginal degree, from British sovereignty. As for the growth of pluralism in the south, both domestically and in relation to the unionist tradition in the north, the events of the past quarter of a century have if anything tended to push Northern nationalists in the opposite direction to their Southern counterparts. The more purely domestic aspects of the growth of Southern pluralism find only limited echoes amongst Northern nationalists, living in a society whose internal tensions have not encouraged more liberal and open attitudes to other traditions.

All in all, while Northern nationalists' sense of Irish identity has not been threatened in the same way as Northern unionists' sense of Britishness, the events of the past quarter of a century have certainly challenged preconceptions. Another factor disturbing for Northern nationalists is the evident conflict between the cultural and political aspiration to a united Ireland and the economic reality of the extreme dependence of the Northern economy upon massive transfers from Britain within the United Kingdom context. This economic reality must in considerable measure constrain Northern nationalist preferences for a united Ireland as against a United Kingdom.

This is so for two reasons. First, because the Irish state, while it has been catching up with Britain in terms of output and living standards, still has some distance to go before attaining parity with Britain. Second, and more important even if and when such parity is attained, the Irish state's much smaller size in absolute terms — its population is one-sixteenth that of Britain — means that its ability to afford significant financial transfers to the north would never come anywhere near matching that of Britain.

The truth is that in economic terms a union of north and south would be feasible only if and when the level of *per capita* output of Northern Ireland came close enough to that of Britain to make such transfers unnecessary. Given the amount of economic ground lost by Northern Ireland as a result of the violence of the last twenty-five years, decades must elapse before that point could be reached. Thus the IRA campaign has certainly postponed by many years the time when Irish unification could become conceivable even in purely economic terms.

Consciousness of these economic facts inevitably impacts upon Northern nationalists so that they have to operate on two tracks: one of reality and one of aspiration, with complex psychological implications for their sense of identity.

The different identity problems of both communities in Northern Ireland are also quite distinct from the identity problems of the inhabitants of the Irish state and of the people of Britain. The second half of the twentieth century has in fact seen the emergence of what might be described as an archipelago of identity problems in these islands which provide the complex web within which a resolution must be sought of the outstanding relationships between the peoples involved.

◉ CHAPTER 4
ISSUES FOR IRELAND

NORTHERN IRELAND: A NEW RELATIONSHIP

This chapter explores two major issues for Ireland arising from Britain's European prospects and policies: finding a new relationship with Northern Ireland, and Ireland and EMU. The issue of differing British and Irish perspectives on the 1996 intergovernmental conference and on integration generally is examined in subsequent chapters.

There is a profound paradox in the north-south relationship in Ireland. On the one hand the people of the south, in principle committed to the political re-unification of the island, have in practice tended to identify exclusively with their own state. On the other hand the unionists in Northern Ireland, although bitterly opposed to political unification, have in fact never ceased to think of themselves in all-Ireland terms as a threatened minority in the island of Ireland, rather than as a secure majority within a stable Northern Ireland polity. The fact that in each case a deeper psychological attitude diverges so starkly from an overtly stated position has not made it any easier to resolve the problem posed by the division of the island.

For Northern nationalists in particular — all too conscious of the underlying partitionism of so many of their Southern compatriots — this paradox has been a painful and disturbing one. Their sense of insecurity and alienation within a Northern Ireland social and political ethos with which they cannot readily identify has been intensified by this Southern factor. In fairness it has to be said, however, that despite the prevalence of partitionist attitudes in the south, most political leaders in the Irish state since the late 1960s — in contrast to many of their predecessors during the first half-century of independence — have given a high degree of priority to the Northern crisis and have sought to devise peaceful and agreed solutions to the conflict there.

The Sunningdale Agreement of 1973; the New Ireland Forum of 1984 and the negotiation of the Anglo-Irish Agreement of 1985; the handling of the peace process in 1992-23; the negotiation of the Downing Street Declaration and of the Framework Document; and the effort to salvage the peace process after its breakdown early in 1996; all these bear witness to a Southern political commitment that has often run well ahead of public opinion in the Republic. This public opinion has indeed at times shown signs of impatience with the scale of the time and effort invested by successive Irish governments in the Northern problem.

During this quarter of a century a number of preconditions for a durable Northern settlement have gradually emerged. One such precondition was that Southern opinion should shift radically from a commitment by all constitutional parties in the Irish state — as well as the vast majority of the electorate in the south — to an irredentist stance, to an unambiguous rejection of this thesis by all parties and by a similarly overwhelming proportion of public opinion. This shift has in fact taken place: the vast bulk of Southern opinion has become firmly and unambiguously committed to the principle 'no re-unification without the freely given consent of a majority in Northern Ireland' — a consent which it is accepted does not now exist and is unlikely to come into existence in the foreseeable future.

A second precondition for a durable settlement has been an ending of violence: all efforts to secure agreed settlements during the 1970s and 1980s foundered in part at least because of the absence of peaceful conditions. After August 1994 such conditions began to prevail, but were unhappily not sustained, leaving many unionists unconvinced of the permanence of the peace, especially after the resumption of violence in February 1996.

There is a third precondition which the fulfilment of the first two should in time bring into existence. Hitherto the siege mentality of Northern unionism induced by their sense of being under a threat internally from the nationalist minority and externally from the Irish state, has inhibited recognition by them of the fact that, objectively, their own interests require the taking of steps to end the nationalist alienation from a Northern Ireland polity. For it is this nationalist alienation that has been the ultimate source of the instability threatening unionist security.

But, if accompanied by permanent cessation of violence, the erosion of Southern irredentism would create the conditions in which for the first time it would become *possible* to envisage unionists identifying this reality for themselves and in their own interest actively seeking a settlement that would end this nationalist alienation. While in this context the initial reaction to the Framework Document from political unionism was not encouraging, the fact that for the first time a Northern Ireland settlement can now be conceived on terms that would not threaten the identity and security of unionists within the United Kingdom should in time facilitate a rational re-thinking of unionist attitudes towards the nationalist community.

Key elements of a settlement, built on an unambiguous acceptance of the 'consent' principle, and, pending the emergence of such consent, upon explicit acceptance of the continuance of Northern Ireland within the United Kingdom, would need to include:

* The creation of a new north-south relationship which, while unthreatening to unionists, would satisfy nationalists' sense of Irish identity, thus helping them for the first time to identify with a Northern Ireland polity

* Agreement on a process of internal self-government in Northern Ireland that would command the assent of both communities and, as a sub-set of this, the development of a Northern Ireland security system with which both communities could identify.

The second of these objectives relates to the internal situation within Northern Ireland, in which as a neighbour potentially affected by violence in the North, the Irish state has a vital interest, but with which it is not itself *directly* involved. With the first, however, it has a clear responsibility to engage itself.

Most Northern unionists suspect that nationalist pressure for new north-south links involves a hidden agenda: that it is part of a move to draw them subtly and by degrees into a united Ireland, within which they would be a vulnerable minority. That they hold such a belief is, perhaps, scarcely surprising (despite the evidence of changing attitudes in the Republic, dating back at least to the proposal of the Constitution Review Committee of 1966-67 to amend Article 3 of the Constitution), given the Irish state's past irredentism, together with its Supreme Court's interpretation of Articles 2 and 3 of its Constitution as representing a 'constitutional imperative' to seek such re-unification, and, above all, the IRA's prolonged campaign of violence.

Now it may well be the case that some Northern nationalists *do* in fact see north-south links in just such a light. However, the interests of the Irish state do not lie, and are not perceived by its leaders to lie, in such a direction. The interests of that state, and its concern for its own security, lie rather in achieving a permanent cessation of violence in the north and in creating conditions conducive to the subsequent political stability of that part of the island within the United Kingdom.

Such stability clearly depends upon the Northern nationalist minority being able to identify with the political structures of the Northern polity — and politicians in the Republic have come to realise that this will require the creation of north-south links to balance in some measure acceptance by Northern nationalists of the indefinite continuance of Northern Ireland within the United Kingdom.

For some in the south such links are not intrinsically desirable; on the contrary, because they will limit the exercise of the Irish state's sovereign control over certain matters previously under its exclusive authority, such links have hitherto tended to be viewed in the south with little enthusiam — as was evident, for example, in the preparation for the 1973 Sunningdale Conference*.

Up till now Southern support for north-south institutional links has in fact tended to reflect a somewhat reluctant recognition of the need to accept such structures because of their potential stabilising effects within the Northern nationalist community. More recently, however, this rather negative Southern attitude has begun to change because in the context of the peace process expectations developed of a potentially dynamic spin-off emerging from a closer north-south economic relationship.

Thus a more positive climate for an intensified north-south relationship has been created in the Republic because of a combination of a recognition at political level of the positive contribution this could make towards nationalist attitudes to a future stable Northern Ireland polity within the United Kingdom, and a new belief in business circles and amongst public opinion generally that significant economic benefits could accrue to both parts of the island from a north-south link with new institutional elements.

However, perhaps the most interesting feature of the debate on this issue in the aftermath of the cessation of violence in August 1994 has been the reaction of the predominantly unionist *Northern* business community to the possibility of closer north-south institutional links. Thus, despite the clear advance signalling of disapproval of the Framework Document proposals by Northern unionist politicians, it was striking that, in their statements immediately after the publication of that document, all three Northern business organisations — the Northern Ireland CBI, Institute of Directors, and Chambers of Commerce as well as the Northern Committee of the ICTU, were strongly supportive of the kind of north-south links envisaged.

The emergence in the Northern Ireland business world of this positive attitude towards a future closer north-south relationship reflects a recognition in that quarter of the change in the economic balance between

---

* For opposition within the Republic's administration to a transfer of functions to a Council of Ireland, see FitzGerald, *All in a Life*, p. 203.

north and south that has taken place since the 1960s. During this period the Northern economy has been significantly weakened by a number of factors, including the direct and indirect effects of the violence that has afflicted the area. This period has at the same time seen a rapid expansion of the economy of the Republic, the growth of which has since the early 1970s been more rapid than that of any other EU country.

During the past quarter of a century both parts of the island have had to face a rapid decline in vulnerable sectors of industry — vehicles, clothing and textiles — the decline in the latter sector affecting Northern Ireland much more severely. But in the Republic this process has been more than offset by the inflow of foreign investment especially into high-tech sectors, such as electronics and computers. The result has been that manufacturing employment in the Republic is now 10 per cent higher than in 1966 — whereas in Northern Ireland it has fallen by no less than 40 per cent since then.

As a consequence the Republic is now more heavily industrialised than Northern Ireland — in marked contrast to the situation a quarter of a century ago. It is especially notable that whereas in 1966 over half of Irish employment in metals and engineering was in Northern Ireland, today that proportion has fallen to little more than one-quarter.

During the past quarter of a century a huge, but in the long run, unsustainable, expansion of the public sector in Northern Ireland has for the time being offset the employment consequences of the de-industrialisation process there: the public administration and security sector has more than doubled in size and direct employment in the public sector as a whole now accounts for 32 per cent of employment in Northern Ireland, as against 24 per cent in the Republic.

This shift in the economic balance between the two parts of the island, together with the dynamism of the Republic's economy, provides the context for the recent emergence of Northern business interest in a much closer economic relationship between north and south, and for a growing recognition that such a relationship might be facilitated by the creation of new institutional links that did not prejudice Northern Ireland's position within the United Kingdom.

There are three different dimensions to this developing Northern business interest in a new economic relationship between north and south.

First, there is the opportunity for some Northern producers that is provided by the rapid expansion of the market in the Republic and for the Northern tourist industry by a growth in the number of visitors from the south in conditions of peace.

Second, joint promotion outside Ireland of tourism, exports and industrial investment would have clear benefits for the north. The tourism and industrial promotional bodies in the Republic operate on a larger scale, in a more sophisticated way, and with greater success, than those in Northern Ireland, and in these sectors joint promotion on an equitable north-south basis would have clear benefits for the north. It is notable, however, that industrial promotion was excluded from the areas mentioned in the Framework Document for possible joint action; this may well have reflected an unwillingness by the Republic to share its skills in this area — precisely because the north would be likely to be such a clear beneficiary of joint industrial promotion. This is, however, a matter that could be further pursued by Northern negotiators.

In the export promotion area Northern Ireland industry is dependent upon the efforts of the relevant British agencies. While this is clearly advantageous for products such as military equipment, for many other products, and especially for those that have a specifically Irish character, Northern producers would be much better served by a joint north-south body. (It should, perhaps, be said that joint north-south promotions are already being undertaken by the Republic's trade promotion board.)

The third area in which the north could gain from a closer involvement with the Republic is in its relationship with the European Union institutions. A measure of co-operation in respect of this relationship already exists, especially in the agricultural sector. But given the common European Community interests of north and south in relation to a range of EU policies, and the frequent divergence between Northern Irish and British interests in many of these areas, it could be in the interest of Northern Ireland to be able to formulate and pursue common policies with the Irish state on many EU issues.

The common interests of the two parts of the island in many EU matters is in fact recognised and provided for in the Framework Document, and the issues involved are raised in some detail in the concluding section of the paper given by David Fell, Head of the Northern Ireland Civil Service, to the IEA Belfast Conference which is included in the accompanying volume.

David Fell speculates about the merits and feasibility of treating the island of Ireland as a single entity for at least some aspects of the relationship with the European Union. He suggests that Northern Ireland's best interests may be served by aligning in different policy areas with the Irish or British positions, raising the question of whether perhaps 'a Northern Ireland administration might be in the best possible position if it could choose, issue by issue, in some form of ingenious political geometry, whether to align itself with the Irish or British position — the best of all possible worlds'.

Among the questions which he sees as being raised by this possibility are whether and how north-south structures might represent Northern Ireland's interests, given that these structures would be composed of the nationals of two separate member states — and also how the European institutions might react to such a development — or the British Treasury, should Northern Ireland as a result secure an outcome involving a higher level of public expenditure!

Moreover, he goes on to ask: 'Given the problems that might arise in establishing a common north-south position on some issues, could the two administrations contemplate, politically and practically, devolving or delegating the management of the relationship with European institutions to some form of north-south body? ... And, how would all this be affected by the persistence of two separate currencies north and south, should Ireland join the EMU and Britain remain outside?'

The latter question, of course, lies at the heart of the potential dilemma facing the Irish government. But the issues posed by the concept of a north-south body undertaking the management of the Irish relationship with the EU institutions is, perhaps, even more fundamental. For what would be involved here would be a sharing with Northern Ireland of the Irish state's sovereignty in EU matters which could, possibly, indirectly involve a measure of devolution of British sovereignty to the north in respect of some aspects of public expenditure. Whatever about Britain, no greater test could be devised of the Irish State's commitment to achieving a Northern Ireland settlement. Although a sharing of its promotional capacity in relation to tourism and export promotion is evidently acceptable, it would appear — from what is *not* in the Framework Document — that at this stage a sharing of its industrial promotion skills is regarded with less favour. Against that somewhat discouraging background, how willing would the Irish state be to share with Northern Ireland its sovereignty over the most crucial area of its foreign policy?

Most people in the Irish state have given no thought to this issue because the possiblity of having to face the kind of decision thus hinted at by David Fell is currently obscured by the still-negative attitude of political unionism to north-south bodies. But in the period ahead, if the possibility of the disappearance of the perceived threat to the existence of the Northern polity begins to be grasped by political unionism, and with unionist politicians gradually coming under increasing pressure from the Northern business community to take advantage of the potential opportunities provided by a new north-south relationship, they may at some stage find it opportune to raise this issue of sovereignty-sharing by the Irish state in a key area of external policy. From a rational unionist viewpoint that kind of north-south structure would be all gain and no loss — because under David Fell's formula Northern Ireland would continue to have access to Brussels through London where that suited its interests. Thus no price would have to be paid for gaining a crucial influence on the policy of another EU member state, Ireland.

For the Irish state this would be a very big step to take; but its vital interest in a Northern settlement that would ensure peace and stability in that part of the island, together with the embarrassment involved in rejecting a new north-south dimension of considerable substance, might leave it with little option in the matter if and when this issue were to be seriously posed.

In the meantime a somewhat different choice may present itself. If by the Maastricht date of 1999, or perhaps somewhat later, Germany and France agree to the establishment of an Economic and Monetary Union with a single currency, and if Britain does not join that Union, at any rate at the outset, how will the advantages of Irish membership of EMU be balanced against the potentially disruptive effects of two such different currency regimes within the island of Ireland?

IRELAND AND EMU

It is, of course, somewhat over-simplistic to present Ireland's potential foreign policy dilemma solely in terms of a possible British decision not to participate in a single currency.

First of all, there are other aspects of EU policy in respect of which Britain's negative attitude may create problems and pose choices for the Irish state in terms of its possible new relationship with Northern Ireland.

Second, even in the area of monetary policy there are other member states which in terms of their economic performance are unlikely to participate in a single currency at any rate at the outset, so that the choice for Ireland in relation to EMU has wider implications: rather than involving a decision as to whether to remain with Britain outside a monetary union of all the continental EU states, the actual choice might, initially at least, be between two EU blocs — a hard-currency bloc and a soft-currency bloc.

Nevertheless from an Irish viewpoint it is the British decision that is crucial — and in any event almost three-quarters of Irish exports to continental EU countries go to the 'hard currency' group — Germany, France, the Netherlands and Austria, which together represent a bigger market than the UK, although some of these exports are up against competition in these markets from 'soft currency' producers, as is pointed out by Lochlann Quinn in Chapter 8.

The first point that has to be made in this connection is that the potential benefits for Ireland of participating in a single currency within a European monetary union are very great.

At the European level such a currency would provide more favourable economic conditions because it would reduce the present negative impact on overall European growth of uncoordinated national macro-economic policies. Aggregate demand management could thus become more effective and efficient, and in these conditions interest rates should be correspondingly lower. Moreover, because Europe could then speak with a single voice in international discussion of monetary matters, co-ordination between it and Japan and the US would be facilitated, thus contributing to a more stable international exchange rate regime.

So far as Ireland is concerned, because at its present stage of development it has a greater *potential* for growth than its EU partners, it has the greatest interest of any member state in low interest rates — which are widely viewed as the single most important determinant of economic growth.* It is almost impossible to over-estimate the importance of this factor.

Second, within Europe, Ireland, with Belgium/Luxembourg, has by far the highest ratio of trade and external payments to GNP. Even deducting from the value of exports in 1994 the share of export receipts accounted for by profits subsequently remitted abroad, their value in that year was £18.5 bn., and on the same basis total external receipts were £25 bn. The latter figure is equivalent to over 80 per cent of a 1994 GNP of £31 bn.

For an economy as open as the Irish economy, the removal of the obstacle of varying exchange rates and the achievement of exchange rate stability vis-à-vis its principal customers would be of exceptional importance. First of all, this would create a much greater degree of certainty for business, as it would provide conditions favouring trade between states that would benefit consumers through increased competition and greater economies of scale.

---

* The study of EMU by the Economic and Social Research Institute suggests that the level of Irish interest rates within the EMU would initially be 2 per cent and ultimately 1 per cent lower than if it remained outside with Britain (ESRI, 1996).

Moreover, for a country with such a high foreign payments ratio, savings in transaction costs would be especially significant (Chown et al., 1994).

Finally, for individuals crossing borders, the problem of exchange conversion costs would be eliminated. The impact of this in Ireland would be more significant than in many other countries as Irish people have an exceptionally propensity to travel outside their island: in 1995 visits by the 3.6 mn. residents of the Irish State to places outside the island of Ireland totalled 2.55 mn. — two thirds of them to or through Britain — in addition to which, of course, there is substantial cross-border traffic. Total expenditure on travel outside the state is over £1.1 bn. or almost 5 per cent of consumer expenditure — well above the EU average of about 3 per cent.

The disadvantage of participating in a single currency is clearly the loss of the power to influence a state's economy by varying the terms of transactions with other states. In particular, joining a single currency involves giving up the right to devalue in order to compensate for a higher rate of domestic than external inflation — or to match competitive devaluations by significant trading partners. In the past — when Irish inflation rates were higher than those of some continental EU countries, Japan and the US — this was an important economic weapon, although so long as wage rates were closely linked to inflation, such devaluations tended to perpetuate an inflationary spiral as trade unions sought pay increases to offset the consequences of increases in import prices caused by devaluation.

If, however, as now seems to be the case, Ireland has definitively broken out of this vicious spiral and has joined the low inflation countries of the EU (see Table 3 below), the power to devalue in order to offset the consequences of domestically-generated inflation may have lost some of its importance.

TABLE 3: CONSUMER PRICES (ANNUAL PERCENTAGE INCREASES)

	Ireland	Germany	EU
1988	2.1	1.3	3.7
1989	4.1	2.8	5.5
1990	3.3	2.7	5.7
1991	3.2	3.6	5.1
1992	3.1	4.0	4.2
1993	1.4	3.6	3.3
1994	2.3	2.6	3.0
1995	2.5	1.8	3.1
Average	2.75	2.85	4.25
Cumulative Average	24.1	24.6	38.6

Source: OECD, 1995 a

There remains, however, the problem of Ireland's relationship with the UK if that country stayed, whether temporarily or permanently, outside an EMU of which Ireland was a member. As will be seen from Table 4 below, since Ireland joined the Communities the proportion of its exports shipped to the UK has steadily declined — even during the periods when in the mid-1980s and again between 1992 and 1995 the UK growth rate exceeded that of continental EU countries. Nevertheless, that country remains, and will certainly continue to be, Ireland's biggest customer — and also its biggest supplier.

TABLE 4: SHARE OF IRISH TRADE WITH UK

	1972	1983	1993	1995
Imports	51.5*	45.5*	36.0	37.0
Exports	61.5*	37.5*	29.5	26.0

Source: Irish Trade Statistics

* It should be noted that figures for pre-1993 trade with the UK seem to have been exaggerated by one or two percentage points as a result of goods to or from the Far East and the United States trans-shipped in Britain being wrongly attributed to the UK.

In interpreting the figures in Table 4, account should be taken of the fact that in 1995 over £4 bn. of a total merchandise export value of £26.5 bn. will have been accounted for by royalties, licences and profits of multinational manufacturers. As the proportion of the exports to which these profits relate going to the UK was only one-fifth, that country's proportion of Irish export value *excluding this repatriated profit element* was probably somewhat higher than indicated by Table 4, viz. about 27.5 per cent and the other EU proportion was probably about 45 per cent.

On the other hand, as many of these exports were priced in dollars, the proportion of Irish export value that was vulnerable to the sterling/Irish pound exchange rate was probably at or below 25 per cent. This is in fact the average figure that emerges from a mid-1993 Bord Tráchtála Survey of 600 firms responsible between them for 60 per cent of Irish exports; the Survey also showed that one-third of exports were priced in dollars and only one-fifth in EU currencies other than sterling.

However, significantly, this survey also revealed that in some sectors sterling pricing was on a much larger scale. Thus smaller firms, which accounted for one-tenth of exports and one-fifth of employment, quoted in sterling for 36 per cent of their exports — a figure that in certain sectors, employing about 5 per cent of the manufacturing labour force, even went as high as 60 per cent.

The vulnerability of many such firms in traditional sectors of industry to a fall in the value of sterling is greatly increased by a lack of sophistication: one-third of them had no foreign currency bank accounts and almost two-thirds failed to hedge against their foreign exchange exposure — despite the fact that forward buying of sterling for a year ahead would provide a very considerable protection against a fall in the value of that currency.

This is so because under normal circumstances — which as it happens did not apply in 1992 — domestic and export prices in Britain would rise significantly in the twelve months after a devaluation. As a result, in addition to providing a breathing space, hedging would help ensure that by the time an Irish firm eventually had to face the effects of a sterling devaluation, a significant part of the benefit accruing to UK traders would have been eroded.

A high proportion of Irish exports to the UK are goods manufactured by domestic producers with lower profit margins, and these goods also have a much higher labour content than the exports of foreign multinationals. This is evident from the fact that although these firms accounted for 25 per cent of manufactured exports in 1990, they employed 45 per cent of the workers then engaged in the export sector. And in that year these Irish-owned firms shipped 43 per cent of their goods to the UK, as against 22.5 per cent in the case of the foreign-owned exporting firms.

On the import side there is also a potential vulnerability to a sterling devaluation that could reduce the prices of consumer goods from the UK — for in 1995, 55 per cent of imports of consumer goods came from the UK, as against 33 per cent of materials for further processing and 20 per cent of capital goods. However, it is notable that during the 1992-93 crisis there were few signs of such price competition from British goods; UK exporters to Ireland seem to have preferred to take their advantage from the devaluation in the form of wider profit margins.

Clearly, therefore, Irish participation in a European single currency from which the UK excluded itself, retaining the possibility of devaluing vis-à-vis the European currency, could pose potentially serious economic problems for Ireland.

On the other hand self-exclusion from a European monetary union could carry a heavy penalty for Ireland in terms of higher interest rates, reduced competitiveness and a consequent less attractive climate for investment. A negative signal would be given to financial markets, which would have implications for the country's credit rating, and would involve the loss of much of the hard-won ground gained over the past decade.

Given the benefits for Ireland of participation in a European Monetary Union with a single currency, and the losses that might be incurred by staying out of such a union, it is obviously desirable that in the years immediately ahead policies be pursued that would leave open the possibility of EMU participation when the moment of decision arrives.

This requires: (1) That steps be taken to ensure that when the time comes Ireland meets the criteria for membership; (2) That domestic policies be pursued to minimise problems which could arise from a combination of Irish membership and British non-participation, followed by a subsequent devaluation of sterling against the single currency.

STEPS TO ENSURE THE CRITERIA ARE MET

Ireland currently meets most of the criteria for EMU membership including the inflation rate and interest rate level — and maintaining this performance in the couple of years ahead should not pose serious problems. The only problem that could arise here — which would be likely to affect other EMU aspirants also — is the possibility that three of these states would achieve inflation rates below 1 per cent thus bringing even a 2.5 per cent rate of inflation outside the range of the criteria.

As for its debt/GDP ratio, between 1987 and 1994 this fell from 117 per cent to 81.5 per cent and is expected to fall to around 75 per cent by the end of 1996 — a performance that has not been paralleled in any other EU country and one which reflects a combination of a high economic growth rate and a low rate of exchequer borrowing in recent years. With economic growth at over 7 per cent in 1994 and 1995 and forecast at 6 per cent in the current year (Dept. Finance 1996, p.6), and 4.5 per cent in subsequent years (ESRI, 1994, Table 4.3, p. 47); with a borrowing target of 1.8 per cent in 1996 which is unlikely to be allowed to rise above this level in the years ahead and may indeed be reduced; and with inflation currently in the region of 2 per cent and unlikely to rise significantly above this level, the debt/GDP ratio would be at or below 70 per cent in 1998. At such a level, and having achieved such a rapid and sustained record of reduction throughout the preceding decade, the Irish debt/GDP ratio would on any reasonable assessment be judged to have been 'sufficiently diminishing and approaching the reference value at a satisfactory pace' (Maastricht Treaty Article 104c. Par. 2), especially as the continuance of these conditions over a prolonged period would eventually reduce this ratio to around 30 per cent (ESRI, 1996, p. 79).

The Maastricht Treaty also requires that in order to qualify for EMU membership in 1999 a country's currency must remain in the ERM band from 1 January 1996 onwards. Since the re-alignment of early 1993 the Irish pound has at all times remained within 5 per cent of the central rate, i.e. well within the wider band that has existed since the currency crisis of 1992. It is, of course, impossible to predict what pressures on the Irish currency may emerge during the years immediately ahead, but short of a new crisis of the kind that blew up in 1992, the Irish pound should not come under the kind of pressure that would make it difficult for it to remain within the present band. Clearly the Central Bank will be concerned so to manage the currency that it meets the EMU criteria in this respect.

STEPS TO PREPARE FOR POST-EMU PRESSURES SHOULD BRITAIN NOT JOIN THE SINGLE CURRENCY

Relevant Moves at European Level
Before looking at specific measures that could be taken to prepare for the contingency of British self-exclusion from an EMU in which Ireland participated, it should, perhaps, be remarked that this is not just an Irish problem. The large devaluations between summer 1992 and summer 1995 of currencies such as the lira (30 per cent) and the peseta (15 per cent) have created problems for their EU partners, leading to the decision of the Cannes European Council to ask the Commission to report speedily on action that might be taken to deal with asymmetric shocks and to establish a robust framework for ordering future exchange rate relationships between an EMU core and other EU members not participating, in its early stages at least, in the single currency — what has come to be called 'co-habitation'. Ireland's specific problem in relation to a stronger and historically dominant partner currency is not unique either: Finland in relation to Sweden and Portugal in relation to Spain have closely associated dilemmas.

The problems posed for a common market by devaluations on this scale, which may confer competitive advantages on the countries concerned, have highlighted the severity of the problems posed by trying to operate a single market *without* a single currency — but also the extreme difficulty of getting all participants in such a single market lined up together at the same moment in a fit shape to merge their currencies successfully.

It would be unwise to expect too much to emerge from this study being undertaken by the Commission; it will not be easy to solve the conundrum posed by the need to establish a stable relationship between a single EMU currency and a major EU currency, such as sterling, which does not participate in it.

Steps Ireland Could Take

If Ireland is to have the capacity to make a free choice in due course between joining the EMU or remaining outside with Britain — and Northern Ireland — steps would have to be taken to introduce greater flexibility into its economy. Even before we reach the point where the EMU decision has to be taken, such flexibility may be needed in order to cope with any divergences that may occur between sterling and the DM during this intervening period.

One part of the problem is the need to tackle the redistributive effects of an appreciation in the real exchange rate that would arise from a sudden and major sterling devaluation. This appreciation would increase the living standards of those remaining in employment at the expense of a loss of jobs by a minority of workers in some more vulnerable industries.

At the same time the need to improve national competitiveness in order to be ready to absorb the shock of a sudden and major sterling devaluation before or after entering the EMU without Britain increases the urgency of reforms in the tax system designed to phase out poverty traps, as well as the need to complete the process of rationalisation of utilities in order to bring costs into line with those of our European competitors, and in particular Britain.

Finally, it would be important that an element of flexibility be built into the public finances, and possibly also future pay rounds, so that in the event of a sterling devaluation the government could play its part in easing the transition to a new exchange rate situation. The gradual building up of such a contingency provision is in any event necessary in order to have domestic funds available to substitute for the inevitable reduction in EU structural funds after 1999.

If steps along the lines just suggested could be taken, then Ireland could enjoy freedom of choice in relation to EMU membership when the time comes, even if, as seems very possible, the UK does not join, at any rate at the outset. Without such steps, and unless a broader European solution to the 'co-habitation' problem can be found, participation in a single currency without Britain would clearly carry considerable risks for the Irish economy.

This chapter has examined how the Republic's relation with Northern Ireland and its decision on joining an EMU will be affected by Britain's European policies. The conclusion to Part I of this book and subsequent chapters in Part II explore in more detail how Britain's approach to European integration compares with that of Ireland and its expected impact on Irish policies.

▣ 5 Conclusion

The Implications for Ireland of Britain's European Policies

It cannot be assumed that even if Britain's economic interests, as articulated by its main interest groups and established by objective analysis, point in the direction of greater European integration, political decisions to pursue those interests will be taken rapidly or categorically. If, as we argue, Britain faces a crisis of identity in its global, transatlantic and European relations after the end of the Cold War, as well as in its internal political structure and its relations with Ireland, then this could be a traumatic and protracted period in which political conclusions may well follow economic interests, assuming they do so at all, only with considerable delay.

The present period is as important a transition as any in Britain's modern history. It could take at least 10-15 years to play out, during which time Irish decision-makers will have to make working assumptions about the direction of British policy and about the extent to which it will have to face stop-go political shifts as well as the more familiar stop-go shifts of economic policy. Even then, we cannot assume that the change of policy will be unidirectional. Strategic decisions, such as Scottish and Welsh devolution, if taken by a possible Labour government, could be reversed by a returning Conservative one. This would be turbulent and could provoke more radical consequences, such as, for example, a surge of support for Scottish independence. Britain is therefore likely to remain, in Stephen George's term, an 'awkward' partner — both of Europe and Ireland — over this middle- to long-term period. Irish policy-makers could face a more prolonged period of transition — two to three parliamentary terms — than might have been expected simply from the need to decide on EMU.

Such a time-frame must also inform discussion of the relationship between the government's Northern Ireland and European policies. To what extent, for example, does a north-south convergence of policy, arising from greater insular integration, necessitate greater east-west integration between Britain and Ireland over, say, 10-15 years? As Dublin negotiates with London and

Unionism over a period of several years, there could be some pull back towards anglocentric outcomes and away from continental ones.

Over the next five years the balance of interest and perception on EU matters for Ireland will also be changing in a profound manner. In its report on the inter-governmental conference the Institute for European Affairs has painted a 'malign scenario' for Ireland in the following way:

> 'The majority of member-states would decide to deepen the integration process by, for example, extending qualified majority voting, adding new competences, confirming the deadlines for EMU and fleshing out the end objectives of European Union. The UK, and possibly some others, would refuse to agree to these measures or objectives or both. The impasse would be broken by a formula whereby two or more tiers of membership would result. In that case Ireland would have to choose between two options: continue its membership of the EU core group or elect to accompany the UK (and perhaps others) into some as yet unknown relationship with that core' (IEA, 1995, p.246).

The report concludes that 'since either option would carry penalties, the obvious ploy is to avoid making a choice' by Ireland proposing or supporting more unitary models in the negotiations and using its influence and alliances to head-off such a stark set of options. From the perspective of this study, it can be seen that such an effort might have to be sustained over quite a prolonged period. Possible changes in the Common Agricultural Policy, in the flow of structural fund transfers to Ireland, in the EU budget and in European security arrangements could shift the balance of Irish public perceptions of the EU, conceivably in a more anglocentric direction. Similar pressures would be exerted by the opening up of integration on this island. Depending, therefore, on how Britain's own crisis of identity works out, concealed within it are significant implications for Ireland.

It is also clear that a dialectic of dependence-independence-inter-dependence in the totality of relations between Ireland and Britain must inform these choices. The historical cycle which saw greater Irish economic independence from Britain achieved through Irish EC/EU membership could be coming to an end. There may be a conflict of interest involved between a Britain which sees an opportunity to reestablish a new Irish economic and political dependence and an Irish aspiration towards a new interdependence within the wider European scene. It is clearly in Ireland's interest to have Britain as a full and willing participant in the EU. It is in Britain's interest to attract Ireland back towards her orbit, in order to avoid isolation and to cultivate alliances with a neighbouring small state, as well as to maintain and deepen relations with an important trading partner. London has never lost the habit of looking at Ireland as a whole and this is now all the more apparent in the three-stranded talks. One can see a vocabulary emerging to describe it, not least the alleged 'satellite' status of the pound against sterling and renewed discussion of Ireland's role as a regional section of the larger economy of these islands, notably in the retail sector.

There is a contradictory pull between the Republic's political imperative in seeking a Northern Ireland settlement, which would bring it closer to the UK, and the economic imperative to join an inner core group launching the transition to EMU. This will be reinforced by the dichotomy between indigenous and multinational industry in the Republic; the labour-intensive indigenous industry is much more attracted to the British market — and up to the mid-1980s was encouraged by exchange rate policy to restrict investment to these islands. The debate on Ireland's early participation in EMU tends to be influenced by these economic groupings, with representatives of indigenous and smaller industry, and now the Irish Farmers' Association, more cautious about entering EMU if Britain does not join, whereas the more international sector of the economy is happier to proceed independently of Britain. The interdependence of the Irish and British economies is now better appreciated by policy-makers, however.

Much depends on an analysis of where the British economy is going. One should beware of assumptions that it is still in decline and that the best course for Irish policy should be to escape dependence on such a terminally-ill economy. Suppose, on the other hand, that it became the most competitive economy in Europe, Britain would then attract even more inward investment — and so would a peaceful Northern Ireland which has a lower cost base than the Republic, and which could well be in competition rather than in harmony with Dublin. Would it follow perhaps that such a strengthened British economy would see sterling strengthen as the markets responded to better performance? Or would it instead be penalised by not participating in a monetary union?

Much depends also on the economic model adopted by Britain — is it a competitive devaluation one, or is it one that can hold its own in competition with the social market economies of western Europe? It is precisely this uncertainty that underlies the opt-out from EMU of which Mr Major makes so much: has the institutional shift in the market place during the 1980s gone far enough to guarantee competitiveness in a stable monetary framework? Or does Britain need to maintain policy flexibility for another five or more years?

The papers in the accompanying volume by Colm McCarthy and Philip Halpin are useful for this discussion. McCarthy points out that a crucial factor is the relationship of sterling to the deutschmark — had the Irish pound not devalued against the DM on eight separate occasions, roughly every two years since 1979, following sterling, the punt-sterling exchange rate today would be 1.69. Lochlann Quinn makes a similar point in Chapter 8. The crucial issue here will be how to create a stable relationship between DM/sterling/US$ which will in turn stabilise the smaller currencies in an EMU. The dollar is important because its movements disproportionately affect those of sterling. Ensuring stability in euro/US$ relations will require much closer EU concertation with the US authorities than has yet been contemplated on either side of the Atlantic.

There is a methodological problem running through any discussion of Britain's prospects and policies: at crucial points one's conclusions will mirror the contours of the ideological and political debate in Britain itself. This rages around the necessity/danger of constitutional and institutional change; the achievement/non-achievement of a competitive economy and the escape from economic decline; the desirability/danger of isolation in Europe. The important point here is to identify all the possible outcomes rather than unthinkingly succumb to one particular model or scenario.

We do not know and cannot predict the outcome of forthcoming political conflict, such as whether Michael Portillo, John Redwood or someone like them might emerge as Tory leader should Mr Major suffer an election defeat. The Tory party is definitely hardening up its nationalist approach as the election nears. After an election it could split; if that possibility loomed, would it then opt for a healer or a warrior? The internal, just as much as the external, conflict will dictate British policy, which may therefore be politically driven over the medium- to long-term. Internally this situation is reminiscent of the Home Rule issues of the period 1885-1914. Externally Britain is tempted to seek to return to its classic European position as head of an alliance opposed to the strongest European power, i.e. Germany — but with what allies? Ireland faces difficult choices in any polarisation of EU politics between Britain and Germany. The implications of this are explored further in the following Chapters and in the Summing Up and Conclusions of this book.

Part 2
Commentaries

◼ CHAPTER 6
BRITAIN IN EUROPE: THE POLITICS OF IDENTIFICATION

PAUL GILLESPIE

God has ceased to be British, and Providence no longer smiles.

— Linda Colley

BRITAIN'S CRISIS OF IDENTITY

Britain is facing a crisis of identity after the end of the Cold War. Debate on this question has become more and more explicit and now suffuses much of its political discourse. Four rearrangements are under way, each of which will have a bearing on its international and national postures and role. They are: changing global and transatlantic relations after the end of the Cold War; changing political and economic relations between Britain and Europe; pressure to change Britain's own constitutional structures and political institutions; and changing relations between Britain and Ireland.

Given their interpenetration and accumulating intensity, it is realistic to speak of a crisis of identity, both internally and externally. This has created a 'crisis of identification' in Britain's relations with its European neighbours. The term describes both external and internal difficulties and moments of decision, which are appropriate in analysing the new politics of European interdependence. It has been used to good effect in the analysis of Canadian federalism, 'in the sense that the citizens who advance demands cannot identify with and give their allegiance to the Canadian federation until their cultural differences are recognised and affirmed in the constitution and legal and political structures of Canada' (Tully, 1995 a, p. 78).

The concept seems applicable in a wider setting of Britain's relations with Europe, which are beset with uncertainty about the recognition of national identity. Hence the stress on subsidiarity and diversity in its leaders' political rhetoric. Rather than treating this as a rationalisation for semi-detachment or semi-commitment in the classical British tradition of relations with the continent, it should be recognised as a dilemma which might best be addressed by examining how and whether the vocabulary and institutions standardly associated with the European Union and the nation state should be revised in order to accommodate demands for recognition of national as well as cultural diversity.

As Tully points out: 'Many culturally diverse, post-colonial societies face similar crises of political identification in one form or another. Whether in former Yugoslavia, Israel-Palestine, the multiculturalism and multinationalism of the United Kingdom, the European Union, the Maori of New Zealand, or the culturally and linguistically diverse United States, the politics of cultural recognition is one of the most common and difficult problems of the present age' (ibid, p. 80).

He suggests that 'deep diversity', a term coined by the political theorist Charles Taylor, is useful as a means of tapping into the multiple political identities characteristic of many of the most developed societies caught between the nation state and an emerging international society. This would replace identity as uniformity, homogeneity and assimilation with a concept that stresses family resemblance, criss-crossing similarity and difference — and that would allow for the legitimate emergence of multiple identities and citizenships that better express the realities of today's world. Standard nationalist and imperialist usage has suppressed this type of pluralism. Three constitutional principles, of mutual recognition, continuity and consent, that were central to consitutional theory when it was being constructed in the seventeenth and eighteenth centuries but which were disregarded in national and imperial practice, need to be resurrected to cater for the contemporary world's demands for cultural recognition and diversity (Gillespie, 1996 b; Tully, 1995 b).

It would be an appropriate irony if the working out of Britain's own relations with Europe should make its contribution to transcending many of the polarities its own imperial and national history and political practice have helped to create. The point applies *a fortiori* to relations between Britain and Ireland. The issues are not confined to Britain and its international relations, although the British ones are very distinctive, given its particular history. Similar crises of identity affect other developed nation states in Europe — Spain, Italy and France, for example — which confront the twin disintegrative forces of fragmentation and globalisation, and the need to absorb migrants from their former colonies (Schnapper, 1994). One of the most interesting and challenging tasks facing the European Union is to find the appropriate vocabulary and concepts to describe its own original approach to this task. The passionate political debate over Europe in Britain has been as much about its own future as that of Europe as a whole; but it does suggest models of international association and integration that can teach other states — a fact that is easily obscured by the overlay of introversion in which it is often cast. Jeremy Black concludes his illuminating study of Britain's historical relations with the continent of Europe on a similar note: 'In defending the configuration and continuity of British practices, politicians are fighting not for selfish national interests but for the sense of the living past that is such a vital component of a people's understanding, acceptance and appreciation of their own society and identity' (Black, 1994, p. 270).

HISTORICAL AND POLITICAL PERSPECTIVES

There is a clear continuity between Britain's classical posture in relation to Europe and that of today. The eighteenth- and nineteenth-century British model sought to create a stable balance among the continental powers, which would allow Britain to pursue its worldwide imperial interests hindered as little as possible by European competitors or continental entanglements. London avoided lasting alliances with individual European states, instead concentrating on supporting a balance of power against first Spain and France and then Germany (Meier-Walser, 1994; Kissinger, 1995 b). The importance of military mobilisation against the great European Catholic powers — and therefore against their supporters in Ireland — was central to the construction of British identity as a Protestant state in the seventeenth and eighteenth centuries. In this sense, Europe — and Ireland — became Britain's 'Others' (Colley, 1992; Marquand, 1995, p. 22).

The classical statement of the balance of power policy was made by Lord Palmerston to the House of Commons on 1 March, 1848: 'We have no eternal allies and we have no perpetual enemies. Our interests are eternal and perpetual and those interests it is our duty to follow.' It was encapsulated memorably by Sir Eyre Crowe as follows: 'The maintenance of this balance by throwing her weight now on this scale and now on that, but ever on the side opposed to the political dictatorship of the strongest single state or group at a given time' (quoted in Blair, 1995 c).

The system of relations between the five European powers, Britain, Russia, Germany, France and Austria-Hungary, constructed in the post-Napoleonic period, underwent substantial development as the century developed. It was radically changed towards its end as each of the powers took to the competitive road of the new global imperialism and then constructed a series of rigid alliances and an arms race which rendered balance of power diplomacy increasingly inflexible (Kissinger, 1995 b, pp. 166-200; Kennedy, 1988, pp. 194-256; Hobsbaum, 1987, pp. 302-327). The system proved incapable of coping with these strains and broke down into global war. Likewise, in the 1920s and 1930s there was a failure to reconstruct a balance of power system, and the alternative League of Nations system of collective security also failed, with the same result.

Dispute continues among historians and international relations specialists as to whether balance of power systems per se, or the fact that they broke down because they were unable to contain the inherently expansionist tendencies of some players, are to blame for the collapse into war (Howard 1994). These methodological disputes are more relevant to current European politics than they might seem at first glance. They pit proponents of the state system of international relations, 'realists' or 'neo-realists', against those who argue that interdependence and globalisation have fundamentally altered the balance of power assumptions on which nation state-centred theories are based. Where one stands on these arguments may substantially affect one's attitude to further, quasi-federal, European integration — and one's attitude to British insistence that the traditional sovereign role of the nation state can be preserved.

In this century, then, Britain remained undefeated and unconquered, unlike France, Italy and Germany, as Langellier points out in his contribution to the accompanying volume of seminar papers. Jean Monnet put it like this in his memoirs: 'Britain had not been conquered or invaded; she felt no need to exorcise history' (Barnett, 1995, p. 116). As a result of these historical experiences and in addition to the insularity that is geographically fixed, Britain has had a very different attitude towards pooling sovereignty and creating supranational institutions — and also towards radical reform of its own governmental and civic institutions.

GLOBAL AND TRANSATLANTIC RELATIONS

Instead of defeat Britain suffered relative post-imperial decline. This was masked for many of its population by its post-war special but dependent relationship with the United States, 'a junior partner in an orbit of power predominantly under American aegis', as a British diplomat put it in 1945 (Curtis, 1995, p. 146). The transfer of hegemony from London to Washington was one of the most important in the history of the great powers (Taylor, 1993 b). It was traumatic for those involved. The US pursued a ruthless objective of prising open access to British markets organised in the sterling bloc and imperial trade preferences, assets and colonies.

Lend-Lease aid was secured strictly against the surrender of bases, the forced sale of British companies in the US, Canada and Latin America, restrictions on exports, and the removal of currency and trade controls. It was cancelled precipitously a week after the end of the war with Japan, a decision 'which fell on Whitehall like a V2, without warning', according to Alan Bullock's biography of Bevin, and gave great trouble to the financially-stretched new Labour government. A further emergency loan negotiated in December 1945 reinforced US conditions for access to British imperial and colonial markets and assets and insisted on sterling convertibility. As Michael Howard has put it: 'The Congress of the United States saw no reason to do any favours to a former ally which appeared to be squandering its loan money on socialist experiments at home and the maintenance of imperial hegemony abroad' (Howard, 1995, p. 707). The terms of the junior partnership negotiated between London and Washington included continuing close military, security and intelligence cooperation, which was put readily at the disposal of the new hegemon, especially in colonial and Third World settings.

Some authors suggest that Britain's activity in creating the Cold War between the USSR and the US was an essential means of maintaining its role as a front-rank power (Ryan, 1982; Taylor, 1990). Others, among them a lively group of (mainly conservative) revisionist historians, are re-evaluating Britain's war and post-war record, especially relations with the US, in the light of this humiliating transfer of power (d'Ancona, 1994; Porter, 1995). Several writers argue that Britain should have settled with Hitler in the spring of 1941, allowing him to concentrate on defeating Russia, and Britain to retain its empire and avoid going into debt with the Americans (Charmley, 1994). The attack on Churchill's role broke a 40-year-old taboo and is a clear signal of a more fundamental change in public attitudes towards Britain's place in the world.

It serves to highlight the continuing belief in the British governing class after the war that, despite the shift of power to the US, the empire and the global reach it represented were still fundamental interests and elements of its identity as a 'world island'. In a famous memorandum to the incoming Labour government in 1945, Lord Keynes warned that the resources were simply not there to sustain Britain's great imperial role without deep borrowing from the US. This echoed continuing warnings from the Imperial General Staff that Britain could not afford to fight a war on two continental fronts — a classical example of imperial overstretch (Kennedy, 1988, pp. 423-25).

It was nonetheless decided to attempt to hold on to much of the empire, despite the concession of partitioned independence to India, Pakistan, Israel and Jordan. This locked Britain into a continuing presence in the Middle and Far East and Africa which was not abandoned until after the Suez humiliation (again at US hands) in 1956. Inevitably, this coloured attitudes towards the early projects of European integration, which were treated with a combination of indifference and hostility. The feeling was reciprocated. Monnet noted after the Coal and Steel Community had been decided upon that 'the essential point had been won, irrevocably. Europe was on the move. Whatever the British decided would be their own affair' (Barnett, 1995, p. 116).

The very success of the subaltern special relationship with the US meant that there was in successive post-war governments a failure to perceive, or a systematically delayed perception of the consequences of post-imperial decline for British interests in global and European terms (Wallace, 1992; George, 1994). The management of decline was an explicit (if for the most part exclusively internally acknowledged) objective of the Foreign Office. The following outburst of a British ambassador somewhere in central Europe captures the mood well: 'For 40 years, we have been the rearguard. For 40 bloody years, we in the Foreign Office have covered Britain's slow, step-by-step retreat from power and influence. And we have never allowed that retreat to become a rout or to lose the appearance of dignity and purpose. Does anyone appreciate what we have done for Britain? Nobody — and that is precisely the measure of our success!' (Ascherson, 1995 a).

At a joint FCO/RIIA conference on 'Britain in the World' on 29 March 1995 the Foreign Secretary, Douglas Hurd argued that the task of managing decline was fully accomplished by the mid-1980s, that the special relationship with the US is now redundant, having been overtaken by a continuing close alliance, but that it has taken a decade to come fully to terms with these facts in European as well as global terms (Hurd, 1995 c).

Dean Acheson's remark in 1962 therefore remains apposite: 'Great Britain has lost an empire but has not yet found a role.' Hurd was impatient to emphasise the necessity of holding on to the continuing assets of Britain's continuing liberal internationalism, including its military and security strength, its seat on the Security Council, its trading and investment skills, its worldwide cultural and linguistic reach and its inherited global perpectives. Cable listed them out in a paper prepared for that conference: 240,000 servicemen and women; 215 overseas missions; world-class companies in chemicals, pharmaceuticals, oil, food-processing, aerospace; strong service sectors in advertising, retail communications, aviation and music publishing; English spoken by some 20 per cent of the world's population, the official or semi-official language in 70 countries and undoubtedly the most important world language; the BBC's worldwide audience of some 130 million listeners (Cable, 1995 b). To them can be added its performances in the economic and financial fields: it is a nation of traders and travellers, which exports 25 per cent of its manufacturing output; it is the third largest outward investor, the largest in the US; its banking and financial services are truly global in reach, in keeping with a long history of strength in these respects (Sutherland, 1996). Argument continues over whether post-war economic decline has been reversed, specifically by the radical policies followed under the Thatcher government. The evidence is mixed, with Britain performing well on some criteria, more weakly on others (McRae, 1995 b); in several important respects the jury is still out (Crafts, 1992, 1996, 1996 a).

Whether Britain can hold on to these assets depends on how it responds politically to its current dilemmas, internal and external. There is still a widespread perception in the US, to quote Charles Kupchen, senior fellow in European studies at the Council on Foreign Relations in New York, that 'Britain has not responded very well to this diminution of its role. One option would have been to accept it; another to make your influence felt by playing the role of spoiler. They've done that with the United States and Europe. They end up making it worse than if they had just let geopolitics take its course. They react in such a way that it pisses people off' (Black, 1995 a).

There has also been a British failure to perceive, or a delayed perception of, changing US interests in EU integration after the end of the Cold War. The US attitude towards European integration has become more clearcut in the past few years. Throughout the Cold War it was seen as a means of reinforcing western European solidarity, but strictly within the limits set by US hegemony in the political-military sphere. 'Western Europe was America's Europe' (Wallace, 1995 a, pp. 59-60). The new position reflects Washington's conviction that Europe must now take on more responsibility for its own security as the US reorients towards the Pacific and the Americas and comes to terms with its own new role. There is a much greater readiness to reach a partnership arrangement with a strengthened EU across the broad span of political, economic and security affairs, as was formalised at the signing of the US-EU New Transatlantic Agenda in Madrid on 3 December, 1995 (Eizenstadt, 1995 b). The US itself has lost hegemony after the successive blows of relative industrial and economic decline and military overstretch, notwithstanding the collapse of the Soviet Union. It requires a different constellation of alliances with its main allies (Cox, 1995).

The developing US-EU relationship is not without tension, based as it is on an assymetrical interaction between a fully developed US federal system and an EU association of states undecided as yet on whether to develop in a classical federal direction. EU competences are varied, strong on trade and agriculture, much less developed on foreign, monetary and fiscal policy and on justice and home affairs. Precisely because these are contested among the member-states involved in the 1996 IGC, there are opportunities for the US to exploit differences of opinion among them if this suits its interests. Many French commentators are convinced that precisely this is happening on monetary union, from a combination of 'Anglo-Saxon' and Eurosceptic opponents whose interests may be affected by the loss of the dollar's role as a reserve currency (Gillespie, 1995 b; Pfaff, 1995).

The same applies in the security field, where there is a reluctance on the part of the Europeans to take on a regional military role, combined with an evident frustration in Washington that they have not done so. The consequences could be seen in the reassertion of US military thrust and brokerage that brought together the Dayton accords to end the Bosnian war. Similar tensions underlie the discussion about whether and how to enlarge NATO without antagonising the Russians. The British have been reluctant, but not vocally so, about this; the Germans and French have a similar approach. This may be why France signalled a readiness to rejoin the NATO integrated command in January 1996 — as much to influence a new alignment from within as to change the basic orientation of its foreign policy for the past 30 years.

There is a congruence between the French and US positions, but not between those of Washington and London, on Germany's role in the new European order. Washington believes that Germany has come to the centre of affairs. The best means of accommodating it is to have a wider and deeper European Union, officially seen as decisively in the US security interest (Eisenstadt, 1994 a; Frankenberger, 1996; Kissinger, 1995 a; Wallace, 1995 b). 'There is a simple observation that if Britain's voice is less influential in Paris or Bonn, it is likely to be less influential in Washington,' was how Mr Raymond Seitz put it on the occasion of his retirement as US ambassador to the court of St James in 1994.

Changing transatlantic relations after the end of the Cold War, as we have seen, mean that Washington's interests propel it much more in favour of European integration rather than relying on a special relationship with Britain to fulfil its security interests. The EU gives it a 'single address', all the more important in dealing with worldwide uncertainties now that the bipolar east-west axis has gone. It embeds Germany in Europe within a Franco-German axis; it accommodates Europe's democratic impulse. Mr Malcolm Rifkind's enthusiasm to reinvigorate the transatlantic relationship is expressed in European rather than exclusively British terms, but may well underestimate Washington's more positive orientation towards the EU.

The option of keeping Europe at arm's length which appealed to Britain during the imperial and Cold War periods has become redundant as relative political and economic decline has proceeded. Insofar as US pressure is a determining factor on British policy it would tend to propel London more decisively towards the heart of Europe. A free-standing role, as advocated notably by David Howell, chairman of the House of Commons Foreign Affairs Committee, is seen by many as no longer realistic, given changing British economic interests, and would not be supported by the Americans (Howell, 1995 a, b).

This is not to deny that Britain has extensive international economic, political and cultural interests far beyond Europe, but to acknowledge that without influence in the heart of Europe it would not be able to defend them most effectively. It faces a very difficult choice between becoming the Hong Kong of Europe, through exploiting competitive advantages in deregulation, free trade, labour market flexibility and international investment, or getting to the heart of a Europe that must deepen if it is to remain coherent. Resisting such a stark choice, the British government proposes instead a variable model.

Dr Kissinger, in his address to the FCO/RIIA seminar, spelled out the lessons of recent geopolitical change. The US needs a special relationship with Europe as a whole, not with any one of its larger states. Britain has an essential role to play in forging a new relationship, he said. While war between strategic partners in Europe is inconceivable, rendering the former balance of power model of intra-European relations itself redundant, the fact remains that the balance of *global* power, with six or seven centres, continues to mirror the nineteenth-century European pattern (Kissinger, 1995 a, b). Commentators have welcomed the opening-up of these issues, but the British government may not relish the possible direction the debate might take. In an editorial *The Independent* (29 March 1995), asked the following questions: 'Can Britain afford the Trident nuclear deterrent and keep it out of strategic arms negotiations? Is our permanent seat on the Security Council worth the cost in international commitment? Is it truly the wish of the British people that our troops should be promoted as if commodities for export?'

The *Financial Times* was even more blunt: 'While the Cold War continued, a UK shorn of empire could cling to the remnants of greatness as the loyal henchman of the US. That role, too, is at an end.' Britain faces a choice between being a 'modest, self-governing offshore island' shorn of international representative status, converging towards a role 'similar to that of, say, Korea', or accepting a role in the EU that multiplies influence but requires shared sovereignty. After its relatively short-lived role as 'arbiter of Europe, ruler of the seas, imperial power workshop of the world and its financial centre' Britain now needs to come to terms with, in Adam Smith's words, 'the real mediocrity of her circumstances' as a small island off the coast of Europe (Editorial, 27 June, 1995).

In contrast *The Times* argues that the 'edge of Europe' is 'a more comfortable place to be in than the heart' — in fact with EMU 'the heart of Europe is no longer a friendly cliché; it is a trap,' which does not suit British interests (Editorial, 13 June, 1995). Cable told the FCO/RIIC conference that the 'hollowness of Britain's belief that it has a special relationship with the US has been brutally exposed' in the row over Gerry Adams's visit to the White House. The way in which Irish-American and Anglo-American interests intersected and competed under the Clinton presidency brought it forcefully and painfully home to British opinion that the special relationship with Washington as defined throughout the Cold War had come to an end. It had lost its salience when they tried to pull levers of power to little avail in order to prevent Mr Adams from travelling to the US (O'Grady, 1996; O'Clery, 1996; Guelke, 1996). The rift was even more apparent over Bosnia, which was in several respects reminiscent of the Suez affair (Cox, 1995, pp. 78-9; Traynor, 1995 a; Cable 1995 b). The sense of a transatlantic identity in crisis pervaded the British media in 1994-96 and as we have seen has provoked a far-reaching reappraisal of the historical record as well.

BRITAIN AND EUROPE

The continuity of British attitude and policy is more visible after the end of the Cold War, despite the end of the empire on which balance of power doctrines were predicated. The commentator Andrew Marr argues that continental observers fear a reversion to the nineteenth-century pattern in what they see in British proposals as 'a hankering after a return to the Europe of Metternich and Castlereagh, of shifting and unstable alliances between nation states manoeuvering ceaselessly for advantage' (Marr, 1994 a). But now Britain has fewer allies with which to balance.

The EU's transition to continent-wide concerns has led to a debate about widening and deepening in which Britain is perceived, for the most part accurately, as favouring a wider and looser arrangement rather than a more closely integrated one. George makes it clear in Chapter 11 that this has been a consistent approach by the Conservative government over the past seven or eight years.

Political leadership in relation to the European issue was markedly absent in the post-war period, in contrast to the situation on the continent. From the outset British politicians underestimated the inherent dynamism of the European integration project. It took the shock of the Suez crisis to convince Macmillan that the British approach should be reconsidered, leading to the negotiations in the early 1960s, the outcome of which was subsequently vetoed by de Gaulle. When Ted Heath successfully negotiated entry ten years later, he had to stress the overwhelming economic case for entry, and the EC as an economic enterprise, a common market, rather than a political one, an emphasis that proved enduring in British public opinion. Britain's subsequent failure to reap the economic benefits of membership, on which entry was predicated in spite of the Common Agricultural Policy, was, indeed, an expression of its industrial decline. 'No-one expected 20 years ago, when Britain joined the Common Market, that one of the main benefits would be to have the Japanese in Britain,' earning the dismissive French sobriquet *porte-avion Japonais* (Steele, 1994).

It is not at all clear whether the UK's undoubted success in attracting the lion's share of inward investment to the EU in recent years — some 40 per cent of the overall total — is an expression of economic recovery or weakness (Cassell, 1993). The failure to generate British exports in response to EC membership in the 1970s led to the prolonged argument about its budgetary contribution, which reinforced the public image of the EC as a technocratic-bureaucratic force remote from everyday concerns. Heath's policy failure is seen by the foremost authority on British relations with the EC/EU as having 'undermined the commitment to European integration that he had made a cornerstone of his modernisation strategy for the British economy' (George, 1994 c, p. 59). Subsequent prime ministers have all in some measure minimised the supranational elements of existing membership and failed to convey the advantages Britain secured from being inside rather than outside.

Nevertheless, as George argues, there are very substantial elements of continuity in British attitudes towards the EC/EU and its inter-governmental conferences. He lists seven principles common to the approaches of Mrs Thatcher and Mr Major towards the EC/EU: a belief in a Europe of nation states; pragmatism rather than a teleological federalism as the benchmark for considering the desirability of further integration; the need for relevance rather than doctrine as the touchstone of its involvement; an abiding emphasis on the European competiveness in the global economy; equally, an insistence that Europe must be open to the world; a commitment to NATO and the US role in Europe; and a consistent demand for financial probity in the conduct of EC/EU affairs.

It can be convincingly argued that Britain set the pace and the agenda in the Single European Act IGC, following Mrs Thatcher's reluctant conversion to its necessity; and that the clear diplomatic victor in the Maastricht Treaty on European Union was Britain, with its opt-outs and the inter-governmental pillared structure of the treaty. The modest British agenda for the 1996 IGC could have found allies, despite German impatience, had not the 1996 beef crisis intervened. The German representative on the IGC negotiating committee, Mr Werner Hoyer, concluded that Britain's policy of non-cooperation had backfired, by convincing many of the smaller member states to back more majority voting (Hort, 1996). Most British voters concluded that Britain lost the 'beef war', according to an opinion poll in *The Daily Telegraph* (King, 1996).

Malcolm Rifkind's Chatham House address in September 1995, his first elaboration of his approach to foreign policy as Foreign Secretary, invoked another Palmerstonian maxim: 'The furtherance of British interests should be the only object of a British Foreign Secretary.' Mr Rifkind went on to distinguish between influence and interests, saying that 'occasionally it may be right to accept less influence in specific areas [of the EU] in order to protect key national interests ... We will not accept proposals that would damage Britain's interests on the spurious grounds that otherwise we will lose influence, create a two-speed Europe or be left out in the cold' (Rifkind, 1995 d). His speech emphasised transatlantic and global links both for Britain and Europe and was widely seen as taking a more Eurosceptic line than might have been expected after Mr Major's leadership victory in July 1995. Critics were unconvinced that the distinction between influence and interests was valid — in what circumstances would a loss of influence be in Britain's foreign policy interests? (Ascherson, 1995 b).

There are fears once again that Britain will pursue a balance of power strategy and by her influence if not her power encourage other large European states to do likewise. Kissinger, for example, although he is sympathetic to Britain's position, warns that circumstances have changed after the end of the Cold War. In some respects the emerging pattern of world politics will be more like the European state system of the eighteenth and nineteenth centuries than the rigid patterns of the Cold War (Kissinger, 1995 b, p. 23). But in those circumstances Palmerston's advice would surely be that in global terms Britain's interests would be best served by maximising its European influence. This has certainly been Washington's approach as it has changed its attitude to Britain and Germany. Dr Kissinger concluded: 'What I would like to avoid is Britain being fixed in a Europe where Gaullist policies will be pursued by British methods. That would be a lethal combination' (Black, 1995 a). As Garton Ash puts it: 'Britain might actually find itself doing worse in a Europe in which Germany and France started behaving like Britain than in a Europe in which Britain and France have to be a little more like Germany,' (Garton Ash, 1996, p. 28).

The German CDU/CSU paper in September 1994 explicitly warned against such an outcome because it would expose Germany to the historical temptation to go it alone in central Europe, which led to two catastrophes this century (CDU/CSU, 1994; Lamers, 1994). This geopolitical perspective on the necessity of Germany being bound into Europe should be contrasted with a British government view that continues to regard the EU largely from a pragmatic, predominantly economic perspective and which instinctively invokes NATO and the Americans whenever geopolitical concerns are articulated (Davidson, 1994 b). Part of the British argument has it that the original geopolitical case for the EC has been changed by these events because of their very success: 'The determination of the founding fathers has succeeded far beyond the estimations of most people of their time. Their vision was proved right for its age. But it is outdated. It will not now do' (Major, 1994). The nation state remains as a fixture, central to the evolution of European politics, he argues. This has been a constant theme of Mr Hurd and Mr Rifkind.

The point applies as much to the EU's institutional and decision-making structure as to the deeper geopolitical case made for it. Mr Hurd told the IEA's Dublin conference in March 1994: 'The technique [the EC's founding fathers] used was perhaps inevitably centripetal, that is to say it moved decisions towards the centre and away from the nation states ... But it does not follow that this centralising process ... has to continue indefinitely in our Union. Indeed it seems to me that it should not if we are to act with the grain of history because the needs and instincts of this generation have changed.'

Britain therefore proposes a distinct model of European integration, in Hurd's words, a 'multi-track, multi-speed, even multi-layered approach, which will increasingly be the way of the future'. It is a 'matrix model', in which member-states would be free to pick and choose in an *à la carte* fashion from the policies and structures on offer. The phrase 'multi-core' has also been used to describe it. Subsidiarity, decentralisation, inter-governmentalism, possible renationalisation of policies would characterise it. But there is little evidence that the model appeals to many other member states, partly because of the variable geometry it provokes.

Mr Major may be in danger of talking himself into the second tier he argues against; other leaders, especially in the six founding states, reject the model as a recipe for disintegration and unravelling (despite the quite widespread mood of Euroscepticism through the Fifteen, including Germany, Spain, Italy and the Netherlands, now a net contributor) — while the cohesion states, the new EFTA members and the Visegrad applicants wish in their various ways to preserve a greater unicity than is envisaged in the British model. Britain's tendency to dismiss Germany's special pleas about the temptations of its past are equally not shared by other member states. These issues must be clarified over the course of the IGC negotiations, which will put the various models of integration to the test.

They were dramatised by a speech Dr Kohl delivered at the University of Louvain on 1 February, 1996. Its central message, and the one that attracted headlines and hostile comment in Britain, was that 'the policy of European integration is in reality a question of war and peace in the twenty-first century'. He warned about the dangers facing Europe if the 'slowest ship', i.e. Britain, were permitted to dictate the pace of integration at the IGC.

The speech was unexceptionable, in that its main themes have been delivered many times by Dr Kohl, most prominently at his party's conference in October 1995; on this occasion it did not attract much attention in Germany. In Britain, however, it infuriated Eurosceptics and Europhobes, but alerted others to the fundamental issues at stake in the current debate on Europe's future. In that sense it was a very useful exercise. It provides an opportunity to assess what is arguably the most interesting polarity in contemporary European political discourse — between German Christian Democracy's social market and quasi-federal model of European politics and British Conservatism's institutionally-diluted, socially-deregulated and, by way of rapid EU enlargement, defederalised one.

'Nationalism — that is war,' Dr Kohl said, quoting François Mitterrand's speech last year to the European Parliament. He went on to question the role of the nation state. 'We have no desire to return to the nation state of old. It cannot solve the great problems of the twenty-first century.' He is afraid that a hegemonic Germany, free from the shackles of common European rules, would provoke protectionism and nationalism among its neighbours and return the continent to the balance of power politics, the nationalism and the trade and military wars which 'brought great suffering to our continent'. It is important to remember, in interpreting the British response to Dr Kohl, that, as George puts it in his paper, 'because Britain was undefeated in the Second World War, and did not experience occupation, nationalism was not discredited as it was in parts of continental Europe'.

Dr Kohl was referring to the imperial nationalisms of the large powers, rather than to the more defensive nationalisms of those they invaded and occupied. His warnings bring out, nonetheless, a defensive nationalism in Britain, particularly on the English right wing, which is reminded forcibly of previous German ultimata and *faits accomplis* in Europe.

One Tory MP, Mr John Wilkinson, put it this way: 'Wars have usually ensued from hegemonic ambitions on the continent. It has been Britain's duty to maintain a balance of power in Europe, and to do that we have got to keep our distance.' It can be a dialogue of the deaf, in which a German leadership pleading for help to suppress the historical demons of its European past by way of a more integrated Europe is seen to be just as menacing to British interests as a Germany going it alone. Either way Britain is confronted by German hegemony, so the argument goes — either from a German dominated federalised Europe or a Bismarckian or even a Hitlerian one (Beedham, 1996). It is better to keep the distance, emphasising global interests, continent-wide concerns rather than a pooled sovereignty which would undermine that central institution, the nation state.

The problem here is that the Kohl plea is disregarded. This response begs the large question of whether the nation state is indeed capable of handling these issues. Can it avoid the twin forces of sub-national fragmentation and supranational globalisation that afflict it? European integration has often responded to these dilemmas in the best British fashion — pragmatically — in such a way as to use the pooling of sovereignty to shore up rather than to undermine the nation state (Milward, 1994). Dr Kohl's argument is that this will no longer be possible in an EU with up to 30 members and in a world economy and political system where Europe must compete with the US and Asia. He sets out four areas in which Germany wants to see progress at the IGC: a strengthened common foreign and security policy, in with there is much more majority voting; an improvement in cooperation against crime and drugs; greater openness and efficiency in decision-making; and more powers for the European Parliament.

Underlying this rather dry list is the more fundamental geopolitical requirement of avoiding retrogression to the balance of power pattern of European politics earlier this century. It goes with a conviction that if the opportunity is lost on this occasion to make qualitative progress towards more integration, 'it will take considerably longer than one generation before we are given such an opportunity again'. These are the words of an old man in a hurry, of course, as his British critics are quick to point out. But Dr Kohl is now expected to stand again in the 1998 federal elections. And he is determined to create the conditions that would enable a core group of states to make progress faster than the others who are unable or unwilling to join them. However, nobody wants a European superstate, he says, which 'does not and never will exist'.

Dr Kohl said that 'we can only protect our common interests if we speak with one voice and pool our resources'. His assertion is based on the premise that balances of power between nation states are no longer capable of guaranteeing a stable equilibrium in Europe. Linked with another theme, variable geometry, it takes on a different colour: 'If individual partners are not prepared to participate in certain steps towards integration, the others should not be denied the opportunity to develop increased cooperation.' This strategy of differentiated integration is being pressed by an influential group of German policy-makers and political theorists and has been taken up by the French and German governments (Janning, 1996). They take it for granted that monetary union and security and defence union are fundamental requirements for membership of the core group; and they are prepared to face into a political crisis, possibly during the Irish EU presidency, to clear the decks (Friedman, 1996). It would cover economic and monetary policy, strategies for EU enlargement, and majority voting. At the conclusion of the Florence Council in June 1996 Mr Major said he would welcome a speeding up of the IGC negotiations, in the belief that German support for Mr Blair's positions could backfire on the Labour leader in the election campaign. But such political tactics are reported to have reinforced the determination of the German Government not to give the British Government any domestic advantages, in the belief that such attitudes are inimical to the EU interest (Helm and Rentoul, 1996; Davidson, 1996).

It is a function of political hegemony to set agendas in this way, which should not occasion too much surprise (Wallace, 1995 b). But within Germany, as the more acute British observers point out, there is also a lively debate about whether Germany's best interests are served by more integration, including monetary union, or, as a group around the historian and political scientist Hans-Peter Schwarz, a critic of the Maastricht Treaty on European Union, argue, that 'Germany is doomed to remain a nation state and doomed to live with all the (uncomfortable) consequences' after the end of the Cold War (Janning, 1996, p. 35). Schwarz has not the same kind of agonised doubts about German normalisation as afflict Dr Kohl and his main advisors. This adds point to the argument that it all depends which Germany you are listening to. But it should be no excuse for dismissing Kohl's fears as self-serving, as British Eurosceptics, egged on by the revisionist historians, are inclined to do. Just because Germans disagree is not a good reason for not evaluating carefully which of their policy lines are more convincing guarantors of European stability.

Mr Major's speech about bringing Britain 'to the heart of Europe' was made in Bonn, but he has failed to develop relations with Germany, leaving Paris and Bonn still uncertain as to where precisely Britain stands (Frankenberger, 1996; Lamers, 1994; Langellier, 1996; George, 1994 b; Moraeu Defargues, 1994). The Labour Party leader, Mr Tony Blair, makes much of this failure. 'Forfeit a central role in Europe and we forfeit our opportunity to play a substantial role in the world ... The fact is that Europe is the only route through which Britain can exercise power and influence. If it is to maintain its role as a global player, it has to be a central part of the politics of Europe' (Blair, 1995 c).

There is no good reason to expect that the US would be interested in encouraging a Britain that had isolated itself from a more integrated Europe. Indeed the French sought to improve relations with the US partly as a means of balancing Germany within a more Europeanised NATO. The French nuclear test results were reportedly shared with the US and Britain (*The Guardian*, 10.9.95). France's suggestion that its nuclear forces should be shared within the EU framework was badly received by most member states, but welcomed by Britain. The French and British share many military and security interests, not least the ability to 'punch above their weight' in world politics, symbolised by their nuclear weapons. If there were to be a deterioration of transatlantic relations, over Russia, for example, Britain would have little option but to opt for closer EU integration led by security/defence concerns rather than economic ones.

Recent discussions between France and Britain on defence cooperation, the dulcet refusal of the British government to criticise the 1995 French nuclear tests, which greatly impressed Mr Chirac, and the British proposals for developing the CFSP and its relations with the WEU at the 1996 IGC strongly suggest that London is keeping its options open. Langellier talks of flirtatious glances — oeillades — being directed at Paris. This mirrors the potential love affair between British and French Gaullism (Rees-Mogg, 1995). France and Britain play a a leadership game in the hard core of European security and therefore with the US. It is important not to underestimate it from the perspective of a small, neutral state such as Ireland, with very different historical experiences and traditions.

Cable's fear that Britain's Trident-based nuclear system 'might simply have to be dumped' if it got in the way of a comprehensive nuclear disarmament deal between the US and Russia would reinforce the urgency of cooperation with France. But so far Britain is not prepared to contemplate the scale of expenditure needed, especially on satellite communications and missile lift-off capability, not to mention the radical changes that would be required in the EU's political system to cater for such a common defence. The continuation of NATO and of the US presence in Europe remains a central British policy objective. Nonetheless, a recent authoritative commentary on Britain's security interests concluded: 'The only way Britain is going to influence world events in the future is as a major European power working closely with France and Germany, and dealing with the US as a power committed to Europe' (Sharp, 1996).

From Ireland's point of view it is much preferable that Britain should indeed be at the heart of Europe, as Dick Spring has argued and Hurd, Rifkind and Major continue to reassert. An isolated or marginalised Britain would present grave policy difficulties for Ireland — and pose a challenge of how best to prevent a polarisation between variable German and variable British models of integration which would have this outcome. Indeed, the Benelux states originally favoured British membership of the EC precisely to counter-balance the dominant Franco-German axis — and they still do, as Leo Tindemans told Jonathan Steele: ' "It's often said that Kohl is the best European in Germany, but after him, who? what? And in five years' time?" Europe, he argued, needed Britain as a counterweight' (Steele, 1994). The argument stands 30 years later, despite the failure of the British political elite to address it, and the conclusion of a recent Dutch policy paper that the British have disregarded this crucial interest.

Ireland is again at the centre of these arguments about Germany's role, just as in the 1990 EU presidency following German unification, during the IGC and the 1996 presidency. If the Germans do indeed press the issue and force a polarisation in the IGC between their model and the British Conservative one of integration, Ireland faces hard choices about whether to aim for, and align with, the core group, the British one, or some intermediate category.

BRITAIN'S DEBATE ON CONSTITUTIONAL AND INSTITUTIONAL REFORM

The United Kingdom's own constitutional and institutional structures are in need of more or less drastic rearrangement, according to a widespread view among commentators and opposition parties (Hutton, 1994; Jacques, 1994; Jenkins, 1995; Marr, 1995 f; Rogaly, 1994). Opinion polls show that this view has widespread public support (Riddell, 1995 a). Its state is (next to Ireland's) the most centralised in the EU and is badly in need of devolution, they argue. Its institutions — monarchy, established church, House of Lords, parliament-citizen relationship and electoral system, state secrecy and economic short-termism — sorely need modernisation (Siedentop, 1995). 'Britain's low investment economy is rooted in the character of its institutions,' according to Hutton. 'We have a winner takes all economy and polity' (1994 a). His book, *The State We're In*, which proposes a radical agenda of constitutional, institutional and economic change, was on the best-seller list for 23 weeks in 1995, eight of them at the top of it, and has sold over 150,000 copies. According to Anthony Sampson, one of the most prominent British commentators, only the army and the Bank of England appear relatively undiminished and unchallenged by an increasingly intrusive and profit-driven mass media; 'But they wield the crudest forms of power — the gun and the money — which need little mystique to support them' (Sampson, 1994); unfortunately this was written before the *Sunday Mirror*'s memorable story on the 'Bonk of England'.

Under successive Conservative governments since 1979 Britain's democratic accountability has been severely compromised by a proliferation of quangos; and its class and educational systems still inhibit economic growth and development (Crafts, 1992; FitzGerald, 1996 b; Hutton, 1994 a, b). There is a real deterioration in its social fabric; one of the principal historians of modern Britain, Keith Robbins, concludes that the enterprise culture of the Thatcher years is perhaps inextricably linked to such social divisions. 'Those very incentives and deregulation initiatives of which the government was so proud served to deepen divisions of wealth, health and welfare. These in turn were related to poor skills, poor opportunities and the breakdown of family life ... and illegitimacy rates' (Robbins, 1994 a, p. 400).

Anyone following British political debates will be struck by the vehemence with which such views are held — and contested. The debates tend to follow rough party lines, so that it is necessary to be cautious about taking criticisms from one side of the political divide, specifically the Labour and Liberal Democrat, as characteristic of the entire British political spectrum, when in fact the existing constitutional arrangements are defended by the Conservatives and their supporters. There is significant agreement across political divides about the need for renewal and reform, however, which tends to bring 'one nation' social democrats and conservatives together in criticism of Mrs Thatcher's legacies; or to impel Mr Major to propose a new committee system for governing Scotland rather than relying only on outright opposition to Labour devolution plans, which he says will break up the United Kingdom.

An observer from Ireland cannot but agree with the argument that in recent years the nature of the British state has come back to the centre of political controversy in a way that is reminiscent above all of the period up to the Treaty in 1921. For the generation before that, Ireland had been at the centre of British political debate, along with battles over the suffrage, reform of the House of Lords, and the social reforms of 1906-11. From the 1920s, controversies about the social and economic responsibilities of the state were the stuff of politics; controversy about its relations to the multinational structure of the United Kingdom were little heard (Marquand, 1995).

The wheel has now come full circle. After the end of the Cold War in 1989 there has been a rolling questioning of the structures that were previously taken so much for granted (Mitchell, 1996, p. 61). That war not only masked the changes in Britain's international position, it provided a rationale for the continuation of its governing structures, or *ancien regime*, as Marquand describes them. The two are intimately connected. National identity among these larger European states has been constructed — invented, imagined — externally as well as internally; nowhere has this been more true than of the United Kingdom. It has always been closely bound up with the evolution of threats from abroad and the construction of foreign policy to deal with them, from the union with Scotland in 1707 to the partition of Ireland in 1920. British identity, it is now better understood, is very much a function of its eighteenth- and nineteenth-century history; its Protestantism, expanding commercial, trading, financial and naval imperialism and its cultural identity pitched against successive continental, mainly Catholic, enemies, have intimately moulded its political fabric. It now faces the task of reconstructing, reforming or discarding the elements of that identity in the full glare of international involvement.

Historians, political geographers and journalists increasingly debate the following questions: 'Is the United Kingdom still viable? Can "Britain" survive the stresses and strains which participation in the European process inescapably entails? ... What is "Britishness" now that its collective external expression — the British Empire — has faded into the past?' (Robbins, 1994 b). The question of British identity looms large in what is a very lively and critical, if ill-focussed, discussion. Identities are questioned and invented at crucial historical turning points, Dodd argues. 'Driving the debates around the curriculum for History or English,' for example, 'are arguments such as: Who are the British? Which history should be taught? How national should it be? What are the crucial dates and events? Should literature in the English language be the subject of study or literature produced within Britain?' (Dodd, 1995, p. 9; Ascherson, 1996; O'Toole, 1996).

The historian Linda Colley has put Britain's identity crisis in a longer historical context. It is worth quoting the conclusion from her book, *Britons, Forging the Nation 1707-1837*, at some length, since it encapsulates so many of the issues in what has become an influential formulation:

'Since virtually every major European state is currently under pressure from a resurgence of small nationalities which once acquiesced in being a component part of a greater whole, today's increasingly strident calls for a breakup of Britain should not be attributed exclusively to this island's own peculiar development. But we can understand the nature of the present crisis only if we recognise that the factors that provided for the forging of a British nation in the past have largely ceased to operate. Protestantism, that once vital cement, has now a limited influence on British culture, as indeed has Christianity itself. Recurrent wars with the states of continental Europe have in all likelihood come to an end, so different kinds of Britons no longer feel the same compulsion to remain united in the face of the enemy from without. And, crucially, both commercial supremacy and imperial hegemony have gone. No more can Britons reassure themselves of their distinct and privileged identity by contrasting themselves with impoverished Europeans (real or imaginary), or by exercising authority over manifestly alien peoples. God has ceased to be British, and Providence no longer smiles' (Colley, 1992, p. 374).

The resulting doubt and disarray have taken many forms, including a return to older loyalties of Englishness, Scottishness or Welshness. The symbols of Britishness arising from the past 300 years, such as the royal family and parliament, are debated as never before. Most importantly from our point of view, British national uncertainty is highly evident in the apprehension with which so many Britons regard increasing a more integrated Europe. Whereas the Germans and the French, who are more confident about their unique identity, see a Europe without frontiers in terms of opportunity, 'the British are far more inclined to view it as a threat. This is partly because they have fought against continental European states so often in the past; but their apparent insularity is to be explained also by their growing doubts about who they are in the present. Consciously or unconsciously, they fear assuming a new identity in case it obliterates entirely the already insecure identity they currently possess' (Colley, 1992, p. 375).

Nairn argues that the monarchy's 'enchanted glass' has been an essential means of ensuring the coherence of British identity in the century and a half after the period covered in Colley's volume (Nairn, 1994). In the first edition of his equally influential book, published in 1988, he assumed that the monarchy was more or less intact as an institutional and symbolic system conferring legitimacy on the British constitutional structure. In the Introduction to the second edition six years later he acknowledges a profound change in popular attitudes. 'The fact is that in that spiritual or ideological sense which the book's main argument saw as crucial to the way British identity functioned, the House of Windsor is dead.' Its glamour has been destroyed, the glass shattered, by a series of events in the early 1990s, including Queen Elizabeth's decision to pay income tax, the Windsor Castle fire and the breakdown of two royal marriages.

But the explanation goes deeper than this accumulation of unfortunate events. Invoking Mr Michael Portillo's celebrated speech in January 1994 attacking nihilism in politics and the media (Portillo, 1994), Nairn argues that Thatcherism itself, so passionately espoused by Mr Portillo, is the real source of the collapse of that consensus which has been so central to the monarchy's appeal. 'The "Thatcher revolution" Mr Portillo wishes to continue set out to restore British grandeur. What it actually did was to break the back of British identity' (Nairn, 1994, p. xxiii). This is because Thatcherism was a contradiction in terms, liberation of a civil society with no change in its political state. She assumed that inside British society there was an American society of small capitalists waiting to break out from the straitjacket of the management of decline. Her refusal to contemplate constitutional change, indeed her continuing urge to centralise when confronted with resistance, is reminiscent of the top down reforms promoted by Gorbachev in the Soviet Union; it may end up in the same way, if account is taken of the unintended consequences for the United Kingdom, in which the monarchy became a '*sui generis* formula for reconciling four different nationalities within a single imperial state'.

A central contradiction in Thatcherism was its determination to reduce the links between the state and the citizen, while still demanding unconditional loyalty, Wallace argues. The UK was built as a multinational state, held together by its prestige and the importance of Britain in world markets. Socio-economic integration was achieved in the nineteenth and early twentieth centuries by mass education, cheap newspapers, the postal and railway services. Local government and the provision of early rights and benefits in two great stages, by the Lloyd George Liberals and then the post-1945 Labour government, gave the working class a stake in the UK 'in return for the loyalty — and military service — expected of them'. The run down of local government, the railway system, public education and the health services, along with deindustrialisation and privatisation, have 'made Britain a much less united kingdom than it was a generation ago', in which 'market forces disintegrate the nation state' rather than release entrepreneurial energy (Wallace, 1995 c).

He also points out that 'the Conservative Party loses its head most completely when its sense of English identity is thrown into confusion'. Another unintended consequence of the Thatcher decade was the emergence of what Nairn terms a 'half-explicit nationalism whose substance was English rather than British'. It has become increasingly recognised as such, with a roll-on effect in Scotland and Wales (Ascherson, 1996; Neil, 1996; O'Toole, 1996). As Ascherson puts it: 'The fiction of a British "nation" has kept English nationalism in check ... . We can begin to see a confluence ahead. The river of Eurosceptic xenophobia is beginning to converge with the river of intolerant English nationalism.' The consequences have been plain to see during the BSE beef crisis, which brought out the worst element of both sentiments, egged on by a press owned in large part by foreigners.

Robbins concludes his book with a survey of this unity and division. He underlines how much it has been exacerbated by an electoral geography which concentrates Conservative support and increasingly its ruling cadres so markedly in England, especially in the south-east. 'The Conservative ascendancy was an English ascendancy,' he writes. 'It is scarcely surprising, therefore, that a sense of alienation from the United Kingdom, as it existed, was widespread' (Robbins, 1994 a, p. 397). Labour and the Liberal Democrats continue to draw their support disproportionately from Scotland, Wales, the north of England and in the south from the 'multicultural' first- or second-generation Asian and Carribbean immigrant sections of the population from which many Labour activists are drawn. A Labour MP points out that 'the European debate in Britain tends to be an inter-English debate by men and women obsessed with a sense of loss, actual or potential. It is also a southern English debate, taking place mainly within the Conservative Party. In Scotland and the English regions, where a renewed perspective of identity is offered on Europe in opposition to the London centralisation which is the hallmark of recent times, the discussion is more relaxed' (MacShane, 1996).

Clearly this rearrangement or disintegration of British identity poses especially difficult problems for Northern Ireland unionists. Their dilemma is that they remain loyal to an imperial identity in retreat but cannot identify with the mawkishly sentimental alternative English one on offer. This lends credibility to unionist calls for the negotiation of a new British-Irish agreement, to substitute for the Anglo-Irish Agreement from which they feel excluded, and which would 'reflect the multiplicity of relationships within these islands and recognise the reality of the economic interdependence between the two sovereign states' (Donaldson, 1995; see also Loughlin, 1995; Todd, 1995). Contemporary Anglo-Britishism has great difficulty in adjusting; it tends to be 'metropolitan towards the peripheral countries in its archipelago, nativist towards Europe and alternately superior and servile towards America' (Nairn, 1994, p. xxxiii).

BRITAIN AND IRELAND

Many of these themes concerning state, national identity and regional identity have been worked out in the history of the United Kingdom and between Britain and Ireland. Kearney's masterly survey of over 2,000 years of interaction in *The British Isles, A History of Four Nations* is an indispensable corrective to the systematic elision of Englishness and Britishness in the mainstrean historiography in our neighbouring island. Established in the Victorian age, a period in which British uniqueness was taken for granted, the discipline of history 'encoded the values of that age. History was then, in large part, the account of the rise of the British constitution to perfection and of the British empire to greatness' (Black, 1994, p. 1). Kearney believes that a 'Britannic' dimension remains necessary, nonetheless, in that 'the histories of what are normally regarded as four distinct "nations" appear more intelligible if they are seen first within a general British Isles context and secondly if they are seen in terms of "cultures" and "sub-cultures" '.

Kearney concludes his panorama by stressing the continued dominance of the south-east in economic, political and cultural life and in communications; he cautions that class and regional, as well as national lines of difference continue to play their part. But 'there is no sign that the British Isles is ceasing to be an enduring historical unit, of which the Republic of Ireland forms part, and to which new, non-European ethnic groups are now making a contribution' (Kearney, 1989, pp. 212, 216).

A relatively unified English state was well-formed by the end of the medieval period. A combination of the centralising Norman state and the English Church succeeded in laying the foundations of a national culture and national identity, although their full flowering had to await the Tudor renaissance and the Reformation. A crucial factor in this centralisation process during virtually all its medieval, early modern and modern periods was the systematic confrontation between the English state and the Celtic periphery in Ireland, Scotland and Wales, which provided a continuing focus for its military and administrative consolidation. Conquest and control of the Celtic peripheries, expressed through union with Wales (1536), Scotland (1707) and Ireland (1800) to create the United Kingdom was simultaneously a process by which English political, economic and cultural hegemony was established over the other nationalities.

This 'internal colonialism' within these islands bears many similarities to the later external colonial expansion. As A. L. Rowse put it: 'By far the most important conclusion, and one that I had not realised before going into it, was the continuity of the process of expansion within the British islands with that across the oceans, especially the phase of it which is crucial for modern history — Bismarck called it 'the decisive fact in the modern world' — that across the Atlantic to the peopling of north America' (Quoted in Heckler, 1975, p. 63). Many of the same social forces and ideologies were involved in Ireland and the American colony.

While the multinational character of the British state is formally acknowledged in its title the effective historical elision between English and British identity, downgrading that of Scotland and Wales, has created profound problems for British leaders, particularly Conservative ones, after the loss of the empire which was the culmination of British identity; it has exposed the ambiguity of English identity in defining modern Britain's relationship with Europe. Little England is far less at home with Europe than little Scotland, little Wales — or little Ireland. It is no surprise that the two crises should coincide and overlap.

The next few years provide a real opportunity for British political leaders to combine a rearrangement of the union of England, Scotland, Wales and

Northern Ireland with a rearrangement of the relationship between the United Kingdom and the European Union.

It is intriguing to speculate about the potential interaction between these processes of constitutional rearrangement. Asssuming the Northern Ireland talks were to result in a devolved power-sharing assembly with strong north-south links, would there be a knock-on, precedent-creating effect for Scotland, Wales and the English regions? And will the talks process, the necessity of constitutional change and the end of the flow of structural funds trigger a reconsideration of the overcentralism of the Irish state in addition to an amendment of Articles 2 and 3? The 1996 IGC agenda on institutional change, defence and foreign policy and eastern enlargement coincides with the Northern talks. There is an opportunity for radical reassessment of political arrangements in all these dimensions, in which the EU will operate, as it were, as a fourth strand of talks, a quadrilateral dimension, in addition to those within Northern Ireland, between north and south and between the Irish and British governments. Joint representation of Irish interests in Brussels, for example, could throw new light on the regional dimension within Ireland.

Optimistic and pessimistic scenarios are painted of the prospects involved for Ireland north and south. Kearney and Wilson, for example, argue that European identity, citizenship and the new regionalism provide a powerful new framework within which the Irish question is capable of being resolved. It must now be understood as a more normal manifestation of minority-majority, or double-minority conflicts which have mounted in intensity after the end of the Cold War in Europe. Insofar as these are resolved elsewhere traditional zero-sum notions of sovereignty, based on choices between colonial dependence or nationalist independence, can be superseded. 'The idea of European interdependence, combined with the application of the principle of subsidiarity, can, however, for Northern Ireland transcend both. The emerging Europe has a unique opportunity to be truly democratic by fostering notions of sovereignty that are inclusive rather than absolute, shared rather than insular, disseminated rather than closed in upon some bureaucratic centre. Northern Ireland could be a testing ground.' Along with optimism about the 'one-island economy', in which peace dividends, economies of scale and cooperation on economic development, tourism and attraction of international investment, combine, this is an alluring and attractive picture (Kearney and Wilson, 1994).

Anderson and O'Dowd argue, following substantial programmes of research among political, business, official and other interest groups that cross-border bodies, as proposed in the Framework Document, will have to have strong political and institutional expression if they are to succeed. 'Without significant political and institutional changes, there will be two separate economies and only limited scope for cooperation: "making a reality of the island economy", contrary to Dr (George) Quigley's "non-political" posture, is precisely dependent on their being "political agendas" (Anderson, 1994, p. 69). Bradley suggests that determined political initiative will be required if the peace dividend for the all-Ireland economy is to be realised and maximised (Bradley, 1995, 1996, 1996 a).

A 1997 UK election in the middle of the inter-governmental conference provides the political opportunity for a direct linking of the debate over constitutional change and the parameters of Britain's future relations with the EU. It is significant that Ireland should be such a central part of this process. Historically, all Britain's major constitutional developments and many of its continental entanglements have hinged on its relations with the Celtic Fringe and especially with Ireland. A favourable outcome settling both amicably would be as important a transition as any seen in Britain for the past 300 years.

THE POLITICAL DEBATE

The next few years will see these four rearrangements of British identity in its Atlantic, European, internal and British-Irish manifestations proceeding alongside and inter-penetrating one another in what must be expected to be a turbulent and unpredictable debate. This confirms the impression of observers in many EU partner states that it is as much about Britain's own as well as Europe's identity. One MP, a Liberal Democrat, explaining in summary to an IEA group in March 1995 that his party favours 'a more federal UK in a more federal EU', ventured to suggest that part of the English Tory agenda is driven by a realisation of some on the Tory right that they have to resign themselves to losing the Celtic Fringe; but this would allow their party 'to rule England for ever', just as the first past the post system and the existing political structure of the UK allowed them to do for seventeen years. The emergence of English nationalism as the conservative heir to imperial identity gives the debate a peculiar insularity in which xenophobia — especially Germanophobia — is more and more apparent; this is more easy to understand because of the simultaneous threat to the UK identity from European integration and from Irish and now Scottish and Welsh nationalism — and from the new multiculturalism. There are now some five million British subjects whose ethnic origins are outside Europe; they can be seen as the 'last true Britons', replacing the gentry as the authentic British class. But this is one of the reasons why precisely English nationalism has arisen with such passion and resistance to them, (Ascherson 1996, p. 29). In his survey of its impact on British identity Cohen concludes that ' "Race" and

"Nation" have now become elements in a rhetoric of order through which modern conservatism can voice populist protest against Britain's post-imperialist plight' (Cohen, 1994, p. 202).

THE CONSERVATIVE PARTY-STATE

The arguments within the Conservative Party have been bitter and vicious, exemplified by the leadership battle from which Mr Major emerged victorious in July, 1995. The Conservative bloc as a whole is divided in at least three ways. First of all there are the mainstream Europeanists convinced of the need for full involvement in the EU, including in economic and monetary union, albeit according to a model of integration that best suits British interests. They should be distinguished from the sceptics properly so-called, who are not convinced of the merits of full involvement and argue for Britain's global interests, but who keep an open mind on the subject. And thirdly there are the Euro-phobes, who effectively advocate withdrawal and isolation. The second and third categories overlap, including newspapers supporting the Conservatives, where supporters of the first group allege that Canadian and Australian proprietors have tapped into a Germanophobe and Europhobe streak in the young new right that was crystallised in the London *Times* leak of the Framework Document on Northern Ireland.

Supporters of the first position — still the Conservative and Commons majorities, after all — are very frustrated about the British debate on Europe and how it is perceived abroad. Its political and rhetorical frame of reference is skewed, they say. What is predominantly an argument between Euro-enthusiasts and Euro-sceptics is expressed and reported too often as one between Euro-sceptics and Euro-phobes. As a result Britain's European stance is in grave danger of being misinterpreted by its partners — including its Irish partners — and its interests of being misrepresented. It is losing influence with those who ought now to be its allies, in contradiction of Palmerston's maxim.

There is no guarantee that the Conservative Party would not break up in opposition under the strain of accommodating such a range of views; in France, for example, it would include Le Pen through de Villiers, Séguin, Chirac, Balladur and Giscard d'Estaing. Such a realignment, including a Labour deal with the Liberal Democrats, may be the best guarantee that Labour could win a second term to deliver on its promises of institutional change. After seventeen years of Tory rule Britain is seen very much as a 'party-state', whose political adversarialism is fully matched in the media. If

Labour wins the next election the political transition will be brutish, according to another observer, because the winner-takes-all electoral system and the unreconstructed political system combine to frustrate a substantial consensus on reform and European participation. This makes it quite unlike the increasingly consensual, coalitionist and corporatist style of government to which we have become accustomed in the Republic.

The institutional crisis crops up again and again. It overlaps, indeed encompasses the crisis of national and international identity, whether it concerns Britain's special relationship with the US, with Europe, with Ireland or within the UK itself. Scotland is 'seething with dissent'; diplomatic contacts are increasingly aware that they need to represent this dimension of the UK. It is a fragile union on this account, in which these overlapping issues of sovereignty and identity are compounded by Mr Major's slender majority and style of leadership. Since he has opted to make defence of the union such an issue in Scotland and Wales, he has had to fence them off from Northern Ireland; devolution and power-sharing only serves to emphasise how Northern Ireland differs from Scotland (Bogdanor, 1996, a, b). This was much to Mr James Molyneaux's discomfiture — and the same applies to his successor, Mr David Trimble, who is, however, in a numerically better position to influence the prime minister. But the unionist leader is reassured by Mr Tony Blair's refusal to continue the pro- Irish unity line traditionally espoused by his party, or at least to express it in the same way, and by the implicitly unionist asssertion by Mr Blair that Mr Major contradicts himself on Northern Ireland and Scotland (Millar, 1995 d). This provoked Labour's former Northern Ireland spokesman, Mr Kevin McNamara, to resign from the party's front bench in protest amid a furious argument over policy. Following the collapse of the IRA ceasefire, Mr McNamara broke party ranks to criticise his party leadership and Mr Major over it.

THE LABOUR PARTY

The patriotic card is not necessarily a trump for the Conservatives. In an echo of Mr Blair's programme Wallace argues that what is needed is for others 'to develop the themes of community and citizenship, of national integration balanced by regional, and local autonomy, of rebuilding the state and the idea of public service. Why should the devil get all the good tunes?' But he sees the danger that Labour will be labelled as illegitimate by the southern English ruling elite, like its Liberal predecessor a hundred years ago, 'unless it can provide a new rationale which unites north and south, English and Scots: a new British identity' (Wallace, 1994).

It would, however, be a mistake to assume that the Labour Party's programme of constitutional change, devolution, a bill of rights, fixed-term parliaments and a freedom of information act will have an easy victory — or that the party in power would rush to implement it in full.

The Labour Party attitude towards the EC/EU has been transformed in the past eight years; but it remains uncertain — on the fence — about EMU, defence policy and eastern enlargement. And Labour-Conservative disagreements on Europe conceal great areas of real consensus.

Labour's shadow foreign secretary, Mr Robin Cook, who has a sceptical background on European issues, in July 1995 launched a nation-wide campaign for a 'people's Europe' to emphasise the party's greater commitment to European involvement. It is convinced there is a generation gap between Labour and Tory supporters on the issue. The policy adopted at the 1995 Labour Party conference highlights the EU's potential for protecting consumers, forestalling ethnic conflicts and promoting environmentalism. It is backed by a Labour survey covering two-thirds of Britain's top exporters, in which the companies report by a majority of two to one that British membership of the EU has been of benefit to them. It also advocates the following:

* European recovery fund to raise finance for infrastructure and training projects to generate jobs and create skills

* Signing up to the Social Charter

* More public scrutiny of the Council of Ministers and financial controls by the European Parliament

* A common framework of rights for consumers

* A recasting of the Common Agricultural Policy so that subsidies assist rural incomes and green farming rather than guaranteeing higher prices

* Decentralisation of key decisions to regions

* Early agreement to allow the central and eastern European states to join the EU.

On economic and monetary union the document says that 'prior to Britain joining any single surrency, we must be confident that Britain will be able to compete effectively within the single currency area ... any such move must be based on the consent of the British people.' This is far from a ringing endorsement of early British entry to EMU. Labour leaders' published comments on it emphasise the same kinds of reservation as are heard from government and Bank of England spokespeople, including particularly the need for real convergence of economic performance. Implicit in the reference to consent is support for the idea of a referendum on British membership of EMU, but with the implication, too, that the party would campaign in favour of Britain joining when and if the conditions are right. The indications are, too, that an incoming Labour administration would be prepared to reach rapid agreement on the IGC package in 1997. It may well be that this will not be as difficult as many assume (FitzGerald, 1996 a).

These Labour uncertainties on Europe mirror those on electoral reform, where it is tempted to hang on to the existing system because of the promise of a landslide victory; and on devolution, where Labour could deprive itself of its Westminster majority if it failed to apply the experiment to English regions as well as to Scotland and Wales, taking account of the 'West Lothian question', which alleges an inherent assymmetry between the powers of Scottish and English MPs to scrutinise each others' legislation in a devolved polity. Blair's leadership is evidently rethinking its position on this issue, as was made clear by his decision to support referendums, for fear of getting bogged down in it during the first years of an incoming administration. The latest Labour formula proposes that there would be a prolonged period of indirect regional assemblies in England while preferences are worked out.

There is even a nightmare scenario in which Blair would win the next election, make constitutional changes and bring Britain into an EMU, but lose the following one to a Portillo/Redwood-led Tory party, riding to victory on the political ineptitude with which the Labour programme was carried through.

There are uncanny resemblances between the position now and that which prevailed before the 1906 election which swept the Tories from power for almost a generation after their prolonged split on imperial preference and free trade. It ushered in Liberal administrations under Asquith and Lloyd George that were as radical in their social and constitutional reforms as any British government this century. But Lloyd George had fire in his belly taking on aristocratic Britain that Blair would need to match if he is properly to mobilise dissatisfaction with the Conservatives. A notable feature of commentary on his programme is that it needs to move into a much higher gear of conviction and policy differentiation from the Conservatives if it is to prove effective when the election comes.

Hutton says there is a choice of methods between a strategic Labour approach which would choose a few fundamental measures of constitutional reform and a 'brick-by-brick' one, putting through pragmatic reforms one by one, each of them calculated to add a new social group to an accumulating new 'historic bloc' under Labour hegemony (Hutton, 1995; Leys, 1995). Stephens believes that the rapidly emerging timetable of the British election and the run-in to the inauguration of an EMU in 1999 make it highly unlikely that Britain under a Blair government would be ready to join at first even if it were fully committed to doing so (Stephens, 1996 c). The IEA's own work on this subject would seem to bear this judgement out (IEA, 1995; Halligan, this volume).

There will also be a dynamic arising from the EU's emergent combination of subsidiarity and new regionalism, which may pitch it against a centralist defence of the British constitution (Scott et al, 1994). The British defence of subsidiarity conceals a great hostility to practising it at home. In this sense Malcolm Rifkind's suggestion that the EU should adopt the United Kingdom as a model of diversity, not uniformity, is deeply ironic.

CONCLUSION: A VARIABLE EUROPE AND AN UNPREDICTABLE BRITAIN

Two distinct sources of uncertainty therefore confront Irish policy-makers in the medium-term as the new structures of governance and rules of the game in European integration are negotiated. First of all, there can be little doubt that a more variable model of integration will emerge from the 1996 IGC negotiations, and from subsequent ones on EMU, CAP reform, own resources and structural funds, and then on enlargement.

The key questions are whether it will be possible to preserve the EU's 'unicity' — its unity and uniqueness, and an inclusive institutional scope — in this larger and more diverse setting. Systematic variations of objective *capacity* to sustain integration projects, a longstanding feature of the EC/EU, have now been joined by an endorsement of varying *commitment* to do so by the Maastricht Treaty. It seems likely that variability will be further endorsed, but there are rather strict limits to it in a wide setting, especially as regards variations of political commitment and will (IEA, 1995, 97-106, 233-262).

This is where the second great uncertainty comes into play: Britain's role in Europe and the EU. Britain proposes its own distinctive model of integration, a looser, wider Europe, open to the world, with an emphasis on flexibility and inter-governmentalism as keynotes of cooperation between European nation states. Within this model there is room for differences of emphasis on particular areas of policy between the main British political parties, notably on EMU and the social chapter, but also on CFSP and Justice and Home Affairs. But there is substantial consensus between them on the basic framework.

Irish and other negotiators raise the question whether there is sufficient institutional backbone and political commitment in the British model to sustain the ambitious continental tasks of stabilisation, peace and prosperity that the EU has set for itself. Or is this model too weak and flaccid, with the result that, if it were to be adopted, disintegration, regional balances of power, even, as Dr Kohl fears, nationalism and wars, are more likely to result? The polarisation between German and British models is one of the most noteworthy features of the contemporary European scene, which has been given a xenophobic twist by the emergence of right-wing English nationalism. It is not helped by the unfortunate choice of the German metaphor: people in Britain remember only too well what happened to the slowest ships in the convoy during the two world wars against Germany.

A Britain preoccupied with resolving its internal as well as its external crisis of identity after the end of the Cold War is, of course, less likely to see its model prevail. It has less room for tactical manoeuvre because of Mr Major's parliamentary arithmetic, and therefore less influence and fewer allies than is expected to be the case after the next general election, whether it is won by Labour or the Conservatives. This introduces one short-term unpredictable factor into the IGC negotiations. A more substantial medium-term one is the likelihood that whatever government wins will not be in a position to decide its basic European policy, including whether it will participate in EMU, until after the deadline in early 1999.

It is important from the Irish perspective to realise two central facts about the current political transition in Britain. First of all, the balance of its main interest groups — industry, the City of London, trade unions — and its public opinion, are still predominantly in favour of a participative approach towards Europe, despite a discernible shift towards Euroscepticism. But, secondly, such a transition will necessarily take a long time to work itself out, even if Labour wins the next election. Politically mishandled, it could go disastrously wrong.

Ireland's participation in the EU has consolidated independence from Britain both politically and economically. It is essential that this achievement be preserved during the next few years of negotiation over the future of Northern Ireland and preparation for Irish involvement in a more integrated Europe. The temptation to tie Irish fortunes to such an uncertain partner, whether politically or economically, should be resisted during the course of Britain's transition towards a more well-defined European role. It is very much in Ireland's interest that the British debate is so resolved, but by no means inevitable that it will be.

◼ CHAPTER 7
BRITAIN, IRELAND AND EMU: THE CURRENCY DILEMMA

BRENDAN HALLIGAN

INTRODUCTION

The shift from dependence to independence and, latterly, to interdependence between Ireland and Britain is one of the central themes of this study. The tension between independence and interdependence is nowhere more graphically illustrated than in the area of monetary policy. The Irish state, for sound pragmatic reasons, allied its currency and monetary policy with sterling until the establishment of the Exchange Rate Mechanism (ERM) in 1979 but chose, although Britain did not, to enter the ERM as part of a larger strategy of integrating with the other member states of the then European Economic Community.

Although a factor in that decision was concern about inflationary pressures being imported from Britain through the fixed currency link, this strategy was also conceived as part of a policy to lessen Ireland's overall dependence on Britain by diversifying economic and trade relations across a broader spectrum than had obtained up to that point. It could also be taken politically as an assertion of greater Irish independence within the new multi-lateral framework offered by Europe. Nevertheless, the reality from 1979 onwards was that Irish monetary policy became bi-polar. The relationship of the Irish pound with sterling remained important from the point of view of competitiveness but a new relationship, basically that with the DM, had also to be managed if the obligations of ERM membership were to be observed.

Generally speaking, this complex set of relationships was mastered successfully without undue strain but did require periodic adjustment in the central ERM rate so as to avoid serious competitive distortions vis-à-vis sterling. The most notable example of the Irish authorities' response to the latter threat was in April 1986 when the pound was devalued at their request in the face of a serious weakening in the value of sterling. Despite the secular decline in the sterling exchange rate up to the crisis of 1991-92, it can be said that Ireland succeeded in balancing membership of the ERM with the need for competitiveness against its largest trading partner. In that regard, independence (as exemplified by ERM membership) and interdependence (as expressed in the sterling exchange rate) were carefully traded off without undue disruption to Ireland's economic policies, its broad European strategy or its deepening relationships with Britain on Northern Ireland.

Two events have changed the context significantly: Britain's failure to sustain its belated membership of the ERM and the decision at Maastricht to create a single currency by 1999 at the latest. Their conjunction may have been an unfortunate accident of history, but the repercussions were profound for Britain's monetary policy and overall European strategy, and hence for Irish interests. In sum, the third stage of economic and monetary union may well go ahead on schedule while Britain's reaction is, at least, uncertain. The net issue thus raised is simply expressed but difficult to resolve. How can Ireland maintain a central feature of its European strategy, that of keeping pace with the core of integration, while dealing with a key economic and political imperative, that of protecting Irish business from competitive devaluation by sterling and nurturing a bi-partisan policy on Northern Ireland?

This chapter seeks to throw some light on these questions by analysing the rationale and prospects of the single currency, identifying and evaluating possible British responses should it be created, and weighing up the options for Ireland in the light of the independence/interdependence schema developed elsewhere in this volume.

THE PROSPECTS AND TIMETABLE FOR EMU

The Maastricht Treaty laid down a timetable for the establishment of economic and monetary union or what might more properly be called a currency union. The criteria for membership reflected the priorities of the Bundesbank which is required by the German constitution to protect the value of the DM. Sound monetary policy is the overriding aim in framing the preconditions for monetary union and the Bundesbank used the full weight of its influence to impose its own domestic objectives on the European Union. The other member states had no option but to comply, given that the ERM was anchored on the DM because of long-term German success in sustaining a strong currency policy and the corresponding failure of a number of member states to do likewise.

The Treaty provisions on EMU are in effect an invitation to other currencies to adhere to the DM on conditions laid down by the German authorities. Failure to accept them would have resulted in no Treaty provisions, since Germany would have refused to forego the stability and security of the

Bundesbank regime for the uncertainties of a European currency infected by the weaknesses of some others. The Germans, in particular the Bundesbank, hold a veto over monetary union. It cannot happen without them and it can only happen on condition that the stability culture which has underpinned the DM is replicated in the currency union. It is also true, however, that the other member states readily agreed to the inclusion of the convergence criteria in the Treaty on the grounds that they constituted a sound basis for fiscal and monetary policies.

Within Germany itself public sentiment is opposed to giving up the DM, as opinion polls have repeatedly confirmed. Yet, at the same time, the political elite is deeply committed to the achievement of monetary union for higher political reasons, such as those spelled out initially in a CDU/CSU paper on European Union (September 1994). Monetary union is seen as the necessary platform on which to construct political union. In fact, it is regarded as indispensable. Political union, in turn, is regarded as the essential precondition for the security of a united Germany which has found itself unexpectedly at the geographic heart of a democratic Europe, its eastern borders thrust yet again into a zone of instability and uncertainty. The enlargement of the Union to encompass the states of Central and Eastern Europe and the simultaneous creation of a political union which might eventually involve common defence are therefore part of a grand strategic design to ensure the security of the New Germany.

From a German perspective it is hard to refute the logic of this strategy. The problem is that some other member states have been slow to recognise its force or to admit its validity. The speech of Karl Lamers to the Federal Trust in mid-November 1994 reflected this German dilemma of how to convince their fellow EU members of the necessity for this grand design while at the same time reassuring their electorate that monetary union is part of a greater good.

It is in this context that the prospects of monetary union must be evaluated, i.e. as an integral part of a coherent strategy to satisfy the security needs of a united Germany within a united Europe. Initially, since this grand design was little understood, the prospects for monetary union were evaluated on partial information and on an incomplete set of criteria, with the result that both markets and business reacted to the prospects of a single currency in solely economic terms, whereas the fundamental motivation of Germany was essentially political. By the end of 1995 perceptions had changed. The German grand design had become better understood and the Madrid Council (December, 1995) in affirming its determination to introduce the single currency by 1999 added to the belief that the necessary political will existed. Baptising the single currency with the name of the Euro was not only psychologically significant but was seen also as further evidence that the project would go ahead, provided economic circumstances permitted.

The informal ECOFIN Council in Verona (April, 1996) later confirmed a growing belief that the single currency was indeed a real political objective on the part of the majority of member states, notably Germany and France. The debate consequently took on another dimension; a single currency by 1999 might be a real common objective, but was it realistic in the light of the criteria that had to be met beforehand? In Autumn 1996 that question cannot be answered either way with any certainty. The Madrid Council had determined that adjudication on the eligibility of member states would be conducted in the spring of 1998 on the basis of 1997 data regarding member states' public finances and economic performance. That decision, in turn, put the focus on budgetary performance in 1997. Forecasts for German economic growth remain pessimistic and it is conceivable that the criterion for the budget deficit might not be met. Despite that possibility (which some might regard as a probability) the German authorities are insistent that all the criteria will be met in 1997, and are taking steps accordingly.

The position of France is equally pivotal in any assessment of the possibilities for monetary union. Just as it would be inconceivable to press ahead without the DM it would be unthinkable to proceed without the franc. The internal market would be shattered were France to behave as Britain in floating the franc against the DM and/or to abandon the fiscal and monetary policies which have underpinned the franc fort. Any assessment of French economic policy must conclude that for their own strategic reasons the French are determined to lock on to the DM and to follow the policy guidelines laid down by the Bundesbank. The independence granted to the Bank of France, as required by the Maastricht Treaty, is confirmation of that strategic intent, leading to the conclusion that German and French policies on monetary union are moving in tandem, with Germany setting the pace as well as the parameters.

Nevertheless, French policy on Europe underwent an inevitable, and perhaps necessary, re-evaluation following the election of President Chirac in mid-1995. Given that the Franco-German axis is the bedrock on which the integration process rests, any re-interpretation of French priorities would have had repercussions extending beyond EMU and would have decisively affected prospects for the single currency. In the event, it seems that the Franco-German partnership is destined to endure as a result of President Chirac's assessment that it serves the best long-term interests of France and of the emergence of a close personal liaison with Chancellor Kohl analogous to that which prevailed in past decades between successive French presidents and German chancellors.

It can be argued, as a result of these developments, that France and Germany are again *ad idem* with regard to the grand design for Europe, with the single currency as the cornerstone of the next stage of integration. But the question also arises as to whether France, for its part, can meet the budget deficit criterion. Public finance reform at the end of 1995 met with such popular opposition as to put that objective in doubt, a great deal remains to be done if budgetary performance in 1997 is to be successful in lowering the deficit to the required level. There is no certainty that any policy, however vigorously pursued by the authorities, will simultaneously cut expenditure and raise growth in the short period which remains before the crucial Council decision in 1998. It can only be noted that President Chirac and his government are publicly committed to doing so and that their eventual success is being taken as a working hypothesis by other policy-makers.

This assumption was strengthened by a government decision (August 1996) to take the necessary steps in the 1997 budget, such as to freeze public expenditure, in order to meet the Maastricht criterion on the level of the govenment deficit (i.e. not more than 3% of GDP).

Aside from Germany and France, the creation of the single currency is critically dependent on the involvement of the Benelux. This is so for geo-political as well as economic reasons. Furthermore, as President Santer has remarked, the aggregate GDP of the single currency zone should be equivalent to that of Japan if the Euro is to have international credibility and the requisite weight in the markets consistent with its intended role. For that reason alone, the membership of Benelux is an indispensable (although not sufficient) condition for success. It can be argued that, for their part, Benelux countries are pursuing the same strategy as France. This is particularly true of the Netherlands, as a Dutch government position paper made clear as early as November 1994. Not to be outdone, the Belgians indicated their determination to accept the rigours of the DM regime, although with less convincing credentials; in particular the very high level of their debt/GDP ratio poses a serious problem. The speech by Prime Minister Dehaene to the French Institute for International Relations (26 October 1994) bore that out.

While doubts continued to be expressed in many quarters as to Belgium's eligibility or capacity to become eligible, the situation took a dramatic turn in mid-summer 1996 when the parliament conferred special powers on the

Prime Minister in respect of budgetary policy. The message was unequivocal. It was Belgium's ambition to be amongst the founding members of the single currency.

The same ambition is true of the Austrians and in their case is entirely credible in the light of the long-term stable relationship between the schilling and the DM. By mid-1996, it had become generally accepted that Ireland and Finland would also meet the convergence criteria but that Denmark, which would also qualify, would not opt for initial membership because of political circumstances arising from popular attitudes towards membership of the EU as a whole.

The situation could thus be summarised by saying that in Autumn 1996 the Franco-German axis seems determined to proceed with the single currency on schedule in 1999, a group of other member states with strong political, economic and geographical ties with both countries would also qualify, and two of the more peripheral states would be members, but that the economic capacity of the Franco-German partnership to meet the criteria was in doubt and, hence, the whole project still lay in the balance as far as the 1999 deadline is concerned.

Were the single currency to proceed as planned, then the relationship between the participating states and those outside would become the critical determining feature for the medium term. The Verona Ecofin Council was helpful in that regard as it sketched out the broad contours of the system post 1999. All member states not meeting the criteria initially would be expected to do so within four years and so enter the single currency by 2003. In the meantime, their exchange rates with the Euro would be determined on a bilateral basis between the ECB and their respective national central banks, with the ECB having the right to initiate a review of the rate should that be considered necessary. This innovation would remove one of the defects of the ERM which relied exclusively on national authorities to trigger a change in the central rate. Non-participating currencies would be free to fluctuate within agreed bands which would be sufficiently broad to discourage speculative attacks but these bands could be progressively narrowed in step with success in meeting the convergence criteria.

This complex system governing the relationship between the Ins and the Outs represents no more than a series of political understandings on the part of the finance ministers and cannot be taken as definitive; it will be clarified more definitively during Ireland's EU Presidency. But the understandings serve as a pointer to what will most likely emerge and provide the best scenario available regarding the future relationship between sterling and the Euro should the UK decide not to participate as a founding member. It has to be noted, for purposes of completeness, that the UK had previously signalled it did not regard itself as bound by any agreement governing the exchange rate relationship between the Euro and the Outs, and that Sweden has entered similar reservations for the time being. It would seem that these views will be respected in whatever regime is ultimately determined.

BRITISH PROSPECTS

In the context of EMU, the UK emerges as a singular case. It sought and secured a formula in the Maastricht Treaty which gave it the right to opt into the single currency on the decision of its government and parliament. For all other member states, with the exception of Denmark, entry into the third stage of EMU was to be automatic on meeting the convergence criteria (although the decision of the German Constitutional Court introduces a constraint on the German position) but for the UK there was to be no such automaticity. Membership was to be by choice.

The reasons for the UK stance at Maastricht are many and deep-rooted and go beyond the question of EMU *per se*. The more immediate cause lay in the Euro-sceptic rhetoric developed by Mrs Thatcher throughout her premiership which simultaneously reflected and heightened a deep distrust within the Conservative Party towards the integration process. Mr Major, following a brief flirtation with a more mellow line towards Europe, reverted to the language of his predecessor at Maastricht for the sake of party unity and insisted that the UK should be excluded from the Social Chapter and be free to choose membership of the single currency if it so desired. It was on the basis of these achievements that, in the immediate aftermath, he proclaimed 'game, set and match' had been won.

The choice of metaphor was illuminating. It presupposed there was an opponent to be faced, something to be played for, and a victory to be secured. That no other prime minister felt compelled to speak to his or her electorate in such terms reinforces the point that the UK stance on integration was, and remains, unique among the family of member states. It confirms the analysis set out in Part I that the UK has a deep-rooted problem with the European project as a whole, of which EMU is but one example, and that the issue of identity is at the heart of the matter. Opposition to a more united Europe was not just a peculiarity of Thatcherism but is a long-term phenomenon which needs sympathetic understanding if it is to be addressed appropriately by other member states and managed successfully in specific policy areas such as EMU.

It can be held that the misfortune of EMU is that it crystallised in the most dramatic form possible British reservations about sharing sovereignty. The issue could not be fudged, it could only be postponed. At stake appeared to be the sovereignty of parliament, the cornerstone of the constitutional order and itself the most valued and tangible achievement of the long historical evolution from feudalism to a constitutional monarchy. As this evolution is a journey which no other member state has had the privilege of sharing, i.e. shaping and fashioning a parliamentary democracy over a period of centuries, it is understandable that traditionalists or conservatives should look askance at constitutional innovations or at experiments intended to redefine the powers of the nation state; but it is equally understandable that observers in other member states should fail to comprehend the depth of the concerns expressed.

The single currency was seen as striking at the heart of parliamentary supremacy, in this instance at parliament's authority over the Central Bank and the key areas of exchange and interest rate policies. The prospect of yielding up sovereignty to an independent national monetary authority is anathema to many parliamentarians (of both main parties) especially when the prospective independent authority is supranational and not amenable to parliamentary control in any conventional sense. The refusal of the UK to join the ERM in 1979 was consistent with that strongly-held tradition, and Mrs Thatcher immediately regretted the brief period of membership as an aberration. The return to the normality of a nominally independent exchange rate was widely greeted with relief. However, the persistence of the goal of EMU re-opened the wounds and opposition to British involvement was presented as a refusal to countenance any further encroachment on sovereignty. The single currency thus became the battle ground upon which UK participation in deeper integration was to be contested. In this debate, the economic merits of the single currency became secondary to larger political considerations.

While this was true of the Conservative Party, the economic case for monetary union was discussed in business and financial circles. Differences of opinion have proved to be sharp but there are discernible elements of support for UK membership, predictably from business engaged in international markets. The City of London, the great financial centre of Europe, has already seen the European Monetary Institute sited in Frankfurt and may anticipate with good reason that this presages an unattractive loss of influence and business, should the single currency proceed. Nevertheless, within financial circles there is no clear-cut majority either way, although the realisation (as of Autumn 1996) that the timetable may be met by a core group of states could begin to exert its own influence. In any event, it can be said that the divisions which have convulsed the Conservative Party are not mirrored across the broad spectrum of British business. The debate has generally been pragmatic rather than ideological and any government decision to stay out or go in would not meet with overwhelming opposition. On the other hand, because the voice of business was muted it was consequently not very influential (although by mid-1996 the CBI had begun to express doubts about the wisdom of staying outside the single currency). The debate about UK membership thus remains predominantly political.

That being the case, the position of the Labour Party is crucial in view of the possibility that it might form the next government. Here again, the situation is more complex than would appear at first sight. Labour had previously committed a future government to membership of the ERM and while it has not overtly reversed that policy with the election of a new leader, neither has it vigorously re-endorsed it, nor has it pronounced unambiguously on EMU. Instead, there has been cautious expression of what may be best called a holding position. Probably this is for good political reasons related to the election campaign, but it is also possible that demands for a referendum on EMU membership, which are embarrassing for the Conservative Party, have caused Labour to be circumspect about its intentions. Furthermore, there is a residue of opposition within the party towards Europe for precisely the same reasons concerning parliamentary sovereignty as excite their Conservative counterparts; and also a traditional reluctance, reiterated by the Labour Party last year, to accept an independent role for the Bank of England – a *sine qua non* of EMU participation. The true scale of that opposition within Labour is unknown because of self-imposed discipline designed to minimise any evidence of internal party divisions but it would be unwise to dismiss it as irrelevant or insignificant.

The generality of the Labour Party may well be less reverent than the Conservatives towards the conventions of the unwritten UK constitution but it harbours its own version of traditionalism and has yet to exhibit broad enthusiasm for the European project. It too has to resolve the identity crisis identified in Part I. In the last analysis it is probably better positioned to do so, more cleanly and quickly than the Conservative Party, because of economic considerations. The aim of re-invigorating the economy will be predominant in terms of its government priorities, and EMU membership will be evaluated on the basis of what it can deliver as an antidote to the cycle of booms and recessions which bedevilled and undermined past Labour governments. Pragmatism could overwhelm sentiment and the logic of sharing sovereignty in monetary policy could eventually be followed vigorously, with side effects in other policy areas. On balance, it can be expected that a Labour government would eventually opt to enter the single currency after a period in office, but with the caveat that it solves beforehand the conundrum of whether a decision by parliament is sufficient in itself or must be complemented by a referendum. Should a referendum be deemed necessary there is no way, at this distance, of forecasting the outcome with any degree of confidence.

FUTURE UK SCENARIOS

In the light of all these uncertainties, it would be prudent to assume that the most likely scenario is that Britain will not be a participant in the single currency should the 1999 deadline be kept. From an Irish viewpoint two questions arise. When, if ever, will Britain enter the currency union? And until it does, what will be its exchange rate relationship with the Euro?

As to the first question, it would seem improbable that Britain would remain indefinitely outside the single currency; this would be true even for a Conservative government beset by divisions on the matter. Following the establishment of the third stage of EMU, facts rather than theoretical possibilities would have to be faced, some of which might prove to be unpalatable if an interest premium or exchange rate volatility (or both, seeing that they are a function of each other) were to be the cost of nominal independence. At best, the UK monetary authorities could attempt to shadow the Euro and perforce follow the same macro-economic disciplines as the participating member states. In that case, the question would arise as to whether virtual membership without a voice was preferable to real membership with one. Alternatively, a policy of competitive devaluation would be punished by the markets and opposed on internal market grounds by the member states within the single currency. Strategically, staying outside would not seem to make sense for the long term.

The most likely answer to this question is that Britain would ultimately be compelled for reasons of economic self interest to exercise its right to opt-in and so become a participant. As to when this might happen, it would be anybody's guess, ranging from the run-up period to 2003, when all other currencies are expected to join, to the more distant prospect of enlargement when a new batch of currencies would become potential members. In that eventuality splendid isolation might be portrayed as courageous political defiance but also dismissed as indefensible in terms of economic logic. In so far as international policy is ultimately concerned with the defence of national interests, then economics would be likely eventually to prevail. The late-joiner syndrome, set out in the Summing-up and Conclusions of this volume, would thus be repeated.

Regarding the second question about the likely exchange rate relationship between the Euro and sterling, the answer has been partially given above. Even though the UK does not feel itself obliged by the Treaty to enter a structured relationship, one option is to behave as if it did. This would have the merit of incorporating the convergence criteria into domestic policy with a consequent pay-off in terms of inflation and interest rates. By implication, it would introduce and sustain exchange rate stability. This strategy would furthermore leave open the possibility of British entry at any appropriate moment, since Treaty requirements would be honoured (with the likely exception of independence for the Bank of England). It should be recalled that there is in any event a Treaty obligation on all member states to coordinate macro-economic policy, and this strategy would also satisfy that requirement. The main doubt over this scenario is whether it is feasible, i.e. have Britain's economic weaknesses been cured to the point where the exchange rate would no longer be under threat?

It is frequently argued that a second option is to pursue a course of competitive devaluation, but the conscious choice of such a policy is vigorously contested by the authorities as representing neither their past nor their current intent. They have not chosen to devalue; rather the markets have imposed their will on the value of sterling. While this begs the question as to why the markets have so chosen, these protestations have to be taken at face value. Nevertheless, past events leave open the possibility that history could be repeated, and it is this fear, more than any other, which exercises Irish analysts in assessing potential competitive threats should Ireland enter the single currency while Britain remained outside. It need hardly be said that a competitive devaluation policy, whether by choice or circumstance, would eventually be deemed incompatible with the provisions of the internal market. At some point a choice would have to be made between the two. Consequently, the option is not a runner for the long term (although in the short to medium term it could cause damage to trade partners, like Ireland).

A third British option would be to follow a wait-and-see approach, in which the markets would determine the sterling exchange rate while the authorities would seek to balance domestic political and economic objectives against the need to maintain a secure footing within the internal market. Such a strategy would be no more than a medium-term one at best; ultimately the issue of membership would have to be confronted.

Another option, which is not widely supported, might be to declare emphatically that membership is to be ruled out for the foreseeable future and that the intent is to accelerate and intensify past policies based on a deregulated competitive economy. If it were to be genuinely competitive then that reality would be reflected in a strong currency (thus obviating Irish fears) but if it were not, then a secular downward trend in the exchange rate would be inevitable (thus heightening Irish fears).

This latter option is often presented as part of a larger scenario relating to British withdrawal from the EU apart from trading relationships and would be the most extreme representation of the identity crisis examined in Part I of this volume. As such it does not command widespread support in British political or business circles, although it does attract disproportionate attention in the British media. In fact withdrawal represents the least likely outcome of the resolution to the identity crisis and, accordingly, should be incorporated into Irish strategic analysis only as the most malign and most improbable scenario for the future. It has to be said, however, that the BSE crisis and the British government's response to the ban on its beef and beef products raised the spectre of withdrawal even in minds which had previously dismissed it as wishful thinking.

Finally, at the other end of the spectrum, there is what, in current circumstances, would be the most benign scenario in terms of Irish interests whereby the British authorities would privately decide to gear up for membership, conduct macro-economic policies accordingly and opt-in at the first opportunity. There is reason to believe that an implicit strategy along these lines best explains the posture of the Conservative government and the future plans of Labour. It might be explained away publicly as doing no more than what is sensible, but communicated in confidence where it matters as being tantamount to the Danish strategy, i.e. let the single currency happen, watch it succeed, admit it is a fact of life and submit to the inevitable. This would be the late-joiner syndrome at work but its importance could lie in the fact that if they believed this was the undeclared policy of the next British government, whatever its composition, the markets and other member states might in the interim treat the UK as a virtual member of the Euro.

These options have necessarily focused on Britain's choices but it is also true that the European Union will have its own range of responses which could counteract or complement whatever Britain decides, so that the end result might be even more complicated. There could be a dynamic in the bi-lateral relationship between the Euro and sterling, either of a positive or negative nature, and it would indeed be strange if there were not. The point here is that in relation to membership of the Euro, Britain is not a free agent but part of a large club where minimum rules and behavioural norms have to be respected.

All these scenarios (and they are not intended to be exhaustive) must be subject to one overriding consideration, which has been previously mentioned. The issue of putting British membership of the single currency to the test of a referendum is being debated with increasing vigour and may eventually be accepted by either or both the main parties as an integral part of the decision-making process. That a referendum is at odds with the very principle of parliamentary sovereignty they purport to defend has not deterred those who wish to uphold it. This inherent contradiction will thus not prevent a referendum from being held should the dynamics of the election campaign push the debate in that direction.

Were a referendum to be held, it is inevitable that the question for decision would become much larger than that appearing on the ballot paper. The real issue at stake would be Britain's continuing participation in the European Union and not just its membership of the single currency. As such, the outcome would be impossible to predict as it would depend on too many variables, such as the complexion of the next government, the fall-out from the electoral process, the state of the economy, not to mention the extent to which the identity crisis had been resolved. If the role of Britain in Europe is not settled until the debate about the nature of Britain has itself been put to rest, the timing of the referendum would, clearly, be crucial.

BRITAIN'S ECONOMIC PROSPECTS

Embedded in the political debate about the single currency is an argument about Britain's economic prospects, an argument which is at the heart of the identity crisis. One view claims that British performance throughout this century has been that of long-term secular decline, which may not have been arrested even in the past decade. A contrary view is that the economy has now been transformed into one of the most competitive in Europe, and stands poised for success. On the one hand, sluggish growth throughout the nineties, is advanced as evidence of continuing deep-seated structural defects. On the other, impressive statistics regarding productivity gains and cost reductions are presented as proof that the worst is past and the future brighter than it ever was. Both sides of the case were argued persuasively at conferences on which this volume is based and are represented in the papers published in the accompanying one.

A value judgement either way must influence economic observers in their interpretation of what is best for Britain in the context of the single currency, and is accordingly of interest to an Irish audience. For on the issue of what policy Britain should pursue, the two schools diverge; structuralists would tend to favour membership while exponents of the competitive model would prefer freedom outside the currency union. Both have a valid point of departure in that Britain still suffers from structural problems but has also modernised its competitive base; that this is so gives little comfort to those who would wish to predict with reasonable confidence where the logic of economic interests will lead in the long run, as distinct from the political debate in the short term.

What can be said, however, is that for the short to medium term the British economy will continue to be a strong competitor for Ireland not only in world markets but also within the two domestic markets. Interdependence with Britain has to be factored into any assessment as to the nature of Ireland's economic interests.

THE TRIANGULAR RELATIONSHIP

The currency crisis of 1992-93 revealed that the Irish authorities had less freedom in managing the exchange rate than had been believed. The period between 1979 and 1992 had come to be regarded as one in which the trade dependence on the UK had been progressively reduced to the point where the shock of a sterling devaluation could be absorbed. The markets reacted otherwise and irrespective of the validity of the arguments on which that perception was based, the reality is that it influenced their behaviour and ultimately forced the Irish authorities to devalue.

The initial consequence of this was effectively to restore the direct linkage with sterling which many had believed ended. For a period the Irish exchange rate more or less shadowed sterling and Irish interest rates again became a function of those in the UK. It seemed that the link between the Irish pound and the DM had been broken. But the Irish authorities subsequently restored the main features of the bi-polar exchange rate policy that had been in place throughout ERM membership and the pound appreciated somewhat against sterling and stabilised vis-à-vis the DM, with interest rates tending back towards the German level. In so far as there was ever a status quo, it has been restored. The markets now take a calmer view of the Irish currency, and the particularly strong economic performance in the past few years has done much to sustain and enhance their confidence in the fundamentals. Nevertheless, the relationship with the UK in terms of trade remains an issue.

The belief that Irish dependency on the UK had been brought to an end was based on an analysis of trade flows which indicated progressively lower exports going to the UK and a corresponding increase to the rest of the Union. During the national debate on exchange rate strategy in the latter part of 1992, it was increasingly argued however that the trade statistics masked a high degree of continuing dependency in terms of jobs, specifically in the more labour intensive and lower value-added indigenous industries. Analyses were produced which supported this claim and were in the end broadly accepted as representing economic reality, however unpalatable. Majority opinion among the indigenous business community was to the effect that from a competitive standpoint the exchange rate at the end of 1992 was unsustainable. Some economists added that the dependency was even greater than at first appeared since UK imports competed on the home market and if sterling were to devalue could displace Irish products. The negative effects could extend into the services sector, such as tourism and retailing.

The main aspects of this debate were summarised in the Institute of European Affairs's *Maastricht – Crisis of Confidence* report (1993) and were also the subject of the Institute's project on EMU, which concluded that the degree of exposure for the indigenous manufacturing sector over the short term was such that another sharp sterling devaluation of a magnitude similar to that of 1992-93 would have to be offset by innovative domestic policies.

An added complication of recent origin is that because of political events in Northern Ireland dependence on the British economy could increase rather than lessen. The peace dividend, should it transpire, was seen by some commentators and business people mainly in terms of greater north-south trade. There are differences as to the extent of the potential trade increase, but what is not in dispute is that policy-makers in Dublin could be reluctant to adopt measures likely to discourage or prevent the emergence of an all-Ireland economy. This ambition could push Ireland towards greater economic interdependence with the UK and perforce would work contrary to what has been an implicit policy objective since joining the EEC in 1973, i.e. to lessen dependency on Britain by diversifying European trade to the point where its distribution between different markets corresponded to the EU norm (presuming there is one). The end result of these divergent pressures could be a classic political dilemma; the national interest in one key area of policy would run counter to that in another.

The view in Northern Ireland is sometimes expressed quite differently. The argument goes that the Northern economy is so integrated with the British that the potential for increased north-south trade is actually quite limited. The small size of both economies is advanced as a further argument for not expecting any significant increase in the volume of trade either way. The conclusion drawn is that a triangular relationship between the Republic, Northern Ireland and Britain is unlikely to emerge to any significant extent and that the relationships are more likely to remain predominantly bilateral.

On the other hand, the combined view of the Northern CBI and the Irish Business and Employers' Confederation (as expressed to the Forum for Peace and Reconciliation in December 1994) was that potential for increased north-south trade existed and could create about 75,000 net new jobs. However optimistic this forecast may appear the Irish government has no alternative but to take account of it as a political fact – if there is a peace dividend to be realised. In these circumstances, the dispute between economists could be secondary to the more general belief that employment opportunities had been created and the government would have to react appropriately. In summary, decision-makers in the Republic might be required to re-assess their European policy in the light of its possible impact on north-south relations. This could be the case until such time as the argument about the potential of an all-Ireland economy were resolved but it is hardly likely to be answered conclusively before 1999. The result, it would seem, is that for the first time since 1973 the government may well be confronted by a Northern dimension to its European strategy. The triangular relationship cannot be ignored, albeit for political rather than economic reasons.

SHOULD IRISH ECONOMIC POLICY TRACK THE UK?

The exchange rate crisis of 1992-93 and the Northern peace process raise policy issues of unexpected (and unwonted) complexity. If neither had happened then Irish strategy on European integration would presumably have followed a predictable course. The line laid down by ERM membership in 1979, support for the Single European Act and opting for membership of EMU at Maastricht would doubtless have been continued by actually joining the monetary union whenever it was created. Indeed, the conduct of the public finances has been governed by a determination to meet the Maastricht criteria, especially the reduction of the debt to GDP ratio to 60 per cent by 1999. Furthermore, the authorities have repeatedly expressed their intent of being part of the single currency from the outset. This determination to be part of the EMU is consistent with a larger strategy of supporting and participating in moves towards the goal of an ever-closer Union. On the presumption that this formulation of the issue is accurate then the question to be addressed is whether Irish policy on European integration should be continued or, differently expressed, whether the degree of dependency is such that Irish policy-makers should cut their losses and resort to tracking the UK economy, specifically the exchange rate, for reasons of competitiveness and hence, employment. The arguments on both sides are weighty.

It has been assumed earlier that on the balance of probability monetary union will be created and will lead inevitably to some deeper form of political union, possibly arising from the outcome of the 1996 inter-governmental conference. Should the Conservative Party remain in power up to the point of decision on EMU membership then the most likely scenario is that the opt-out clause in Maastricht will be invoked by Britain or that the issue of membership (and possibly of the next stage of integration) will be put to the British electorate in a referendum.

The arguments against Irish membership of the single currency are predicated on continued UK opposition to monetary union. If, in these circumstances, the authorities in Ireland concluded that the economy could not afford to run the dangers of an uncompetitive exchange rate, Ireland would exclude itself from monetary union as an actual or potential member, compromise its participation in a political union, and submit to UK exchange policy. The main preoccupations of Irish policy would then be the maintenance of competitiveness with the UK by broadly following movements in sterling and would require a regime of low inflation, high productivity and moderate pay increases. If implemented it would have the positive knock-on effect of sustaining competitiveness in other European markets.

There would, however, be costs. In the first instance they would be political. By removing oneself from the mainstream of integration, influence would be lost in the various Councils. Secondly, there would be economic consequences jeopardising Irish benefits from the common agricultural policy (CAP) and other transfers. It could also be argued that the economic costs could include slower growth as a consequence of being tied to British growth rates, but this too is open to dispute.

Other economic consequences would necessarily arise. Should Britain remain outside the single currency for a protracted period and if Ireland were to follow suit it would imply that Irish exchange rate policy would be dictated in effect from London, a return to the pre-ERM position. That possibility would require careful evaluation, especially if it were to be believed that it would have wider implications for economic growth and for the consensual model constructed for macro-economic management during the past decade.

Moreover, choosing to stay outside the single currency until such time as Britain decided to opt-in would be a judgement on Ireland's interdependence with Britain, which others might interpret as continuing and unavoidable dependence.

The argument for Ireland joining the monetary union in circumstances where the UK opted out is mainly grounded on the proposition that membership of a broadly-based European Union is politically and economically more advantageous than strengthened links with Britain and some indeterminate relationship with the rest of the EU. In political terms there is an expectation that a deeper union will adopt over time some elements of fiscal federalism. These might include a larger budget, although this is open to argument. In any event, enlargement to Central and Eastern Europe will increase competition for transfers. It could also be held that membership of the core or *avant garde* confers a better entitlement to some quantum of the EU budget and stronger access to settled common policies, such as the CAP. A place at the Council table is better than none and could be used to maximise opportunities and minimise threats. Continued participation in the single market would also be a valuable asset in developing the export potential of the Irish economy. Hence, benefits in terms of job protection could be at the expense of losses in transfers and the political ability to defend national economic interests within the Councils of a hard core monetary and political union.

A decision to honour the provisions of the Maastricht Treaty as they apply to Ireland could also be justified by an assumption that Britain's non-participation would be temporary rather than permanent. In those circumstances the threats to Irish competitiveness would be faced and the costs borne, should they arise, on the grounds that they would be outweighed by long-run advantages. This would be a fine judgement call involving many of the variables identified in this volume. A decision to proceed with Ireland's membership of the single currency would furthermore be an assertion that interdependence with Britain has to be seen in a larger European context and that dependence on its economy is much less significant than in the past. It would also represent an Irish judgement on the future resolution of the identity crisis in Britain grounded on the belief that British interests are indissolubly linked with its European neighbours.

The complexity of this analysis, covering a wide range of scenarios, led to proposals that the economic implications of EMU for Ireland should be examined more thoroughly, especially in the context of the UK remaining outside the single currency. The government initiative in late 1995 to commission an expert analysis on these issues met those demands and the resulting report by the ESRI was published in the following July (ESRI, 1996). Amongst its conclusions was the somewhat surprising comment that the quantified benefits of EMU membership were smaller than might have been expected. Not unsurprisingly, however, it confirmed that a large sterling devaluation would be damaging, especially for the sectors most exposed to currency risks, such as clothing, food processing and textiles. But, in a point worth much reflection, it added that in the longer-term the more rapid adjustment and lower interest rates associated with being in the EMU should lead to an earlier and stronger industrial recovery "than if Ireland were continuing to operate as an independent currency".

The comprehensiveness of the ESRI analysis did much to fill the information gap which many believed made debate on the vexed question of "Ireland in, UK out" more a matter of rhetoric than informed discussion. But the report also had the merit of reminding public opinion that there were unquantifiable benefits associated with EMU membership which ultimately fell to individual judgement as to their weight and importance. In effect, there is more to the argument than economic modelling and the quantification of identifiable effects: in the end, the issue is one of political economy rather than economics. Whilst it will be some time before the full import of the ESRI Report can be fully digested, its value to a more measured debate can hardly be underestimated.

CONCLUSION

The debate in Ireland regarding membership of the single currency is predominantly economic rather than political. In Britain it is the reverse. For Ireland the objective of a single currency is one to which virtually all policy-makers have subscribed as good in itself and there are few if any reservations about the loss of monetary sovereignty. Criticism has rather been focused on the governance of the proposed common regime and the absence of employment policies to complement a coordinated monetary policy. Doubts about the feasibility of participation, in the absence of UK membership and a stable exchange rate relationship between sterling and the Euro, have been the centre of debate.

In the meantime, the authorities have successfully continued their strategy of strict fiscal disciplines and sound monetary policy to the point where Irish membership of the Euro in 1999 is taken as given, should the date be met and should Ireland so decide. In that sense, the authorities and the social partners have created what was called 'the necessary fiscal space' to allow them to exercise whichever strategy they thought best at the European Council in 1998. This has been buttressed by repeated declarations that Ireland will be amongst the founding members of the Euro.

But the dilemma, of course, remains. Interdependence with Britain is now a political as well as an economic reality, admittedly in a new and more benign form than at any previous point throughout independence. It will require subtle and complex responses to resolve that dilemma optimally. As of Autumn 1996, solutions are still in the making.

Amongst those offered, in the context of organising the economic affairs of Northern Ireland, is the imaginative proposal set out in the paper by David Fell in the accompanying volume, to the effect that Northern Ireland might be treated as a special case for purposes of EU policy. This would, if accepted, partly answer the dilemma of how best to realise the potential benefits of an all-Ireland economy should Britain opt for a more detached relationship with the rest of the Union. It would simultaneously allow economic co-operation to underpin the peace process, viewed by some as a pre-condition for its eventual success.

Needless to say, not even the most novel proposals relating to the future of the Northern Ireland economy deal satisfactorily with the question of how best to arrange long-term relations between Ireland and Britain as a whole, both economically and politically. The point at issue throughout this chapter is how best to marry two forces which may pull in opposite directions: independence inside the European Union and interdependence with Britain. While no conclusions of a definitive nature have been reached, the following argument emerges.

Britain's crisis of identity is a multiple one, with Europe as the most dramatic manifestation of its depth and intensity, but it is not fundamental in the sense that it is an effect rather than a cause. The roots of the problem lie in questions about Britain's own vision of itself as a society, a polity, an economy and as a participant in international affairs. Despite appearances to the contrary, the debate is moving towards resolution. Facts exert their own logic and politics are ultimately shaped by their weight and presence. In the case of Britain, the facts point in one direction, the necessity of finding an accommodation with a continent of which Britain is a part. Politics can only follow in due course. Interests will prevail.

Irish interests have depended upon their own set of facts since independence. They have not been static, for underlying realities have undergone change. That those interests are currently in a state of flux can hardly be disputed. Europe and Northern Ireland, together with a more balanced economic and political relationship with Britain, are the dominant factors for Ireland at the end of this century. Reconciling them is the new Irish dilemma, the issue to which this chapter has been devoted in the context of EMU.

8 EUROPEAN SOCIAL POLICY, EMU AND COMPETITIVENESS

LOCHLANN QUINN

This chapter examines the impact on the Irish economy of a possible UK opt-out from the Social Chapter and also from Monetary Union. The reaction in Ireland to the Green and White papers on European Social Policy has been characterised by two contrasting attitudes and it is not clear that there is — based on the papers and discussion documents produced — any prospect of a consensus viewpoint.

The arguments of IBEC, representing the business community, start from the presumption that the competitiveness of the European economy is the bedrock for subsequent policy and that it is only with a competitive economy that the principal problem facing all European economies — unemployment — can be addressed. Europe is perceived as losing the economic race compared with the US, Japan and the Pacific Rim countries. The thrust of the argument is that we are putting the cart (social policies) before the horse (the needs of the economy). One sentence in IBEC's submission sums up the position: 'The reform of the European labour markets so as to make higher employment possible is not seriously on the Green Paper agenda'.

The alternative — or the opposite view — rests on the premise that high social standards cannot be seen as an optional extra or a luxury that can be eliminated in tough times but are in and of themselves an integral part of a competitive economic model. Further, there is also the assumption that the Irish people entered a Europe that had as a priority a commitment to the raising of incomes and living standards and that these benefits (enhanced social policies) are *owed* to us by Europe.

There is a large gap between these two positions but it is probably fair to say that this argument is repeated to some extent in every European country — it is not unique to Ireland. The recent new entrants to the Union are wealthy countries with highly developed social systems, but the next group of members from Eastern Europe have significant economic difficulties and will bring these to the Union.

It is difficult not to believe that the concept of the Social Chapter was put together during the booming 1980s when the economic outlook in Europe was buoyant. The collapse of asset prices at the end of the 1980s, the developing recession and the rapid growth of unemployment might well have led to something less ambitious if the project were to have commenced in the 1990s. It is also clear that the US model of massive job creation at the cost of a deterioration in real incomes, extremely basic social services, and minimal employment rights has little relevance to Europe — there would not be in any member state any significant level of popular support for such a change in attitude. The UK comes in for a share of demonisation for operating a low-wage, low-skills strategy. This is somewhat unfair in that the UK appears to seek a flexible labour market assuming that the increasing globalisation of many industries will establish market wage levels. This is certainly true in all financial services (banking, insurance, funds management etc.) which do not give the impression of being low-wage industries.

If the UK had not opted out of the Social Chapter it is reasonable to assume that the argument over which should come first — social policy or the competitiveness of the economy — would have resolved itself over time. Democratic politics are usually practical, politicians respond to voter needs, and it is hard not to see these two options coming together at what are deemed acceptable levels of unemployment and acceptable social policies. Nevertheless, throughout Europe unemployment as our biggest problem appears to be more of a mantra than an expression of any real government action.

At this particular stage there is only one piece of legislation — expected to become law in 1996 — resulting from the Social Chapter and that is the European Works Councils. However, if the Social Chapter is to have any meaning at all then some directives will be issued over the next few years. If they are to be of any relevance it is inevitable that they will impose costs and these costs will be borne in Ireland but not in the UK. In other words, costs will be imposed on Irish industry but not in the UK. If no cost differential opens up we can presume that the Social Chapter remains aspirational and of little relevance. Hence, does the UK opt-out affect us and if so what should we do?

With respect to the first part of that question the answer is almost certainly 'yes' although this has received very little study. The UK is the largest recipient of inward investment to the EU. The reasons for this are related to the fact that the US is the largest external investor in the EU and the UK has a similar language and a not too dissimilar legal and business system. Further, the UK, with an historic global trading history has, in the main, long welcomed foreign investment, unlike, say, France and others who have tended towards an overly protective attitude to incoming investment, which has only recently changed. Japanese and Pacific Rim investment, will, as always, be heavily influenced by the US experiences. Further, these latter countries and the US have a strong antipathy to trade unions and labour rigidity. In the competition for inward investment and jobs it is reasonable to assume that the UK (and Northern Ireland) will use their opt-out from the Social Chapter as a competitive tool. It is difficult to quantify the impact of this argument but it could well be significant over time.

Hopefully the peace process and the unleashing of substantial investment funds will make Northern Ireland very competitive in attracting inward investment. It would be churlish to begrudge them these advantages but there should be little doubt that they will see the absence of the Social Chapter as a significant advantage — as will the Welsh and the Scottish. Finally, existing Irish companies with UK competitors could see their respective competitive positions impacted in a significant way.

But what to do? Is there a consensus available in the country to opt out just because the UK has done so? Unlikely. Is there a perception in government and the trade unions that there is, or could be, a problem they wish to address? Unlikely. In an ideal world the UK would sign up. This is also unlikely — except for change in government, and it must remain an open question that a Labour government, once in office, would sign up for the Social Chapter.

Nevertheless, since this project commenced there has been a perceptible change in Brussels and most EU capitals. The drive to give the Social Chapter real teeth would appear to have declined and one suspects that future developments will be slow unless unemployment levels in Europe start to decline.

THE SINGLE CURRENCY

At the time of writing there are some doubts as to whether the single currency will come into being by the end of the century. However, the policy issue that an Irish government needs to address is what to do if the single currency is implemented and if the UK decides not to join. The single currency will, initially, be limited to an inner core and will probably comprise Germany, France, the Netherlands, Austria, Luxembourg and possibly, Belgium. The UK will not be a member. In this scenario what is the probable effect on Irish industry if Ireland were to join? This chapter does not address the fact that Ireland may have political reasons for wishing to join.

HARD CURRENCIES DO NOT, NECESSARILY, DELIVER STRONG ECONOMIES

It appears that the Irish proponents of the single currency perceive it as a way of disentangling ourselves from the UK economy and thereby joining the faster growing central European economies. Since the 1960s the three hard currencies have been and continue to be, the yen, the mark, and the Swiss franc. For most of this period these countries have grown and developed with low levels of unemployment. They, and Germany in particular, are usually compared with the UK and conclusions are drawn about the performance of the economy and the relationship between that performance and the currency. But throughout this same period other countries have thrived — the US, France, and Italy (the latter two performing almost as well as Germany), and for most of this period these countries have run weak currencies. The hard French franc is a fairly recent phenomenon and as yet remains unassociated with increased economic performance and low unemployment. Many small Third World countries have attempted to run hard currencies with disastrous effects on their domestic economies, although the hard currency in their cases usually has a fair amount of help from other factors. Nevertheless, there is little evidence to support the thesis that a hard currency will transform the economy. The economy will deliver the currency, subject to appropriate fiscal discipline; the currency cannot deliver the economy.

IF WE DO NOT JOIN, WE ARE LINKING OURSELVES TO THE UK

This seems to be a very emotive argument; deciding not to join the *single currency* does not necessarily mean merging with sterling. In the scenario outlined above the following members (including probable members) of the EU that almost certainly will not be part of the single currency are: UK, Spain, Portugal, Italy, Denmark, Sweden, Poland, Slovakia, Czech Republic, Greece and Hungary. Ignoring Ireland, this places about 170 million EU citizens in the single currency and 260 million outside it. There is no need to align with the UK. There could well be a sort of EMS of the outer core. By not joining the single currency we do not decouple ourselves from the majority of other EU citizens; furthermore the maintenance of the Maastricht criteria makes sense in itself irrespective of the existence or otherwise of a single currency. Since we joined the EMS in 1979 the Irish pound has depreciated by some 40 per cent against the DM. The EMS provided no great guarantor of stability — in fact the stability of our currency (on a trade-weighted basis) has only really happened when government policy became unambiguous with respect to deficit and borrowings.

GERMANY AND THE SINGLE CURRENCY

The rise of Germany and also Switzerland, the Netherlands, Austria, and parts of France and Italy in the post-war world has seen a transformation of their economies, where many low-skilled jobs disappeared through engineering as a result of new technology or else migrated to lower-cost economies. This has led to a profile of industry (especially in Germany) concentrating on the top end of each market in areas of technology; in many ways the Japanese experience is similar. These economies can handle — by and large — a hard currency (it may be more correct to say a currency that over the long term consistently appreciates over most other currencies) in that their domestic industries have significant technological advantages and they tend to respond to and gain significant productivity (not just labour but product performance) from investment. This is true over the long term despite the current difficulties both Germany and Japan have with overvalued currencies.

But not all economies command these heights. The profile of Irish industry is not the same as those of Germany and Japan. In the case of our devaluation within the EMS the government subsequently explained that during the period of the crisis (September 1992 to January 1993) they were not in possession of the full facts on Irish industry and its competitors, or of the fact that indigenous companies were high employers with an over-dependence on the UK market. It is not too late to start a comprehensive study of the nature of domestic and foreign industry located here and of what would be the impact of joining EMU whilst the UK and the majority of the EU stayed out. Since this project started in the IEA such a study was commissioned by the government on the economic implications of EMU and has just been published by the Economic and Social Research Institute (ESRI, 1996)

We need to address the issue of what could happen if we do join a single currency. We are not here talking about whether Irish industry is competitive at parity or £1.05. The question to be asked is more rigorous — are we, and can we be, competitive at Stg.£1.50 to the IR£? Since 1979 (the year we joined the EMS) the DM, the Swiss franc, and the yen have appreciated against the US dollar, and sterling and the IR£ by the following amounts.

TABLE 5: APPRECIATION OF SFR, YEN AND DM
(FROM 1979 TO JUNE 1996)
AGAINST

	IR£	Stg	US$
SFR	+40%	+43%	+18%
YEN	+64%	+66%	+51%
DM	+35%	+38%	+12%

If we join, and most of Europe stays out, we need to be satisfied that should the same rate of appreciation reoccur over a period of ten years, we can remain competitive and build employment. It is hard not to believe we might be taking an extraordinary risk.

The current argument against this scenario is that the EU will not permit continued "competitive devaluations" — although what it can do to prevent them is not particularly evident. Whatever is said it is fairly obvious that the vast majority of European economies will not qualify for EMU and that Germany will not admit them. Furthermore, we now live in a GATT/WTO trade environment. The values of currencies outside the EU will be of increasing significance as world trade grows and Europe will have to live with whatever exchange rates the markets find acceptable. There will not be a worldwide single currency and we will not have a fortress Europe. Hence the policy option of saying there will not, and cannot be, competitive devaluations sounds very much like wishful thinking. The implications of this would be that the European Central Bank dictates policy to all EU members, irrespective of whether they have joined the single currency or not!

THE IMPORTANCE OF THE UK

In Ireland we have a domestic market of 3.5 million (or 5 million if Northern Ireland is included). That is small. Some time in the 1970s Irish industry developed a self-confident attitude that Ireland could be a base or a platform for exports. In the past twenty years many Irish companies have developed a presence outside the domestic market — which as a market is about the size of greater Manchester. It is now accepted that economic success requires, in part, the development of significant indigenous industries.

If small businesses are to grow they must, at a very early stage in their life, expand overseas. Unlike small business in the UK, Germany, US, etc., they cannot grow to any significant size in the domestic economy. Going overseas is fraught with risk (all studies from all economies confirm this) and the UK is the most user-friendly for us — the same language, the same business systems, legal and accounting broadly similar, consumer habits fairly similar. Such a situation is not unique to Ireland. Many economies have deep roots with a neighbouring giant (Canada and the US, Austria and Germany, Finland and Russia, Mexico and the US, etc.); that first step (which is high risk step) is easier with a near neighbour. If it succeeds, then one progresses further, for example to France, Germany, Spain, etc. The major Irish companies, such as Smurfit, CRH, all made their first overseas venture in the UK and then used their newly enhanced size to go further. It is the essential stepping stone. There is a danger that we could end up being decoupled from the UK, or that many Irish manufacturers would use the UK to supply the home market.

THE DECISION

The ESRI study, referred to above, which is the result of detailed and comprehensive work, concludes that the balance of advantage, for employment, lies in joining EMU. Their conclusion remains valid even in the event of a significant devaluation of sterling — despite it causing severe short-term problems.

If we join, with the UK and other EU members (including potential members) joining over time the results will, almost certainly, be beneficial. However, if we join and the single currency remains essentially a Franco/German currency zone the outlook must be different. If the UK, most Nordic states, and Eastern and Mediterranean Europe remain outside for the long term then this is a risky strategy.

To remain outside — with the majority — but to continue to operate within the Maastricht criteria and then to join EMU with the second stage entrants could be a very sensible option.

CHAPTER 9
THE NORTHERN DIMENSION
GERARD O'NEILL

The energy that actually shapes the world springs from emotions — racial pride, leader-worship, religious belief, love of war — which liberal intellectuals mechanically write off as anachronisms, and which they have usually destroyed so completely in themselves as to have lost all power of action.

George Orwell, *Collected Essays,* Vol. 2, p. 168

INTRODUCTION

Orwell's typically sardonic observation is an appropriate reminder to those of us engaged in anticipating the future. The past twenty-five years have witnessed a conflict in Northern Ireland that was only marginally about political economy, and which was mainly about conflicting rights and identities, as well as about the distribution of power. We should therefore be mindful of Orwell's implied warning: to confine our analysis of the forces shaping the future relationships on this island to those that are 'intellectually comfortable', such as macro- and micro-economics, is a dangerous mistake.

This is particularly true in light of the 1996 IGC and of subsequent EU negotiations on EMU, enlargement, CAP reform and transfers. Ireland's negotiators will be confronted with an agenda that will in many ways be unique among the participating nations. Not only will they have to deal with concerns about peripherality, size, and relations with Europe's most reluctant member (i.e. the UK), they will also have to deal with the fact that the geographical definition of Irish economic and political concerns are changing due to developments in Northern Ireland.

And, of course, it is not just a question of geographical definitions. There is an emotional context to the EU agenda: patriotism is an emotion, and the question of 'to what we owe our patriotism' will provoke an emotional response. Irish citizens consistently show a level of agreement with statements such as 'I am proud of my country', that is above average in Eurobarometer and other surveys. Our attitudes to Europe have been very positive in a context of mainly economic initiatives: CAP, the ERM, the single market, Maastricht and EMU. But the European policy agenda will shift steadily towards mainly political matters over the next few years (enlargement, federalism, defence), giving full scope to the 'anachronisms' so derided by Orwell's intellectuals.

It is in this context that we must assess developments in Northern Ireland over the next few years. At an economic policy level we could see a major re-orientation of Irish government policies on industrial development, trade promotion and regional planning that would significantly alter the way in which the Irish government goes about defining 'the national interest'. And throughout the IGC Ireland will need a crystal clear definition of the national interest if we are to assess successfully the myriad proposals and counter-proposals that will arise. No other participant in the IGC will be confronted with such a combination of challenges.

This chapter sets out some thoughts on the influences and constraints that Irish negotiators will have to address if the challenges arising from the Northern dimension are to be overcome. The first part explores the issues confronting the south's policy-makers in the the IGC and beyond it. The second part looks briefly at the policy options that will be available to them in light of the alternative scenarios for Europe in the medium term. Finally, we assess the implications of the analysis for the management of future relations between the north and the south.

THE ISSUES

Of course there are important economic forces shaping the future relations between both parts of this island. Progress towards EMU and questions of cohesion will have a direct bearing on the south's future economic policies towards the north. A permanent peace will also raise a number of additional economic issues about future relations. For example, if the peace process is sustained, patterns of inward investment may change; new tourist opportunities should emerge; and the shifting of much public and private sector economic activity from a 'war-time' footing to a peace-time footing will provide space for the realisation of a peace dividend. But these are slowly changing phenomena that will only make themselves felt over the next 5-10 years. Indeed, the timescale of economic changes in Northern Ireland will have an important bearing on the wider context of political and other cross-border issues. It is therefore important to explore the nature and timing of economic changes on this island as they will be the subject of considerable debate and of policy dilemmas in the short and medium term.

However, mindful of Orwell's warning, we must remember that economic issues will not be the only items shaping the south's policy agenda vis-à-vis the north.

Northern Ireland has had 'a good recession'. Its level of manufacturing output growth outpaced that for total UK manufacturing, whilst the numbers in employment in 1993 (as the UK's recession ended) were above those in 1989 (when it started). But the north's main structural problems are still in place as the UK economy enters a recovery phase, namely:

—   a very small tradable sector

—   an overly large public sector

—   a major problem of long-term unemployment (almost half of total jobless).

It is the role of the tradable sector that poses the most problems in the medium and long term for the north's economy. NI's manufacturing sector accounts for only 19 per cent of GDP, and the sector is increasingly comprised of small firms: ten years ago only 20 per cent of manufacturing firms were in the 'small employer' category (i.e., employing fewer than 50 people). Today the proportion is 32 per cent. Nearly 50 per cent of their output is either purchased locally or by customers in Britain. Indeed, employment in manufacturing in Northern Ireland has declined by 5 per cent over the past four years. Moreover, to say that Northern Ireland's manufacturers have outperformed the growth rate of the total UK sector is to damn them with faint praise: UK manufacturing has had one of the worst growth records in Europe over the past twenty years. In effect, Northern Ireland no longer has a sizeable core of indigenous, world-class manufacturers who can confront the challenges of global economic change in the decades ahead.

That said, it must be acknowledged that there are a number of world-class manufacturers based in Northern Ireland, e.g., Powerscreen and Masstock. The problem, of course, is that there is little sign of the 'clustering' of a number of internationally-oriented NI manufacturers, operating in the same industry, and benefiting from the economies of scale recognised in current economic growth theory as generating regional development. The food and agri sector might possess the potential for such clustering, but the north has nothing equivalent to the south's chemicals, computers, software and audio-visual sectors.

The public sector directly accounts for a third of all employment in Northern Ireland, and public expenditure accounts directly for nearly half of GDP (and a higher proportion indirectly). Most of the expenditure is in the form of transfer payments and salaries: thus the public sector provides a large slice of the spending power in Northern Ireland. Not surprisingly, consumer spending accounts for a dis-proportionately large share of economic activity: at nearly three quarters of GDP it is well above the level for the Republic of Ireland or for the EU as a whole. Both these 'dependencies' (public spending and consumer spending) will leave NI's economy exposed to a scenario of below average UK growth in the long term, with the balance of UK economic development shifting rapidly away from both factors as sources of economic growth over the remainder of the decade and beyond. Not to mention the possibility that UK growth may lag behind the EU average in the medium term if the factors responsible for its relative decline are not reversed.

The problem of long-term unemployment reflects not only structural changes in the north's labour market (declining numbers of male and full-time workers, offset by a growing number of female and part-time workers), but also the scale of social deprivation that has at times been 'clouded' by political unrest. The communal 'solidarity' that has arisen from the Troubles is giving way to a recognition of the polarisation that has occurred over the past twenty years within the two communities: intra-community income and social inequalities are now greater than inter-community inequalities. The fall-out from these changes — which parallel similar patterns of polarisation across the UK — will become clearer if the process of 'returning to normality' sets in. However, recent falls in unemployment to levels not seen since the early 1980s are one hopeful sign that the north might be spared the worst extremes of UK urban polarisation.

THE NEAR-TERM OUTLOOK

None of the structural problems outlined above are insurmountable — given time. Renewed inward investment could enable the north's industrial developers to kick-start the clustering process, and even to leap-frog the south in some sectors. Likewise the role of the public sector may decline very gradually, giving entrepreneurs and employees time to accustom themselves to the realities of the marketplace. Similarly, there are several initiatives on the employment front (similar to those now being experimented with in the south) that could quickly transform the north's long-term unemployment problem and the threat of social polarisation.

Moreover, we need to recognise the dynamic nature of the forces at play. Rather than making static comparisons of performance and trends, it must be recognised that the potential synergies that could develop on this island (e.g. through the proposed economic corridor linking Belfast and Dublin) could cause a qualitative transformation in the future of both economies.

For the next few years Northern Ireland will continue to benefit from the momentum behind the UK's recovery. Improving consumer and business confidence, as well as a pick up in borrowing, investment, and manufacturing output, are contributing to a positive trend in NI's GDP both in 1995 and 1996. Growth of around 3.0-3.5 per cent per annum is expected. The impact of possible permanent peace would be marginally negative in the short to medium term — due mainly to cut-backs in security expenditure and on expenditure items such as construction — but would be clearly positive in the long term.

In terms of the wider thrust of UK economic policies, the general trend seems to be one of engineering a shift in the sources of economic growth: going for trade- and investment-led growth rather than public and consumer spending-led growth. Tax policies are designed to price people into work (but not to fuel a spending boom), and social welfare policies are designed to encourage recipients to take up employment (effectively ending the right to long-term benefits). Increasingly, individuals will be expected to use the private sector to access the type of pension, health and education services that have traditionally been provided by the state. Despite all that, the UK's budget deficit (PSBR) is still forecast by The Henley Centre to remain relatively high as a proportion of GDP, declining from an exceptional 6.4 per cent in 1994 to 2.3 per cent in 2000 (which would still be above the pattern in the 1980s). Though the impact of this decline on public spending in the north will not be sudden or severe in the short term, the likelihood is that in line with the rest of the UK Northern Ireland's citizens will be subject to a 'feel okay' rather than a 'feel good' factor over the next few years.

The UK trade balance is forecast to worsen over the next five years (from £5 billion in 1995 to £9 billion in 2000), partially offset by a rising surplus on the invisible account. The total current account deficit will shift from a surplus in 1995 of £0.8 billion to a deficit of £6.5 billion in 2000. The fact that the UK's trade deficit with the rest of the EU has grown in recent years does not bode well for its willingness to be locked into a single currency when it is still benefiting from its last devaluation. A worse than foreseen deterioration of the trade balance could make another devaluation increasingly tempting.

A PROBLEM RATHER THAN A PRIZE

In his June 1994 speech to the Northern Ireland Economic Council, Will Hutton suggested that 'the south has come to regard the north as a problem rather than a prize.' He particularly noted the changes in the relative economic positions of the two parts of the islands in recent decades, as well as anticipating further changes in the future. The south, he expects, is entering a 'virtuous circle' of trade-led growth, controlled public spending, modest wage rises and job creation. The north, on the other hand, he suspects, may be entering a 'vicious circle', characterised by an atrophying manufacturing base, declining ability to compete in world markets, and a dangerous dependence on unsustainably high levels of public expenditure and employment.

This is not, it must be said, the type of prognosis that politicians and others in the south usually use to describe future economic potential on this island. But Ireland's policy-makers will be confronted with extraordinarily difficult choices in the next few years because of the Northern dimension.

DIFFICULT DECISIONS

The emergence of a two-speed Europe in the context of a decision to go ahead with EMU in 1999 would definitely be the worst-case scenario for Ireland vis-à-vis NI (assuming the UK stays outside the core). But it is still the most likely scenario given the Tory government's opposition to EMU and the expected trend in the UK's trade balance. The south has a trade surplus with the north: thus NI 'matters' more to the Republic's businesses than vice versa. A 'peace inspired' rush to build trade links with the north could increase the share of trade going north: in turn exposing the south's indigenous sector in particular to exchange rate turmoil in the light of a potential two-speed EMU.

The reality is that Southern businesses have clearly demonstrated a superior ability to identify and exploit cross-border trade opportunities than their Northern counterparts. This was highlighted in the Coopers and Lybrand survey of NI businesses at the end of 1994; 53 per cent of NI firms were exporting goods to the south in their survey: down from 56 per cent in 1991. Some 61 per cent of NI firms were importing goods from the south, up from 44 per cent in 1991.

Ironically, the price of greater economic integration between the two parts of the island might be increasing economic integration of Ireland into the UK's economic sphere due to a growing trade surplus with NI. But, we have to ask, could the potential for low economic growth in the long term in

Britain and, presumably, Northern Ireland, return us to the long-run decline in the UK's share of our trade?

Similarly, we should not assume that Britain will definitely not join the core. Two factors may force the UK into EMU even if they don't want to join:

- Most inward investors in the UK (American/Asian) have been attracted to the UK as a location because of its membership of the EU (though not solely for this reason). Indeed, much of the improvement in the UK's trade surplus in recent years has been due to the growth of foreign-owned exporters in sectors such as cars and consumer durables which traditionally 'ran up' the largest trade deficits in Britain. Such companies will not be happy to stay outside of EMU, exposing them to unforeseeable exchange rate risks.

- Similarly, the UK's financial sector would be exposed to being pushed down the league table by a strong Euro: a worsening invisible account could make the present, manageable deficit a far less manageable one.

It therefore seems inevitable that Britain will ultimately join the core: but it is not inevitable that they will join it immediately it is formed. If that were to be the case, we would have to ask ourselves whether the Republic should wait for UK to 'see the light' in the early twenty-first century, subject to the inevitable exchange rate buffeting. Or whether it should take the pain of dis-engaging from the UK economy more abruptly than planned, with inevitable consequences in cross-border trade and the whole north-south relationship? In such a scenario the south's political agenda vis-à-vis the north could increasingly clash with its economic agenda vis-à-vis Europe. Therefore, getting Ireland's businesses — and its people — on side will be crucial for those shaping the country's EU policies.

The UK government is consciously going for a 'market share' strategy in Europe: forcing a re-orientation of their economy from one driven by consumption and government spending to one driven by trade and investment, a strategy less evident in its rejection of the Social Chapter. The British people will go through a lot of pain in the next few years as a result: any government may be tempted to 'speed up the process' by further devaluations. Thus their short-term requirements may over-ride their longer-term objectives: the end result could be to present Ireland's policy-makers with difficult choices regardless of the time scale.

THE IMPLICATIONS

The economic background to the remainder of the decade will be crucial. Europe will experience its own 'feel okay' factor over the next 3-4 years. But it will definitely not bear the scale of the 1980s — for there are structural factors that will continue to hold back consumer and investor confidence. These include the wide-scale re-structuring (and downsizing) of Europe's largest companies. This is an important point because it seems that integration makes easier progress in times of economic growth than in times of recession. Much of the enthusiasm for the single market was due to the strong growth experienced in the run-up to 1992. But a substantial proportion of that enthusiasm and hope has since disappeared; hence the feeling on the part of so many that Europe's policy-makers should 'hasten slowly'. Indeed, there are two contrasting scenarios for the long-term future of Europe now exercising the minds of policy-makers and business people alike.

The first might be called 'Completing the Jigsaw'. Within ten years we could see the achievement of full market integration, and a voluntary revolution in European labour markets: adopting the flexibility and commitment to skills development necessary to compete in the global marketplace. This would provide a high degree of currency stability, in turn facilitating currency union across an enlarged EU. Institutional reform and the achievement of the right balance of unity and coherence would proceed smoothly against this background. The feel-okay factor would gradually give way to a feel-good factor as returning confidence and falling unemployment stimulated spending and growth.

The alternative scenario might be called 'Sclerotic Relapse'. Squabbling at the IGC and the triumph of a 're-nationalisation' agenda would severely undermine the willingness of the electorates to tolerate or support further initiatives at a European level. Europe's unemployment problem would steadily worsen as even the gains of the single market were undermined by 'beggar-thy-neighbour' social and economic policies. Europe could re-experience the worst excesses of the Euro-sclerosis era, finding itself entering the twenty-first century as an economic also ran.

The experiences of the single market and of the exchange rate crisis have shown that the economic context for political change at a European level is crucial. They have also shown that it is important to have the business community on side when difficult decisions are required. The same experiences have shown us that the Irish business community and the Irish people in general will be enthusiastic supporters of change once they are convinced of the need for it and the benefits accruing. A dialogue on these issues both north and south of the border should be pursued as a matter of urgency.

In that context, we need to emphasise the wider political context to the future agenda. We need also to recognise the limited ability of economists to predict the impact of peace and economic dynamics on the island. They got it wrong in Germany, and they are likely to get it wrong in Ireland. Most economic prognostications are based on now redundant models using historical measures of economic activity in the separate parts of this island. The real 'economic' factors are not included in their models because these are so difficult to quantify: namely the spirit of innovation, entrepreneurship and hope that can build an economic miracle — one bigger than the mere sum of the parts. It is the vision inside the heads of business people and citizens on both sides of the border that is the most important variable shaping the future for this island. A huge potential exists for enhanced cooperation between companies on both sides of the border, sharing marketing costs as well as investment costs. Such networks, successfully employed in Denmark and other European countries, could be put quickly into place, playing a catalytic role in releasing the potential for trade-led growth. It is people who will build the future, not economic models or international funds. Hence a key priority for policy-makers and businesses will be to build cross-border linkages: between educational institutions and enterprises; between voluntary groups and local authorities; and between suppliers and new customers.

It is this latter point that reminds us of the wider context to future relations on this island. Trade, tourism and inward investment are important elements in building on the peace. But economic growth failed to deliver peace over the past twenty-five years in Northern Ireland, even though the average NI standard of living doubled in real terms between 1969 and 1994. The questions of rights and identities that have been at the heart of the conflict will continue to shape relations on this island and the south's agenda vis-à-vis the north. Europe is already witnessing a growing debate about the future of the nation state; about the sources of its sense of identity, and about the role of its regions. Vaclav Havel described the Maastricht Treaty as 'an absolutely perfect and immensely ingenious modern machine' in his 1994 speech to the European Parliament. But he felt that there was something seriously missing: 'Perhaps it could be called, in a rather simplified way, a spiritual or moral or emotional dimension.'

Europe's future is once again about to be shaped by that same energy that Orwell identified. So will Ireland's, not least because it is the vision of the future shared — or perhaps, not shared — by the peoples on this island that will determine the long-run outcome of the economic, social and political forces that are now unfolding.

CHAPTER 10
BRITAIN IN EUROPE: INTEGRATED SECURITY OR THE REBALANCING OF POWER?

PATRICK KEATINGE

This chapter examines a particular aspect of European policy which is high on the agenda of the European Union's intergovernmental conference, and which is approached by the British and Irish governments from very different starting points. Their joint commitment, expressed in Article J. 4 of the Treaty on European Union, to a common foreign and security policy 'including the eventual framing of a common defence policy, which might in time lead to a common defence', begs many questions as to how this undertaking is to be interpreted. Even the meaning of the terms in which it is cast — 'security' and 'defence' — is not self-evident. Consequently, before exploring the British position and its implications for Ireland, it is necessary to consider what security policy and its hard-edged *alter ego,* defence, entail.

THE RESPONSIBILITIES OF POWER — THE POLICY RATIONALE OF A MAJOR ACTOR

'Security' can be understood in general terms as relating to the need for a stable, predictable and non-threatening environment in which to pursue one's interests. However, 'security policy' remains an ambiguous term which has been subject to a considerable degree of re-definition since the end of the Cold War. Given the different connotations it may have in varying political cultures, it is as well to start by clarifying the sense in which it is used here.

Three elements can be identified (Keatinge, 1995, pp. 6-10). There is an uneasy combination of two long-term approaches, *prevention* (a strategy of reassurance and inclusiveness, based on carrots rather than sticks) and *protection* (insurance against the worst case, based on military instruments). However, in the short term, security policy is more appropriately seen in terms of *crisis management.* In this context governments may deploy a particular, and not necessarily coherent, mix from the whole range of policy instruments available to them, including that of military force.

Ireland, as a small state with low military capacity, is long on prevention and has a niche in crisis management in the form of UN peacekeeping. Its limited exposure to external security threats has given it the luxury of 'abstention' when it comes to protection, which for most other European states has involved alliance commitments. On the other hand, a major actor like the United Kingdom by definition has interests, capabilities and policies across the board, and these will be significant not only from their own point of view but also for their immediate neighbours and their international region. Even if such a state modestly articulates its distinctive role in terms of 'responsibility' rather than 'power', there will be an expectation among others that its policy is framed at least in part in terms of 'leadership' of diplomatic and military coalitions.

The United Kingdom is no longer a *world* power, but in the European context still sees itself as 'a medium-large power with a highly developed sense of international responsibility' (Hurd, cited in Sabin, 1996). Indeed, it might be argued that the less effective its territorial or economic domination, the greater the focus on other aspects of added value it brings to the 'international community' — itself a club which major actors tend to define primarily in terms of other major actors. Hence the importance in British security policy of two classic attributes of power — *diplomatic status* (where permanent membership of the United Nations Security Council compensates for arrears in the economic Group of Seven), and *military capability* (nuclear as well as conventional). In the (west) European triumvirate, which to a large extent determines the political weight of the European Union, these attributes suggest a rough parity with France and on issues to do with force an edge of sorts over Germany.

We should not be surprised, therefore, if the 'great power' mind-set is alive and well in the British debate on security, for supporters and critics alike, and among academics as well as the policy community as a whole. Indeed, the very notion of 'security policy' as a broad category of governmental activity, of which 'defence' is a particular sub-category, does not come easily to the British eye. A recent analysis of British security policy compares it to case law in the Anglo-Saxon tradition: 'an accretion of decisions and events, not to be found defined or described in a single place' (Cowper-Coles, 1994, p. 152). The author goes on to argue against seeing it as 'a coherent subset of foreign policy, within which nestles defence policy, as one Russian doll within another'. He very quickly moves to the core of the subject as he sees it. This is the proposition that armed forces are 'again what they always were: an important, *perhaps the most important,* subset of the larger set of tools which states use to protect and promote their interests overseas' (emphasis added).

Thus Philip Sabin's contribution to this project published in the accompanying volume, in moving directly to a consideration of official defence roles, is within a tradition where 'defence' has a more immediate resonance than the diffuse (and somewhat wimpish?) concept of 'security' (Sabin, 1996). In terms of the tripartite definition of security policy outlined above, the first two roles he refers to (defence of the United Kingdom itself and collective self-defence with allies) clearly have to do with protection, while the third (the promotion of 'wider security interests') implies both long-term prevention and the dilemmas of crisis management. It is arguable that since the end of the Cold War the latter aspect of security policy has been more significant, even in military terms, than the first two. To be fair, it is also arguable that the operational substance of British policy is moving in this direction, though often behind a political rhetoric still strongly coloured by post-imperial (i.e. nationalist) nostalgia.

REBALANCING AFTER THE COLD WAR: MUSICAL CHAIRS AT THE TOP TABLE

Although increasing global economic interdependence has cut across traditional international power games during the past fifty years, particularly by blurring a simple correlation between military capabilities and political influence, it has not eliminated them altogether. There is at least *prime facie* evidence that considerations of 'balancing power' are taken seriously by the governments of major states, however ambiguous the concept or constrained the reality may be. Thus adaptation to the end of the Cold War — in which military capability had been perhaps the central indicator of political influence in east-west relations — is taking place on two levels. The first is a reassessment of power relationships; the second involves attempts to develop a multilateral, rule-bound cooperative security regime. The experience of the past seven years has been paradoxical; although military means are no longer the touchstone of a global ideological confrontation, they have been more widely used as part of the international community's attempts to keep the peace.

In the post-Cold War context, Russia remains the great imponderable and the United States remains the primary reference point of European security policy. Yet the question is increasingly to what extent, rather than whether, the United States will try to disengage from the burdens of superpower leadership. For traditional British policy-makers the special relationship with the US has been a cherished museum piece, revived and deployed by the Thatcher government against rogue states (Argentina 1982, Libya 1986 and Iraq 1990). But it is not an asset much in evidence since the second Gulf war, and least of all since 1994 where the Northern Ireland peace process has been concerned. But then who does have a coherent and durable special relationship with Washington these days? A keen awareness of military dependence on the United States — or rather of the costs of reducing such dependence — remains in Whitehall, and opportunities may arise for an apparent revival of the old firm, particularly in view of the unpredictability of American policy. Thus the United Kingdom still presents itself as the leading champion of authentic Atlanticism; the Foreign Secretary, Malcolm Rifkind, has even summoned up the ghosts of an 'Atlantic Community'.

In continental Europe, France — hitherto the eternal rival — now assumes the role of preferred partner at the hard end of the security policy spectrum, where un-German activities may be indulged. For some this raises the question whether the rest of Europe is to be presented with the gift of Franco-British nuclear collaboration. Something on these lines was implied in French attempts to justify their controversial resumption of nuclear tests in the summer and autumn of 1995. Since 1993 bilateral consultations between the two west European nuclear powers have been formalised, and neither state seems to be contemplating the end of nuclear deterrence in general, nor of their particular roles as nuclear possessors (Quinlan, 1993; Witney, 1994-95). British capabilities have been simplified, and with the most recent modernisation — the Trident submarine-based system — largely paid for, there is little financial incentive to abandon nuclear status.

However, nuclear military power is an enigmatic asset. Even as a symbol of a privileged status, it may lead to diminishing returns as the French government found with regard to their test programme. Dependence on American assistance in the nuclear field is the critical factor in Britain's long-term ambitions, and if a future American administration were to terminate this arrangement it is by no means certain that the United Kingdom would be willing or able to develop a truly national or European deterrent. Even with continued American support, it is not clear whether or in what way nuclear weapons fit into a future European defence.

More to the point in the post-Cold War security environment, there has been an increasing Franco-British focus on collaboration in crisis management, especially in former Yugoslavia. Reinforcing their considerable experience as major contributors to UNPROFOR and as 'natural' members of the Contact Group, the United Kingdom and France are (after the United States) the second and third largest elements in NATO's Implementation Force (IFOR) in Bosnia.

This is no flash in the pan. At their bilateral summit in Chartres in November 1994 the two governments agreed to set up a joint air command, to be used in peacekeeping and humanitarian interventions. This is precisely one of the major areas of European dependence on American capability, and could be functionally significant should American assets no longer be available. In the interim, it will do nicely as a new step in the endless minuet of the Great Powers. However, when the music stops British policy-makers may be unhappily aware that they will still find Germany at the head of the table — a reminder that the economic base of European security, in the broadest sense of that concept, is determined neither by London nor Paris.

INTEGRATED SECURITY OR INSTITUTIONAL GAME-PLAYING?

Even during the Cold War, the balancing of power by the major actors took place within an increasingly complex and durable network of multilateral institutions. Thus their behaviour had to be accommodated to rules, both formal and informal, and the sometimes inconvenient presence of other states. Since 1989, this characteristic of international security policy — an attempt to develop an inclusive cooperative security regime — has been more marked, with an increased emphasis on the role of the United Nations, the Organisation for Security and Cooperation in Europe (formerly the CSCE) and the adaptation of the remaining military alliances in Europe, NATO and the Western European Union (WEU). This is the context in which the European Community/Union has become involved more explicitly than ever before in the politics of European security.

Sabin reminds us that at the time of the last inter-governmental conference in 1991, the formulation of the Common Foreign and Security Policy (especially Article J.4), the role of the WEU as a potential defence organisation for the EU, and even 'noises off' such as the Eurocorps initiative by France and Germany, were all hotly contested issues. There were two camps with contrasting views about the leadership and politico-military organisation of the 'West'. Reflecting an alignment which had existed through most of the Cold War era, and very sharply since de Gaulle's presidency in the 1960s, the United Kingdom stood for the Pax Atlantica under American leadership, and France for a more independent Europe. Germany as ever tried to avoid choosing between the two alternatives; the United States, though strictly speaking a non-playing captain in this game, managed to change the goal-posts early on by warning against the divisive effects of an autonomous WEU. France had to be satisfied with a result in the form of an 'eventual' common defence policy in the Maastricht Treaty which 'might in time' be a common defence — though not necessarily in 1996, when the next game was scheduled.

That line-up has changed. The NATO summit in January 1994, with American agreement on a 'European Security and Defence Identity' (ESDI) and 'Combined Joint Task Forces' (CJTF), put on paper at least the Clinton administration's readiness to live with a future European alliance in the shape of a more developed WEU. Persistent recriminations over policy in Bosnia reinforced the new political reality that the United States, like the Soviet Union five years previously, has succumbed to the giddy freedom of the Sinatra Doctrine ('do it my way'). Although the precise alignment on security and defence in the 1996 IGC is not yet clear, France's traditional position as leader of the European option is much less clear-cut. President Chirac has moved a long way back into the NATO fold, to the point where the WEU may be presented as much as the European pillar of NATO as a potential stand-alone EU alliance.

Nevertheless, we should be under no illusion about British institutional preferences in 'real' security policy (i.e. defence). Above all, an alliance can only be intergovernmental. 'Integration' is all very well when it refers to a military command, and only NATO has that; it may even be valued highly in this context, particularly when new military configurations are under British leadership, as is the case with NATO's Allied Rapid Reaction Corps (ARRC). But the institutional framework at the political level must remain intergovernmental, as it always has been in NATO and the WEU. Thus, it was claimed by a minister of state at the Foreign and Commonwealth Office that intergovernmental decision-making is 'not second best; it is what works' (Heathcoat-Amory, 1994, 135). The minister went on:' 'I do not believe that any realistic observer can think that European governments are ready to delegate decisions on defence, which are ultimately decisions about the lives and deaths of their soldiers, to a supranational body or, even less likely, to majority voting.' The then secretary of state for defence, Malcom Rifkind, reiterated the point in the most emphatic way (Rifkind, 1995 a).

The government's approach to the EU Common Foreign and Security Policy is along the same lines. In Douglas Hurd's view, 1996 is about incremental fine-tuning of a process which is characterised by strong continuity with European Political Cooperation. The former foreign secretary sees (without any evident dismay) the Maastricht Treaty putting a common defence policy a 'long way off', and the 'maintenance of NATO as the essential framework underpinning European security' (Hurd, 1994 a, pp. 426, 428).

Where does this leave the relationship between the European Union and the WEU in 1996? There has been no sign of enthusiasm for merging the two in the British view, but rather an emphasis on the merits of variable geometry. This is described as 'essential to accommodate the different positions and interests of current, and imminent, European Union members in the defence field ... the time is not yet ripe to to try and squeeze these different interests into a single strait-jacket' (Heathcoat-Amory, 1994, p. 135).

In short, to answer the question posed in the title of this chapter — integrated security or the rebalancing of power? — British policy can be interpreted primarily as a form of continuous rebalancing. This is currently conducted within the parameters of incremental adjustments to an institutional status quo, both within the EU and between the EU and NATO, which is taken as given.

THE BRITISH POSITION FOR 1996

The memorandum on the British approach to the defence issue in 1996, circulated among EU partners at the beginning of March 1995, brings together the themes identified above (FCO, 1995). It is a document which at the same time demonstrates the United Kingdom's central place in military collaboration and the limits of its ambitions. Following a 'task-based approach', it is made quite clear that classical defence against aggression, as well as 'major combat operations' such as the Gulf war, are the business of NATO; the WEU, on the other hand, would deal with 'lesser crisis management tasks' on the lines of the WEU's 1992 Petersberg Declaration. The latter include traditional peacekeeping operations and humanitarian interventions, though it is not clear where the dividing line is to be drawn between major and minor combat operations.

The memorandum represents a change in British policy since 1991 in that it does acknowledge the role of the WEU in quite fulsome terms. However, this adjustment is embedded in four 'key considerations': first, the retention of exclusively national responsibilities, such as the Falkland Islands; second, an 'unshakeable conviction' that the nation state remains the basic political unit, and intergovernmentalism the necessary mode of cooperation; third, respect for the varying rights and responsibilites of all affiliates of the WEU, including observers; and fourth, the principle that national contributions to specific operations may vary from case to case. Moreover, although WEU summit meetings (following European Councils) are proposed as a means of enhancing high-level political decision-making, the WEU retains its own separate legal base, secretariat and parliamentary assembly, in 'a reinforced partnership with the European Union'. There is no merger of WEU and EU there, no question of the European Union giving orders to the WEU and not even the introduction of defence as a 'fourth pillar' of the European Union.

Throughout this document and in subsequent statements by British ministers the emphasis has been on improving operational measures. The institutional debate is generally referred to in dismissive terms; substantive cooperation must not be reduced to 'a plaything in the game of European construction' (Portillo, 1995). That of course is consistent with the overall thrust of the Conservative party's policy towards European integration. But what would be the consequences of a Labour government inheriting these guidelines? So far as their general European policy is concerned, the Labour Party's focus on rehabilitating the social opt-out (combined with the emergence of their own Euro-sceptics) might absorb most of their energies.

Nor does the British Labour Party seem to be offering distinctive alternatives on the security front. The circulation of the memorandum was received in a largely bipartisan mood by the defence spokesman, David Clark (*Economist,* 4 March 1995). At the party conference in October 1995 the document on reform of the second pillar of the Maastricht Treaty in the 1996 IGC does emphasise conflict prevention and multilateralism in general terms. However, procedures for the Common Foreign and Security Policy remain firmly intergovernmental and the WEU and the European Union remain at arm's length. Under Labour, the security mandarins would probably be able to carry on pragmatising.

THE IMPLICATIONS FOR IRELAND

Before looking at the implications of the above for Ireland's European policy, it is worth reflecting on the first broad defence role Sabin refers to — United Kingdom 'home defence' — for this concerns us very directly as next-door neighbour. In a cooperative security regime at the European level (which may be presumed to be the current state of affairs, warts and all) the home defence policy sector amounts to what may be described as the 'coastguard role'. This consists of the deployment of sea and air military capabilities to deal with 'low-level' risks (fishery protection, smuggling of drugs, air-sea rescue). These are serious risks; the vulnerability of Irish society to drugs and their associated criminality, and the tensions between Irish fishing interests and those of our EU partners are not yesterday's headlines.

We should be asking ourselves (and Whitehall) whether there is a case for increased collaboration to improve efficiency and cut costs in this context; whether such bilateral collaboration could or should be given a higher public profile in the light of the Northern Ireland peace process; and whether there should be a European-Atlantic seaboard coastguard from Norway to Portugal. The inclusion of Norway, a non-EU state, underlines the need for a 'variable geometry' approach to cooperation. It is also noticeable

that such a European coastguard cuts across the three pillars of Maastricht —
it would protect the internal market through a combination of traditional
inter-state military cooperation and the 'internal' policing of the Union. In
institutional terms, all of this could end up as an activity under the WEU
umbrella, or even — if the United States and Canada were involved —
within a reformed NATO framework.

Mention of the last two institutions, which are still represented by several
Irish politicians and groups as uncongenial symbols of a supposed post-
colonial inheritance, brings us, inevitably, to the 'big issue' — the definition
of a Common Defence Policy (CDP) in and around 1996. It is clear that even
if the United Kingdom wishes to cut a dash on defence it will be far from
communautaire in its approach. Thus there will be no focused pressure
from London on Ireland or other neutrals to sign up for full WEU (and
NATO?) membership as a matter of integrative principle. From the security
point of view there is less incentive than ever for persuading Ireland to
become a 'serious' defence country. Collaboration on coastguarding or
peacekeeping can be developed without treaty revision or the end of formal
'military neutrality' — the participation of Austria, Finland and Sweden in the
Partnership for Peace testifies to that. To that extent, Irish military neutrality
may be a matter of practical indifference to London. However, other partners
may have a less permissive approach, and in any case we arguably owe it to
ourselves at last to examine on its own merits the case for and against
subscribing to mutual assistance guarantees in the context of European
security.

And what of mutual assistance guarantees in the context of the Northern
Ireland peace process? That dog made a good deal of noise in 1949 and as
recently as the early 1980s, but has not barked very loudly, if at all, in the
extraordinary events since August 1994. In the late 1940s, the curious
association of ideas which entwined neutrality and partition into a negative
response to the formation of NATO may have reflected misconceived tactics
on the part of Seán McBride as he tried to exert American leverage on
London, but it subsequently reinforced what was already a 'core value' for
many. As recently as fifteen years ago, a British nationalist, Enoch Powell,
was among those who revived the neutrality-for-unification link in the
context of the 'New Cold War' (Keatinge, 1984).

Was this all just gesture politics? Even at that level, is it possible that
neutrality will be drawn into the Northern debate again, whether out of
mischief by either side, or as an element of reassurance for unionists in the
context of an eventual package deal? If that were to be the case, the end of
military neutrality might be more acceptable to nationalists if it came in

European form. However, there is a considerable distance to travel before such possibilities receive serious attention. In the spring of 1995, there was evidence of some willingness to reassess the psychological gulf between Irish and British nationalism which neutrality represents. The ceremony at Islandbridge on 28 April, where the Irish government formally recognised the significance of the allied victory in 1945, and the part played by Irish men and women, may eventually prove to have been a harbinger of a more profound change in attitude, but that arguably depends on a favourable outcome to the Northern Ireland peace process. In the meantime, the peace process promises one concrete gain for British security policy, in the ability to redeploy military capabilities elsewhere. Indeed, British defence policy is based on the maintainance of existing troop levels, with a view to continuing to be a major player in international crisis management.

Even supposing security and defence were no longer part of the 'great game' of British-Irish relations, we would still probably be left with that corollary of collective self-defence which Irish society sees as intolerable but which is still regarded as essential by the United Kingdom — nuclear deterrence. Nuclear safety, especially with regard to the Sellafield installation in Cumbria, is already a highly visible contentious issue between Dublin and London. Although the question of joining a 'nuclear alliance' may be seen by policy elites as a separate issue, public perceptions are likely to be negative towards all things nuclear. Might nuclear power prove to be the last bone in the British-Irish dogfight?

CHAPTER 11
BRITAIN AND THE 1996 IGC
STEPHEN GEORGE

Britain has acquired a reputation for being an awkward partner in the European Union (EU), for not being fully committed to the project of European integration, for remaining semi-detached from the organisation and its goals. There is plenty of historical evidence to support this view: the initial refusal to join the European Community (EC); the acrimonious renegotiation of the terms of entry under the Wilson government in 1974-75; the even more acrimonious dispute over British budgetary contributions during the first five years of Margaret Thatcher's premiership; the refusal of the same prime minister to accept that the 1992 single market programme should be extended to be given a social dimension, or to embrace monetary union (George, 1994 a).

Margaret Thatcher was replaced as prime minister shortly before the opening of the 1991 IGCs. Her successor, John Major, said that he wanted to put Britain 'at the centre of the debate' on the future of the EC, as 'an enthusiastic participant' (HMSO, 1991). However, he still refused to accept a social chapter in the Treaty on European Union (TEU), agreeing only to the other member states going ahead without Britain under a Protocol to the Treaty; and he negotiated an opt-out for Britain on monetary union.

Subsequently, in the latter half of 1992, Britain held the presidency of the EC. Although there are different interpretations of the conduct of the presidency (Ludlow, 1993; Garel Jones, 1993) it is difficult to argue that it did anything to enhance Britain's pro-EC credentials, particularly because during the presidency the pound was forced out of the exchange rate mechanism of the EMS, amidst recriminations against Germany for the alleged failure of the Bundesbank to support the efforts of the Bank of England to relieve speculative pressure on sterling.

To understand the record of successive British governments in the EC, it is necessary to look at the domestic political constraints that they face. This analysis will also allow an understanding of the position that the government was preparing for the 1996 IGC. First, however, it is important to understand exactly what the bases of British policy in the EC have been.

THE BRITISH POSITION ON EUROPEAN INTEGRATION

Despite frequent presentations in the media of the British position on Europe as being simply negative, it is not difficult to construct a picture of the underlying principles of the policies of successive governments. These have applied to both Labour and Conservative governments in the past, as can be seen from the quotations compiled by Martin Holmes (1991). The continuity of the policies of the last two Conservative prime ministers can be seen very clearly if Margaret Thatcher's Bruges speech of September 1988 (Thatcher, 1988) is compared with an article by John Major that appeared in *The Economist* five years later, in September 1993 (Major, 1993). (A close textual comparison of the two pieces, highlighting their similarities, can be found in George, 1995).

The principles that emerge from comparing these various statements are as follows:

A BELIEF IN A EUROPE OF NATION STATES

British policy has never subscribed to the idea that nationalism is a spent force, and that nation states should be superseded by a federal Europe. Because the language associated with this federalist ideal had become the dominant form of discourse about the EC by the time Britain became a member, British interventions in the debate sounded negative even when they were intended to be positive contributions to building a sustainable EC.

PRAGMATISM

Because British governments never subscribed to the teleological idea of European integration as a process designed to lead to a federal Europe, they always demanded positive and practical reasons for adopting common policies or for changing decision-making procedures. For the British, Europe is a 'journey to an unknown destination' (Shonfield, 1973), and the only justification for taking a further step on that journey is that there are present problems which can best be solved by joint action.

RELEVANCE

Closely related to the pragmatism of the British approach is an impatience with what from a British perspective are irrelevant 'doctrinal' debates. Long before the rest of the EU decided it was a priority, the British government was insisting that action to tackle unemployment was more urgent than endless discussion about how far the powers of the European Parliament ought to be extended, or whether citizens of one member state ought to be allowed to vote in European elections in another member state. As John Major put it, 'Unless the Community is seen to be tackling the problems which affect [the electorates of Europe] now, rather than arguing over abstract concepts, it will lose its credibility' (Major, 1993, p. 23).

ECONOMIC COMPETITIVENESS

Conservative governments always put a strong emphasis on the need for policies to encourage enterprise. Many of the restrictive practices that persisted throughout the EC were swept away in Britain by the Thatcher governments. The single market programme was seen as an opportunity to extend the competitive environment to the rest of the EC, which would be beneficial to the EC as a whole because it would make it more competitive in global terms with the United States and Japan.

A EUROPE OPEN TO THE WORLD

Linked to this commitment to a competitive Europe, but of even older vintage, because it was also a theme of the Labour governments of Wilson and Callaghan, is the idea that the EC should not become a fortress, but should be open to the world. In particular both Labour and Conservative politicians repeatedly stressed during the period of the Cold War that the EC was not the whole of Europe, and that the states of Eastern Europe should not be forgotten.

A COMMITMENT TO NATO

All British governments stressed the importance of the Atlantic Alliance, and resisted any suggestion that the EC should somehow emerge as a 'third force' in world affairs, distancing itself from the United States.

FINANCIAL PROBITY

Finally, a point not mentioned explicitly by either Thatcher or Major, but one that underpinned many interventions by British governments in EU debates, is a consistent demand that EU expenditure be justified in detail, and be accounted for in detail.

THE DOMESTIC DETERMINANTS OF THE BRITISH POSITION

The consistency of British positions on Europe reflect underlying political realities, the values of the civil service, and a cultural pragmatism that pervades the thinking of the political and administrative elites.

Because Britain was undefeated in the Second World War, and did not experience occupation, nationalism was not discredited as it was in parts of continental Europe. The British public remained responsive to nationalist appeals, and political parties never adopted the rhetoric of European integration as part of their political discourse. When Britain applied to join the EC, the reasons given to the British people were pragmatic rather than idealistic; but the fact that membership was not achieved until after the end of the long post-war period of economic growth meant that the EC did not become associated with increasing prosperity in the minds of the British people as it had in the minds of the populations of the original six member states.

As well as reflecting the nationalism of the electorate in their statements about the EC, politicians actually reinforced it. The confrontational attitude to the EC that was first adopted by Wilson in the renegotiation of the terms of British entry, was developed much further by Thatcher. Faced with the need drastically to restructure the British economy, her governments followed policies that precipitated record bankruptcies and high unemployment. In response to the social unrest that this provoked, Thatcher liked to pose as a national leader taking on a common external enemy. One such enemy was the Soviet Union, the 'evil empire'. Eventually another presented itself when Argentina invaded the Falkland Islands, allowing Thatcher to become briefly a real war leader. In between, the EC served as a substitute. In fighting the battle over budgetary contributions, Thatcher was able to call on historically deep-seated British prejudices against the French, and more recent ones against the Germans (Currid, 1995). Her campaign on the issue reinforced the prejudices that she played upon, although it did not prevent British public opinion as a whole becoming steadily more favourable towards membership of the EC (Nugent, 1992).

The association of Thatcher with this nationalistic line towards the EC had different effects in different groups of the population as a whole. It probably helped the Labour Party to evolve in a more pro-EC direction (Seyd and Whiteley, 1992, pp. 47-8); but it left her Conservative successor facing a party membership which was divided on the issue, with a majority strongly negative about further European integration, though with a significant pro-European sentiment persisting among about one-third of the membership, making party management extremely difficult (Seyd, et al., 1994, pp. 57-8).

There are other bases, though, for the consistency of British attitudes. There is also within the British establishment a belief in the importance of avoiding a narrow regionalism in the EU, which dates back to the period of British global hegemony in the late nineteenth and early twentieth centuries. To argue this point fully would require a separate chapter, but it has been developed at length elsewhere (George, 1989). The institutional source of continuity on this issue lies within Whitehall, and perhaps particularly in the Foreign Office, rather than in the arena of party politics, just as the consistent demand for parsimony in public expenditure can be seen as a value of the Treasury. However, it is important not to overlook the importance of such ideas in their own right in conditioning the outlook of British politicians, irrespective of any pressure that they may get from civil servants.

The other important political actors who have not yet been considered are interest groups, and particularly the big economic interests represented by large manufacturing concerns and by the financial institutions of the City of London. Although not always pushing government in the same direction, there has been an adjustment by British economic interests to the reality of membership of the EC/EU, and this has tended to put them on the side of the more pro-European elements in the national debate (Butt Philip, 1992). For example, British industrialists were an important pressure group in favour of the single market programme, and their pressure may have been significant in getting Mrs Thatcher to swallow her principles on majority voting when signing the Single European Act.

On some issues that separated the British government from the governments of other member states, the economic interest groups were on the British side. Indeed, it was not only British industry that was opposed to some of the plans for social legislation drawn up by the European Commission: the Union of European Employers' Confederations (UNICE) was opposed to many items in the 'social charter'. However, it is difficult to argue that business pressure was the real reason for Britain's opposition to the social dimension, as the British government had other, more party political reasons for its opposition.

On the other important issue that followed in the train of the single market programme, monetary union, a gap did emerge between the policy of the Thatcher government and the interests of British economic actors. The government as a whole tried to find a way through the pragmatic doubts of the Treasury about the viability of monetary union and the concerns of industrial and financial interest groups that if there were to be a monetary union, it would be damaging to their business to be left outside of it. John Major, first as Chief Secretary to the Treasury and later as Chancellor of the Exchequer, worked with officials to devise the scheme for the 'hard Ecu' as an evolutionary route to monetary union. Unfortunately, the then prime minister undermined the credibility of her own government's alternative to the Delors plan by stating in the House of Commons that she did not believe that anyone would use the envisaged parallel European currency (*Hansard*,

30 Oct. 1990, col. 878). What was intended to be a genuine and serious contribution to the debate was made to look like a British wrecking tactic.

The gap that had opened up between the prime minister and the rest of her government can ultimately only be explained in terms of ideals. Margaret Thatcher was often described as a 'conviction politician', and one of her convictions was that to surrender monetary sovereignty to the EC would be wrong. As a result she was not prepared to go along with the pragmatic line that the government as a whole was prepared to support. It was against this background that Sir Geoffrey Howe made his famous resignation speech in the Commons in which he expressed the dismay of many supporters of the Conservative Party from business and financial circles about the direction in which Thatcher was leading the party (*Hansard,* 13 Nov. 1990, cols. 461-5). This was the blow from which Thatcher never recovered. However, her successor was faced with a party that still generally backed the Thatcher line on Europe, and so he had to move cautiously in the negotiation of the TEU.

NEGOTIATING MAASTRICHT: BRITAIN AT THE HEART OF EUROPE

In understanding British diplomacy in the approach to Maastricht, it should first be noted that the British view of the nature of the EC was never as eccentric as the media presented it. There was always an undertow of hypocrisy about the *communautaire* statements of politicians from other member states. All states in the EC pursued their national interests, and all were capable of being awkward partners when those national interests were threatened (Buller, 1995, p. 36). However, because European integration was generally considered a good thing in most other states, it was difficult for ministers from those states to oppose even proposals which they knew were damaging to their interests in the forthright way that British ministers could. Indeed, British ministers using the veto in the Council of Ministers were often aware of a widespread sigh of relief around the table before their colleagues went outside to condemn British intransigence to the waiting press.

In other respects, Britain had been in the process of becoming a more normal member of the EC for some years prior to Maastricht. When it first joined, there were certain structural problems that made it difficult for Britain to fit into the EC, but these gradually receded in importance. The most important issue was Britain's budgetary contributions, which bedevilled relations during the first five years of Margaret Thatcher's premiership.

Whatever may be thought of the then prime minister's approach, there was certainly a genuine problem; Britain's partners admitted as much. The problem was solved in one sense by the deal struck at the Fontainebleau meeting of the European Council in June 1984. But in another sense the problem began to solve itself because of changes in Britain's pattern of trade, and changes in the structure of the budget.

Enlargement of the EC brought in three poorer states (Greece, Spain, and Portugal), and led directly to the expansion of the structural funds, which taken together with some reining-in of expenditure on agricultural support produced a clearer division between contributing and receiving member states. Britain remained a net contributor to the budget, but was on the same side of the debate as other contributory states, including both the states that were often seen as the dominant actors in the EC, Germany and France.

During the latter years of Margaret Thatcher's premiership relations with both these countries cooled, especially with Germany. It was certainly no coincidence that John Major's first speech abroad as prime minister was made in Bonn. The Franco-German axis was always central to the unity of the EC, and in order to have any influence on the direction in which the Community would go in the future it was clearly necessary for Britain to be involved in dialogue with both these states. That is not to say, though, that the aim of British diplomacy under the Major government was to break apart the close links between France and Germany. British policy had never involved trying to force France and Germany apart, and officials even saw the special relationship as beneficial. There were issues where Britain was closer to one of the partners, and where it would have been counter-productive for the British to try to persuade the other to modify its policies. On such issues it was sensible for the British to agree a line with the partner to whom they were the closer, and then leave it to them to persuade the other.

Although the Franco-German partnership will always remain important to developments in European integration, it is a mistake to see that relationship as the sole driving force of the EU. This mistake is made not only by the media. In academic writing on the EC, the realist position insisted that the future direction of the EC could be discerned if the balance of power between the big three states was correctly analysed (e.g. Moravcsik, 1991). This position misunderstands the complex nature of the EC/EU diplomatic game. It was probably never an accurate picture, but successive enlargements made it less accurate, as did the introduction of qualified majority voting (QMV) in the Council of Ministers in the Single European Act (SEA).

QMV changed the nature of the diplomatic game. Once a state did not have a veto, it had constantly to be thinking in terms of constructing coalitions with other states, not only to achieve majorities on issues that it favoured, but also to construct blocking minorities on issues that it did not want to see agreed. Such alliances are extremely fluid, changing from issue to issue; and the habit of coalition-building has spread even into those areas that are not formally subject to QMV.

In this fluid diplomatic game it became increasingly difficult for the Franco-German axis to give a lead to the EC. Indeed, many of the other states resented the closeness of the links between France and Germany, and the way in which there was a joint Franco-German position paper presented to every European Council. This made it easier for Britain to enlist other states in support of British positions ahead of Maastricht.

Italian leaders, for example, thought of themselves as representing a big country, and reacted strongly to any slight on Italy's competence, as the British government discovered to its cost in October 1990 when jibes about the competency of the Italian presidency provoked the Italian prime minister to call a vote at the Rome European Council on setting a target date for movement to stage 2 of the Delors plan for monetary union. Despite this incident, Italy was only too happy to join Britain in presenting a joint paper on Common Foreign and Security Policy (CFSP) to the IGC on political union as a counter to the Franco-German paper. Italy was traditionally more Atlanticist than France, but also resented being left out. Admittedly this was the only example of Anglo-Italian collaboration in the Maastricht negotiations, but it was an important intervention in the debate, and showed the potential for alliances in the future.

Spain was another potentially formidable ally for Britain. There is a considerable degree of respect for the professionalism and pragmatism of the Spanish administration amongst their British counterparts. If Spain and Britain could form an alliance, it would carry a great deal of weight. Unfortunately there were not many issues on which the Spanish Socialist government and the British Conservative government could see eye-to-eye. Nevertheless, there was some cooperation behind the scenes during the negotiation of the TEU, no doubt assisted by the fact that the chief British negotiator was Tristan Garel-Jones, a well known hispanophile.

Britain also managed to work closely with Denmark on several of the issues that involved the further surrender of sovereignty. There has never been the total meeting of minds between these two states that British officials sometimes like to pretend, especially on issues of social policy; but

Denmark was the other acknowledged Eurosceptic and the closeness of the alliance between these two was indicated to some extent after Maastricht, when the British government responded to the No vote in the June 1992 Danish referendum by withdrawing its own Maastricht ratification bill from parliament until the Danish issue was settled.

So even before Maastricht the British were not without potential allies. These were not permanent alliances; but permanent alliances are the exception, not the rule in the EU. The coalitions shift on different issues. During the 1991 IGCs, Britain was as centrally involved in the game of building coalitions on specific issues as any of the other member states. The success of this strategy can be seen in the terms of the TEU.

Although represented by Conservative Euro-sceptics as a great defeat for the British view of Europe, it is difficult to see the political union provisions of the TEU, which are the subject of the review in 1996, as anything other than a considerable triumph for British diplomacy, and an indication that the British view was not as eccentric as the media wished to present it.

There were two elements of the TEU with which the British government was particularly pleased: the three-pillar structure of the EU which embodied intergovernmentalism in the areas of Justice and Home Affairs (JHA) and Common Foreign and Security Policy (CFSP); and the writing of subsidiarity into the Treaty as a justiciable concept, so new legislative proposals would have to meet the test of there being a need for action at EU level. In addition, the extension of QMV was largely limited to areas where the government felt it was justified on subsidiarity grounds; and the increase in the powers of the EP was mostly limited to areas where the introduction of QMV indicated a weakening of the democratic control that could be exercised by national parliaments. (In two areas, the multi-annual R&D framework programmes and culture, unanimity was retained but the co-decision procedure still applies.)

Of course there were concessions to other viewpoints. That is the nature of diplomatic bargaining. A Committee of the Regions was created, although only as an advisory body. The role of the EP in most areas where QMV existed was strengthened beyond that agreed in the SEA. There was agreement to review the three-pillar structure in 1996. Overall, though, far from being 'a Treaty too far', as Thatcher insisted, the TEU was nearer to the retreat from federalism which Major presented it as being (*Hansard* 11 Dec. 1991, cols. 859-62 and 18 Dec. 1991, cols. 275-86).

Given this starting point, it is understandable that in its approach to the 1996 IGC the British government intends to negotiate to preserve the TEU from amendments that would undermine its congruence with British objectives. As Douglas Hurd put it in a newspaper interview: 'We shall try to preserve the present architecture [of the EU] which actually suits us by and large' (*Financial Times*, 11/12 Mar. 1995).

BRITISH OBJECTIVES IN THE 1996 IGC

From the outset it was clear that the 1996 agenda would largely be set by other actors. Firstly, this is because of the position of Britain as a *status quo* state, its government being generally satisfied with the existing Treaty whatever Conservative backbenchers (and members of the House of Lords) might say about it. Secondly, given the delay in ratification, 1996 is seen as too early to have a review anyway, especially as three new member states joined only in January 1995. Thirdly, the British government feels there were more urgent issues that the EU ought to be addressing, particularly entrenching democracy in Central and Eastern Europe, and working out ways of increasing the competitiveness of the European economy. Finally, although not unimportantly, the extreme sensitivity of the EU in domestic politics, with a general election due in 1997 at the latest, makes 1996 a very inconvenient time to be forced to negotiate Treaty changes.

As the EU was committed to holding an IGC, the British aim was to turn it in so far as possible into a non-IGC, that is a conference that would not make far-reaching changes to the Treaties, and to use the occasion to anticipate the future shape of an EU enlarged even further to take in several states from Central and Eastern Europe.

It is not anticipated that monetary union will be discussed at the IGC, as there are no further Treaty changes that are needed: all the provisions necessary were laid out in the TEU. The only possible changes are to the target dates, or to the convergence criteria, but it is not the intention of the British government to raise either issue, and it does not expect others to do so.

It is also the view of the government that there will have to be discussions about reform of the budget, including the common agricultural policy and the structural funds, before enlargement negotiations can proceed. However, these are seen as matters to be discussed in parallel with the IGC, not as part of the IGC itself. They might affect the pattern of alliances around IGC issues, though, since the questions involved are of fundamental importance to both net recipient and net contributory states.

The main issues that were anticipated as forming the basis for negotiation in the IGC are: the further extension of the competences of the EU; the three-pillars structure of the EU; defence cooperation; the operation and extent of QMV; and changes to the structure and powers of the central institutions.

EXTENSION OF THE COMPETENCES OF THE EC/EU

In the view of the British government the TEU made all the extensions to the competences of the EC/EU that are necessary. There are three policy areas that were considered at Maastricht for inclusion in the competences of the EC/EU but left until the review: civil nuclear protection, energy policy, and tourism. There is a case for the inclusion of energy in EC/EU competences, and under other circumstances the British government might not have been unsympathetic; but given the extreme sensitivity of the issue of European integration in domestic politics, the government's view is that the less change in the Treaty rules the better because the less ammunition there will be for the Euro-sceptics who are demanding a referendum on the outcome of the IGC.

THE THREE-PILLARS STRUCTURE

At the pre-Maastricht IGC on political union the British government gave a high priority to heading off an attempt by the French and Germans to bring JHA and CFSP under the umbrella of the EC, and to introduce some degree of QMV in those areas. This was not too difficult, because the French government was less committed to it in practice than in rhetoric. It was Helmut Kohl who really wanted this, particularly for the internal security issues that eventually formed the JHA pillar of the TEU.

The British view immediately after the signing of the TEU, with its provision for a review in 1996, was that they had five years in which to prove to the Germans that real progress could be made in these sectors on an intergovernmental basis. Because of the delay in ratification of the Treaty they have had only three.

Making Maastricht work in these pillars was never going to be easy, and it is clear that the Germans are dissatisfied with progress, and will be pressing for the absorption of the intergovernmental pillars into the EC pillar. The British position is that the protection of the three-pillar structure remains a fundamental objective, in line with the general British commitment to building a Europe of cooperating nation states rather than transferring powers to a supranational super-state.

DEFENCE CO-OPERATION

Defence is a more difficult issue for the EU than the generality of CFSP because of the membership, after the 1995 enlargement, of four neutral states (Austria, Finland, Ireland, and Sweden). There is also an underlying question about the role of the United States in the defence of Europe. The British view was set out in a paper presented to foreign ministers at a meeting in Carcassonne in March 1995.

The paper opposed integrating the Western European Union (WEU) into the EU, arguing the advantages of having a forum in which the non-EU NATO members (Turkey, Iceland, and Norway) can participate as observers alongside the non-NATO members of the EU (Austria, Finland, Ireland, and Sweden). It proposed twice-yearly back-to-back summits of the EU and the WEU. The EU would be able to request action from the WEU in the areas of peacekeeping, crisis management, and assisting a regional ally against aggression (as in the Gulf). NATO would remain the vehicle for the defence of Europe itself, but the staffing of WEU would be strengthened, and in a crisis it would be able to use NATO infrastructure, such as communications systems and transport. This is consistent with the long-term British belief that NATO must form the basis for the defence of Europe.

QUALIFIED MAJORITY VOTING

It is wrong to believe that the position of the British government prior to Maastricht was hostile to QMV *per se*. That may well have been Margaret Thatcher's position, but the general position was much more pragmatic. Where QMV could be seen to be needed, it should be adopted. This applied to the single market programme, where even Thatcher could see the logic, hence her signing of the SEA; but it also applied to those other areas that were brought under QMV in the TEU, such as environmental questions where the effects crossed national boundaries. However, the British government does not want to see any further extension of QMV in 1996. On the other hand, it does want to discuss whether the weighting of votes and the size of the blocking minority of votes should be changed, particularly with an eye on future enlargement.

This issue has already caused difficulties. When the accession of Austria, Finland, Sweden and (as it seemed at the time) Norway was under discussion in March 1994, Britain and Spain argued that the size of the blocking minority that was needed to stop proposals under QMV should not be increased from the existing twenty-three. The Commission had proposed that it be increased to twenty-seven, in proportion to the increase in the total votes post-enlargement. Britain and Spain pointed out that because votes were only very approximately proportionate to population size, this would mean that 41 per cent of the population of the EU could be outvoted on any particular issue.

The outcome in 1994 was a compromise to lift the blocking minority (as it turned out to twenty-six because Norway did not agree to join) while accepting that if there were twenty-three votes against a measure it should be withdrawn for a period of reflection rather than pushed through. It was also agreed to consider the issue further at or before the 1996 IGC. It remains important to the British government not to allow the continued dilution of the ability of the larger member states to block legislation, and to get the issue settled before the next round of enlargement negotiations begin so as to avoid being put in the position of having to threaten an enlargement that they wish to see in order to defend a principle that they do not wish to see go by default.

THE EUROPEAN PARLIAMENT

The most ambitious of the EC institutions, the EP indicated in its own position papers for the IGC that it was looking for an extension of the Article 189b procedure, or co-decision. This legislative procedure, introduced in the TEU, gave the EP its strongest basis for forcing amendments to proposed legislation, and ultimately blocking any legislative instrument which did not take sufficient account of its views. It was, however, only one of four procedures applying to legislation, depending on the Articles of the Treaty under which it was introduced (Nugent, 1994, pp 304-23). Ideally, the EP wanted the procedure extending across the board of EC legislation. This also had the implication that QMV would be extended further, as the co-decision procedure was linked to the practice of QMV in the Council of Ministers.

Besides of its opposition to the further extension of QMV, the British government's position on this demand is that it is too soon to consider extension of a procedure that has not yet been adequately tested. The potential for institutional gridlock inherent in the procedure is a possible threat to the efficient working of the EU, which is a fundamental British commitment; and the whole issue of increasing the powers of the EP is likely to be highly controversial in domestic politics.

To counter the existence of a democratic deficit in EU decision-making, and in line with its stress on the importance of subsidiarity, the British alternative to increasing the legislative powers of the EP is to find ways to involve national parliaments more actively in the scrutiny of EU proposals. On the other hand, in line with the British emphasis on efficiency, the government is prepared to propose increases in the EP's role in detecting fraud against the EU budget and ensuring value for money.

It is also recognised in Whitehall that the size of the EP will have to be re-considered, again with an eye on the situation following further enlargement. This is not a controversial issue, though; it is generally recognised in the EU that there will have to be some limit set, with seats being redistributed when further enlargements take place, perhaps more in line with population size than previously (Cameron, 1995, p. 6).

THE COMMISSION

Just as further enlargement will have implications for the size of the EP, it also raises questions about the size of the College of Commissioners. Already the 1995 enlargement has produced a situation where there are too many commissioners (20) for them all to have significant portfolios. Clearly the size of the College of Commissioners cannot simply be increased each time there is another member state, especially as in the British view there are unlikely to be commensurate increases in the competences of the Commission. The British government has since 1986 supported the reduction in the number of commissioners for the large states from two to one; but it also wishes to explore the possibility of not every small state having a commissioner in every Commission, and the establishment of a hierarchy of commissioners along the lines of domestic ministers and junior ministers.

The nomination of the president of the commission caused some discontent when the successor to Jacques Delors was being sought. Moves to involve the EP more at the nomination stage are very likely to emerge from other member states (Cameron, 1995, p. 6). The British government, given the domestic sensitivity of the issue, can be expected to oppose such moves; however, given the British emphasis on ensuring that the populations of Europe are fully involved in developments in the EU, such opposition might put them in a difficult position.

THE COUNCIL OF MINISTERS

In addition to the question of QMV and the blocking minority, enlargement raises the issue of the rotating presidency of the Council. With 15 member states it is already the case that the presidency will only be held by any one state once every $7\frac{1}{2}$ years. Further expansion will reduce the frequency further, making it more difficult to maintain continuity in policy, and meaning that by the time the presidency comes around, any lessons learned from the previous tenure are less likely to be remembered. In response to this the British government favours team presidencies, grouping one large and two smaller member states for a twelve-month period.

THE COURT OF JUSTICE

Having been on the receiving end of a number of recent judgments of the Court which have been costly as well as embarrassing, the British government is in favour of a reconsideration of the powers of the Court at the IGC. It is concerned in general about the implications of the 1991 *Frankovitch* judgment, which empowered individual citizens to sue national governments for their failure to implement EC directives. In more specific terms, the government is upset at the possibility that it will have to pay considerable compensation to the Spanish fishermen involved in the *Factortame* case after the Court followed in March 1996 the opinion of Advocate-General Giuseppe Tesauro which was delivered at the end of November 1995. This is potentially an explosive domestic political issue.

The British government wishes to limit the application of the *Frankovitch* principle to cases where member states show a 'grave and manifest disregard of their obligations', and exclude instances where member states believed in good faith that they were implementing the relevant EC/EU legislation. They also wish to limit the retrospective effect of judgments, with the introduction of some sort of time limit for financial claims by individuals; and to introduce some form of appeal against the judgments of the Court (Watson, 1995).

POLITICS AND DIPLOMACY IN THE IGC

The British government has approached the 1996 IGC with a clear set of objectives, and with a favourable diplomatic context for forging alliances on specific issues. The fluidity that preceded Maastricht has increased with the 1995 enlargement, and the new member states are not favourably disposed towards further centralisation in the EU.

However, the government has problems in making the most of the diplomatic opportunities available to it because of its difficult domestic political situation. With a slender majority in the House of Commons, John Major faces a rebellion from backbench members on the precise issue of membership of the EU. The so-called Euro-sceptics are so hostile to any concessions in the negotiations that there is no chance of the government pleasing them. Indeed, even complete success in defending the TEU will not please them because they have convinced themselves that the TEU itself is a dangerously federalist Treaty.

The domestic problems of the government raise the distinct possibility that the IGC might be completed by a Labour government. There is some sympathy in other European capitals for the idea that the proceedings should be dragged out beyond the British general election, because nobody really wants to see the election fought on a European agenda which might push the Conservatives into adopting an even more intransigent attitude. There might be the hope in some quarters that a Labour Government will adopt a different and more *communautaire* line.

THE POSITION OF THE LABOUR PARTY

Labour has certainly tried to suggest that it is more favourable to the EU than the Conservatives, but on both the broad objectives and the specifics of policy it is difficult to detect any fundamental difference. On most of the objectives outlined earlier, there is nothing in Labour's position to suggest that they will pursue a very different path from the Conservatives.

On the broad objectives of policy, Tony Blair outlined six priorities in a speech in Bonn on 30 May 1995:

- to make the case for Europe from first principles, not taking public opinion for granted

- to address the issue of enlargement to the East and how it is facilitated

- to take on the agenda of reform of the EU, defending what should be defended and changing what should not

- to make the European Union more democratic and open

- to take steps towards building a stronger European foreign and defence policy in harmony with the Atlantic Alliance

- to ensure that the EU remains against protectionism, opens up its markets and becomes a stronger voice for free trade in the world (Blair, 1995 d, pp. 3-4).

This list differs in some respects from those provided by Thatcher and Major, especially in the emphasis placed on a more democratic and open Europe.

However, in other respects it is remarkably similar, especially in the stress on the need for an EU that is a force for free trade.

The similarities came out even more markedly in a speech to a conference on 'Britain and Europe 1996' in which the shadow foreign secretary, Robin Cook, set out what Labour's approach to the IGC would be (Cook, 1995). The basic principles were:

- that European union must be based on a sharing of national interests and not on the surrender of national identity

- that the CFSP should not be merged 'into the bureaucratic machinery of Brussels', but that the existing intergovernmental arrangements should be maintained

- that greater democracy should be achieved by the EP working more closely with national parliaments, with national parliaments having more influence over the Council of Ministers and the EP having wider scrutiny over the Commission

- that the national veto should be retained over matters of vital national interest, and for important decisions on the budget or revision of the treaties, but that it should be used sparingly

- that the CAP should be reformed

- that the creation of jobs should be at the top of the European agenda.

On these issues, some of which go beyond what will be discussed in the IGC, there is no discernible difference between the government and the opposition. In one area, though, there is a clear difference. Labour is committed to ending the British opt-out from the Social Protocol of the TEU. This would mean that the Protocol could be restored to the body of the Treaty as a Social Chapter (which it was in the first place).

The other difference comes back to the matter of the tone in which the negotiations would be conducted. A Labour government would be able to negotiate free of the extremely unhelpful 'voices off' that bedevilled the EU diplomacy of the Major government during 1994-96. Even if there were doubters on the Labour backbenches, they would be unlikely to cause trouble for their prime minister so soon after attaining office again for the first time in over sixteen years.

CONCLUSION

British policy in the EC/EU has shown a remarkable consistency in its objectives over a considerable period of time. The idea that this position is out of line with the rest of the EU is simply incorrect. Even before Maastricht, Britain was centrally involved in all the debates about the future of the EU, and had allies on particular issues. This showed in the outcome of the negotiations: the TEU was much more in line with British policy than with the federalist aspirations of Jacques Delors or Helmut Kohl.

These same consistent objectives inform the British approach to the 1996 IGC. It is an IGC that the British government believes to be unnecessary and even a distraction from the really pressing business facing the EU in 1996. However, given that there has to be an IGC, the British position is well prepared. In particular, the British paper on defence cooperation, presented to foreign ministers in advance even of the meetings of the preparatory group for the IGC, showed real thought about how to address the problem in a way likely to attract support from other member states, particularly from France, the other major player in this policy area.

What apparently threatens to damage British credibility in the negotiations more than any other factor are domestic political constraints. The demands of the Conservative backbench Euro-sceptics are pushing the prime minister into adopting an uncompromising tone that increasingly resembles that of his predecessor before the opening of the 1991 IGCs. As Lord Howe put it: 'A new language of semi-detachment is being created. The world outside Britain is being recast in the hope of making political life at home easier to manage. The UK's capacity to define, articulate and pursue credible, coherent interests at the European negotiating table risks being cast away.' (Howe, 1995, p. 16).

From this point of view an objective observer might come to the conclusion that British interests would be better served under a Labour government which would be likely to follow the same agenda, with the important exception of social policy, but which would be less constrained in pursuit of a satisfactory outcome by domestic interference with the necessary diplomacy.

POSTSCRIPT: MAY 1996

In March 1996 the British Government published a White Paper on its approach to the IGC entitled *A Partnership of Nations: The British Approach to the European Union Intergovernmental Conference 1996*. This did not depart significantly from the positions outlined here.

One issue that had come to the fore in the meantime concerned the powers of the European Court of Justice (ECJ). As a result of a number of rulings that allowed groups or individuals to sue their governments for what turned out to be, in the judgement of the ECJ, improper interpretation of EC law, the government proposed that: some time limit be placed on the retrospective application of the judgments of the Court; that the government of a member state only be liable for damages in cases of 'serious and manifest breach of its obligations'; and that some sort of procedure to allow appeals against judgments be introduced.

Otherwise the White Paper contained few surprises, despite the fact that the domestic political mood hardened against the EU in the early months of 1996. This tendency was strengthened by the crisis that blew up later in March concerning British beef and so-called 'mad-cow disease'. Although the government handled the incident clumsily, there was outrage in Britain when the Commission imposed a ban on exports of British beef world-wide, and refused to lift it even in the face of sound scientific evidence that British beef was safe to eat. As the IGC began at the end of March, opinion polls were showing a majority of the British people actually opposed to continued membership of the EU. These were hardly auspicious circumstances for conducting successful diplomacy.

CHAPTER 12
SUMMING-UP AND CONCLUSIONS

Four key factors are shaping and reshaping British and Irish relations and their joint prospects in Europe, both in the near and long term. These are:

- the shifting content and meaning of 'identity' for all inhabitants in both islands

- the evolving political and economic relations between Ireland and Britain, leading towards greater interdependence, especially in a context of European integration

- the complex and unpredictable nature of change in Britain, coupled with the prospect of a more variable Europe

- the increasing tension between the countervailing demands of Irish economic interests vis-à-vis Europe and political aspirations vis-à-vis Northern Ireland.

These Conclusions sum up the arguments about identity change in Britain, Northern Ireland and the Republic, and end with an assessment of their implications for Ireland in the light of a number of possible scenarios.

BRITAIN'S IDENTITY

Chapter 1 noted that, in the closing years of the twentieth century, Britain is still coming to terms with a crisis of identity arising externally from its loss of empire and its role as a key player in the Cold War, and internally from demands for the devolution of power by the UK regions. Identity is being modified or altered by changes in relationships between:

- Britain and the US

- Britain and Europe

- the nations and regions within Britain

- Britain and Ireland.

The process is further complicated by the fact that each of these elements is in turn influenced (directly or indirectly) by some of the others.

CHANGING TRANSATLANTIC RELATIONS

The United States has become increasingly convinced that Europe must take more responsibility for its own security. From Washington's perspective, the best means of ensuring that Europe does so is to widen and deepen the European Union, with Germany as the anchor of the security framework and with Britain playing a full, but shared, role along with France. This development, which has been in gestation for some time, has affected Britain's self-image as a European state which has a special relationship with the world's leading power.

Relations between Britain and the United States have also been affected by Washington's high-profile participation in the Northern Ireland peace process — not all of it to Britain's liking. The United States has tended to regard both the Irish and British governments as equal players in the process, with neither receiving more 'favourable' treatment than the other. The White House has thereby given a new twist to the special relationship with Britain.

In broad terms, the specifications of the Anglo-American relationship have been enlarged to take account of European developments and of a more pro-active US role in international peace-making, of which Northern Ireland is but one example. British-American relations remain important in their own right and continue to be valued by both parties but are now enveloped in a larger framework. The centrality of a special relationship, complemented by leadership of the Commonwealth, no longer explains or defines Britain's role in the world. Europe must now also be taken into account. This re-positioning in geopolitical terms is far from complete and is contested within Britain itself. In that sense, the change in UK-US relations has made a significant contribution to the identity crisis in Britain.

CHANGING RELATIONS BETWEEN BRITAIN AND EUROPE

Historically Britain pursued a 'balance of power' strategy in Europe but the realities of the late twentieth century have drawn attention initially to the limitations of such a policy, and latterly to its inappropriateness. Europe is no longer the home of great powers with global ambitions and regional rivalries threatening to break into periodic warfare. In that sense, there are no great powers to be balanced. Interdependence has become the order of the day, with the pace set by Germany, France and the Benelux. This new process of integration began without Britain and has been deepened despite its reservations.

In effect, Britain has become a 'change-taker' in Europe, rather than a 'change-maker'. This is a profound reversal of roles which has mainly been imposed by force of circumstances rather than adopted as the result of a strategic re-evaluation. Though its size and military and economic power make Britain a potentially valuable ally of those seeking closer union in Europe, the absence of a shared and coherent vision of Britain's European role among its policy-makers renders any 'alliance' with Britain on European affairs difficult to achieve in practice and even more difficult to sustain in the long term. The prospects of creating greater stability are discussed later.

For Ireland, Britain's propensity to be driven by change from Europe (even if the resulting momentum has been to resist rather than to move with it) means that the implications of further integration must be assessed not only in their own right but also in terms of the implications for Irish-British relations and for Irish-EU relations as a whole.

CHANGES TO BRITAIN'S CONSTITUTIONAL STRUCTURES

Closely related to these two sets of relations are the changes being debated or contemplated in Britain's constitutional structures. Though Britain has engineered the most radical redesign of any society and economy in the European Union over the past twenty years (with the exception of German unification), the effects of an essentially economistic model of national regeneration, while lauded, are also criticised. The surrounding infrastructure of institutions and polity have remained unchanged in their fundamentals. Longer-term societal change has been reflected in the fall in respect for core institutions, such as the monarchy and parliament, which could eventually have significant repercussions for the political order.

The importance of these developments lies in the implications for British culture and identity. The invented nation of 'Britain', comprised as it was originally of three Celtic nations and England, has come under stress in that the bonds of 'Protestantism, war and commerce' — as Linda Colley has identified them — may no longer be sufficient to hold the nations and regions together in terms of shared ethos. The result may range from an English retreat into atavistic nationalism of a 'Little England' extreme (evident in some quarters), to — on an optimistic view — a pluralist reaching out to a new 'British-European' identity, combining a confident Englishness (or Scottishness or Welshness) with a realisation of the positive role the UK can play in a changing Europe. It may also, more probably, lie at some indeterminate point in between.

For Ireland, the resolution of Britain's identity crisis is of crucial importance — not least because it could influence the prospects for a peaceful settlement in Northern Ireland, but also because of its possible effects on Ireland's role in Europe and, hence, on Irish identity itself.

DISPUTED IDENTITIES IN NORTHERN IRELAND

As a particular case of the phenomenon of shifting identities it can be said that both communities in Northern Ireland are 'identities in search of a state'. For the unionist majority, their sense of 'Britishness' is evolving into a home-grown variety as the institutions of monarchy and parliament, which were central to their cultural rationale and self-image, are diminished by scandal and by continuous criticism in the popular media. Northern unionists are in that most uncomfortable and dangerous of places for any group, at a stage where identity is increasingly defined in the negative. In other words, they are what they are not. At the same time, they face the possibility of sharing political institutions with the nationalists in a manner yet to be determined but which would require an adjustment to past values.

The nationalist community is no less challenged. Should the peace process succeed, then their identity will be reshaped through participation in inclusive structures which represent the broad policy goal of both governments. Relationships with their unionist neighbours would be significantly altered as also, of necessity, those with the Republic and Britain. Their identity would perforce be redefined within a more complex context than a Northern Ireland governed by majority rule or by direct rule from Britain.

For both communities, unionist and nationalist, the peace process is intended to replace the contest between identities with a novel accommodation that would respect the integrity of each tradition, threaten neither, but subtly alter both. The 'search for a state' is still under way, proof that the situation is in flux, and corroboration of the argument that a settlement in Northern Ireland is simultaneously part of the constitutional debate in Britain and central to relations between Britain and Ireland.

BRITAIN AND IRELAND

Rapid modernisation is one of the most striking features of the Republic, as was noted in Chapter 3. While the causes are many, membership of the European Union has proved a crucial shaping factor. Economic success has not just produced predictable social benefits but has led to a noticeable self-confidence and a greater sense of pluralism involving a belated acceptance of a multiplicity of Irish traditions. In part, a greater openness has come about as a result of the impact of events in Northern Ireland, which have eroded a partitionist mentality, thereby forcing a re-evaluation of long-held values, as has been evinced by the stance of successive Irish governments in the peace process. Furthermore, a quarter-century of involvement in the EU has added a European element to the Irish identity which, without exaggerating it, has added a new dimension to the sense of Irishness.

The new self-confidence, and the more positive self-image that goes with it, have fed into British-Irish relations, which were in any event in the process of transformation as a result of joint participation in Europe's multilateral framework and the necessity for common action on the north. These two phenomena have been identified earlier as the driving forces behind the latest shift in the political and economic relationship between Ireland and Britain, the consequences of which are considered below.

AN ARCHIPELAGO OF CHANGING IDENTITIES

These conclusions indicate that for quite distinct reasons the nature and content of identity in Britain, Northern Ireland and the Republic are undergoing simultaneous re-evaluation but that, in addition to the circumstances which are peculiar to each, there is a complex interaction at play in that no one identity can be shaped in total isolation from the others. For the Republic there is a consequential political dilemma, the centrepiece of this analysis.

The debate in Britain impinges on that country's relationship with Europe as well as on the scale of the reforms in Northern Ireland. The outcome of each aspect of this debate immediately affects Irish aspirations and, in certain circumstances could impinge upon the exercise of independence in terms of long-term strategy, as the following background analysis suggests.

DEPENDENCE, INDEPENDENCE AND INTERDEPENDENCE

Ireland's economic and political dependence on Britain only partially ended with the establishment of the Irish Free State. Economic realities tied much of Ireland's agricultural sector to British food markets while industrial and commercial activities were mainly allied to the UK; political realities demanded that foreign policy debate revolve around the consequences of partition and, de facto, also led later to a dependence on British European policy (or lack of it) to make progress.

But, as argued in Chapter 2, the 1948 Republic of Ireland Act paved the way for a foreign policy founded more on the politics of political economy. This shift of emphasis gathered momentum through the 1950s and 1960s, spurred by the previous stagnation of the Irish economy — a stagnation that had seeped into the very psyche of Irish society and polity.

Membership of the European Economic Community in the 1970s further re-oriented foreign policy vis-à-vis Britain through the liberating effects of economic integration, primarily because the constraints imposed by British economic and trade policies were progressively removed, thus allowing Ireland to loosen the economic bonds that had previously been imposed by its historical and geographical relationship with Britain. In that sense, economic and political independence (to the extent that any nation state can today be said to be independent of others) were realised only some half-century after the foundation of the Irish state.

From the 1970s onwards the costs and benefits of EC/EU membership have contrasted sharply for Ireland and Britain. While both forfeited sovereignty, the benefits of this sacrifice were unequal. For Ireland has gained materially and psychologically from membership, whereas Britain has gained something under the first but may have lost much under the second. This divergent experience has been a precursor to differences now manifest a quarter of a century later in debates about the EU in both countries.

On the other hand, the need to manage and resolve the crisis in Northern Ireland has brought Ireland and Britain together on a shared agenda, this time as equals (in a European and realpolitik sense), with, however, considerable overlap in desired ends as well as means. Consequently, the two countries have been placed in an interdependent position — both need to resolve the problem of Northern Ireland and each needs the other to feel that the solution is one that can be lived with: the gains must be mutual.

However, interdependence can prove to be a two-edged sword. Ideally it should be self-reinforcing, with tangible benefits all round. In practice, however, interdependence can also be a constraint, for potential benefits cannot be realised fully if the partners diverge on some fundamentals. For Britain and Ireland that could be the case regarding Europe. Here the policy orientation of both countries has differed. Although the potentially contentious effects of this could be, and have been, minimised, the point has now been reached in the integration process where sharply divergent choices may have to be made. From an Irish viewpoint, it means assessing the future of British policy over the long term based on an understanding of the forces at work within British society.

A VOLATILE PARTNER

THE FUTURE BRITAIN

If interdependence has become the defining characteristic of the British-Irish relationship, then the key concern for Irish policy-makers is the kind of Britain to which Ireland will relate in the context of the Northern Ireland issue and negotiations regarding the future of the EU. On the basis of the foregoing analysis, the main conclusion is not reassuring in terms of continuity or certainty. The partner with which Ireland must build stable relations is a volatile one.

At first sight the suggestion that Britain should be regarded as volatile might appear as ill-founded or even inappropriate for a society which prides itself on custom, tradition and continuity. But in relation to Europe, it is accurate enough as a generalisation upon which to base conclusions for the long term. It may be less so for British-Irish relations as a whole.

In so far as Europe is concerned, Britain's approach has for the past half-century veered between distrust and engagement. The predominant mood of the various prime ministerships make the point: indifferent and dismissive under Attlee, hesitant but more engaged under Eden and Macmillan, enthusiastic under Heath, agnostic but pragmatic under Wilson and Callaghan, antagonistic under Thatcher; and awkward and uncertain under Major. This is hardly a record of consistency, but, with the exception of Heath, no prime minister during the past fifty years has been a proponent of Europe, still less an enthusiast. On the contrary, they have all at best gone along unwillingly with a process which could hardly be ignored. The variation has been in the degree of unwillingness, at times bordering on hostility.

The situation in the mid-nineties does little to suggest that the future will differ greatly from the past. The Conservative Party is riven by the question of Europe and the outcome of this internal dispute is virtually impossible to predict. The Labour Party remains untried in the face of European challenges, to which any government must respond as a matter of routine if called upon to do so. There is no guarantee that the divisions so evident in Conservative ranks will not in due course be mirrored within Labour.

Against that background of repeated swings in mood and orientation, and in the absence of a coherent long-term vision broadly accepted across the political spectrum, Britain is more likely than not to be a major source, perhaps the prime cause on occasion, of unpredictability in the process of constructing a more united Europe.

There are too many variables still in play for there to be any certainty about the course of the next two decades. Consequently it would be more prudent to anticipate a series of stop-go policies towards Europe than the measured evolution of a grand strategy, which has hitherto marked German and French approaches.

British government policy at any given point will be dictated by the issues of the day, the personal preferences of the key political leaders and the random happenings of events. Short-term responses will dominate until such time as the larger questions about the future of Britain, externally and internally, are resolved.

A VARIABLE EUROPE

It is still possible, however, to make one prediction with reasonable certainty, although it is an uncomfortable one from the Irish viewpoint. The scene is set for a variable Europe not only because of the prospect of enlargement but equally because of British reluctance to commit itself to core European policies. The UK White Paper (March 1996) confirmed that under the Conservatives Britain intends to restrain integration and, by implication, to remain an outsider should Europe go ahead at a pace unacceptable to it. Moreover, under Labour a minority would wish this to remain so, and could prove to be an influential brake on a more engaged approach. Indeed Franco-German support for the inclusion of a flexibility clause in the Treaties is at once a device to overcome British opposition to a deepening of the integration process and an admission that simultaneous widening and deepening are impossible in practice for the medium term.

Furthermore, the consequences of monetary union are now becoming more clear. The procedures for creating the single currency, if put into effect as planned, will perforce lead to inner and outer circles of member states, the ramifications of which go beyond the mechanics of establishing an exchange rate mechanism between the Ins and the Outs, as they have been described. The relationship between the states creating the single currency will be qualitatively different from that linking non-members to that core, because the stability culture underpinning the single currency will be tantamount to political union. The full repercussions of a 'stability community' have yet to be identified and evaluated but in broad terms they will, at a minimum, require a commonality of political will, economic objectives, instruments, and institutions, in order that the currency union may endure permanently without internal political tensions or economic divergence. In practice, this will prove to be a larger agenda in terms of interdependence than had been previously recognised.

For these reasons, the pressures towards a variable Europe can be said to have intensified even before the IGC reaches conclusions about the future Europe. Providing the third stage of EMU proceeds, then the momentum for deeper integration will be greater than originally expected. It would be consistent with past British policy and with the views of the main parties for Britain to seek to escape the logic of intensified integration by opting-out of various elements of an expanded *acquis communautaire*. Hence, a variable Europe, with member states split into different groupings, is in prospect as a consequence of a move to a greatly enlarged and more diverse Union, the advent of the single currency, and the choices likely to be made by Britain on these issues.

The root cause of all this is that the agenda set for the future of Europe and the agenda being set for the future of Britain are out of kilter with each other. That disjunction lies at the heart of the matter. The logic of these two agendas is pointing towards a differentiated Europe in which Britain will abstain from the core perhaps until it has in the first instance answered fundamental questions about itself. For only then will it be able to address Europe calmly and coherently.

THE PACE OF CHANGE

To a considerable extent, the rationale for this conclusion is based on the analysis in preceding chapters concerning Britain's search for a new identity. No satisfactory formulation of such has as yet been discovered, and none is immediately in view. Hence, Britain's place in Europe or, alternatively, its relationship with Europe, is but a part of a larger conundrum — how to manage a decline in political prestige and economic power. In brief, how is Britain to be re-invented? It is a paradox, tragic for both Britain and Europe, that in the post-war period re-invention has proven easier for the vanquished than for the victorious.

Adaptation to the role of a middle-sized, but still respected, world power, pursuing its destiny within Europe, would be painful even if British society were internally cohesive and at ease with itself in domestic affairs. That such is far from being the case has also emerged as a main conclusion from this study. And so this accentuates the problems of Britain accommodating itself to radical changes in its external relations.

The common point at issue is sovereignty. At European level the question is the extent to which sovereignty is to be shared externally with other nation states. At national level it revolves around the question as to how it is to be shared internally within the state. Looked at from the vantage of the British state as currently constituted, there is a dual concern. Sovereignty could be simultaneously drained from the centre in two opposite directions: outwardly towards Europe and inwardly towards the regions. Britain has a double constitutional problem.

The British dilemma is obvious, and requires sympathetic understanding. To yield sovereignty in one direction could create the preconditions for conceding it in the other. Consequently, a determination to maintain the United Kingdom as a unitary state is consistent with continued resistance towards a United Europe. It also explains why Britain is so insistent on subsidiarity at European level and so averse to it at home.

The key to the double constitutional problem lies in the debate about Britain, rather than the debate about Europe. The solution of the first is the precondition for the solution of the second. It is not easy to undo what has been put together over three centuries or to accept that the experiment in uniting different traditions (or nationalities) needs to be re-examined and arguably renewed. In many respects this experiment has been a success: even an enviable one, given experience elsewhere; but over the past half century there has also been a failure to adapt to change systematically and consensually. Economic performance is one index of that phenomenon, but not the only one. The extent of debate in Britain about the future is testimony to a wide spectrum of concerns going beyond the economy.

The vigour and content of this debate has been chronicled in previous chapters. The analysis suggests that there is still a considerable distance to be travelled before a verdict will be handed down on whether Britain is to remain a unitary state or be transformed into a devolved, rearranged or even a federalised one — to continue the free market economy initiated in the late seventies or to adopt a version of the social market model practised in other European states. The jury is still out on these momentous issues and until such time as decisions on them are handed down, the rest of the European Union must expect Britain to be a difficult and reluctant partner in the probable creation of a Europe which, in terms of politics, is infused with federalist principles and, in economics, is evolving towards a social market.

THE LATE JOINER

The implications of all this for Ireland are hardly encouraging. As new goals are constantly set for European integration, Britain will be at first an opponent and then, as new facts are created, a reluctant participant. On joining, it will be the least enthusiastic of partners, other than where it perceives a distinct national advantage (as was the case with the Internal

Market, its attitude to which was sometimes mistaken for belated Euro-enthusiasm). Should the pace of integration accelerate, then the distance between the convoy and its slowest ship will become greater.

These perspectives give some hint in broad outline of the possible shape of the decade ahead. The flexibility clause mooted by France and Germany as the device for overcoming Britain's late-joiner syndrome will come into play. Differentiation already exists in respect of the Social Chapter, is virtually inevitable regarding the single currency, is latent in the third pillar, is probable in terms of institutional reform, and is conceivable in the security area (unless the nostalgia for the 'special relationship' with the US is finally ditched).

This is not to say that Britain would opt permanently for an outer circle in a Europe of core and non-core states. The historical experience suggests that it will more likely elect to stay outside in the initial stages, but will come in time to accept realities, and then will attempt to shape them to its own interests by participating and seeking to modify what it has joined — thus validating Monnet's strategy of first confronting Britain with facts and then relying on its much admired pragmatism to accept them.

The problem for Ireland is that this scenario implies a lag — perhaps a considerable lag — between EU decisions on further integration and Britain's acceptance of them. The question therefore arises as to whether Ireland must follow Britain for a variety of reasons, not least because of the degree of interdependence which, it has been suggested, now characterises British-Irish relations. Alternatively, will Irish interests perhaps be better served by keeping pace with the core, notwithstanding the costs, political and economic, in terms of relations with Britain?

When put in these terms it seems inevitable that there will be tensions between the Irish strategic objectives identified above, and that trade-offs will have to be made. Until such time as Britain reshapes its own identity, domestically and externally, it will not be possible for Ireland to reconcile comfortably its political and economic ambitions.

TENSIONS AND TRADE-OFFS

Tensions between Ireland and Britain may thus become inevitable, and if so, then trade-offs will arise. With monetary union drawing nearer, the tensions between Ireland's policy objectives are already becoming stronger. A prime economic objective for Ireland is to participate in EMU and to benefit from closer integration. But a prime objective of Irish political policy is to bring about a permanent and peaceful settlement in Northern Ireland that is acceptable to all parties and both governments. The process of underwriting a settlement with a cross-border web of economic, financial and business links accelerated during the 1994-96 ceasefire.

Reconciling these two objectives, the Irish dilemma, could force trade-offs. For example, the debate about Ireland's readiness for EMU raises the question whether Ireland is, or can be, sufficiently independent of Britain that it can afford to pursue diametrically opposed policies in Europe with regard to economic union. There is no inevitability about EMU, or about any aspect of further integration for that matter. Indeed, it is the unpredictability of the medium- and long-term evolution of the European Union that makes the tensions in Irish policies all the more manifest. It is a divergence of views about Europe's future, which will become more evident as the IGC unfolds, that poses the strategic dilemma for Ireland.

Europe's future may indeed be clouded in the medium term by the complex agenda of issues confronting the IGC — including choices about variable geometry or differentiated membership, common foreign and security policy, the institutional balance, justice and home affairs, economic union, and citizenship. In the long run, the Union must undoubtedly respond to challenges arising from further enlargement, from its distribution of resources (including CAP and Structural Funds), from unemployment and social division, and from the competitive challenges of a global economy.

Past experience would indicate that short of an unforeseen catastrophe this range of challenges will be met. The answers may not be satisfactory but they will be fashioned in some form or another. For its part, it can be taken for granted that Ireland would wish to play a full part in determining Europe's responses. But it can be assumed that Britain will be unwilling to do so wholeheartedly, perhaps for as long as the decade ahead.

ALTERNATIVE BRITISH SCENARIOS

In the face of these possibilities, the future of the European Union in terms of British involvement can be reduced to five broad scenarios. The unpredictability of British policy is central to this analysis and from an Irish viewpoint the scenarios range from the malign to the benign in terms of being able to participate in the core or *avant garde* of integration.

Mosaic Europe

The least desirable for Irish interests is a differentiated Europe, consisting of a multi-tiered structure with a mosaic of policies — different member states opting for menus of policies which best suit their individual interests, but no two menus identical, save in the case of those which volunteer for the full list and thereby constitute a core Europe. Differences in the degree of integration would be more or less permanent either because of political will or economic capacity. The unitary structure of the EU would be abandoned indefinitely. In this scenario, Britain would be taken as initially agreeing to no more than the minimum set of common policies and would be precluded automatically from full participation in the institutions, as is already the case under the Social Chapter.

For Ireland, the task in these circumstances would be to participate in a sufficiently broad range to place it as close as possible to the core so as to minimise loss of influence or benefits. The tension between European membership and partnership with Britain would be at its most acute and trade-offs would be concentrated on the minimisation of costs rather than the maximisation of benefits.

The Outsider

The second scenario is one in which Britain pursues a lone strategy in relation to the EU, as was done in relation to the Social Chapter. In this case, the unitary structure of the institutions would be preserved for all other member states, even though there would no doubt be differences in the speed with which they assumed common responsibilities. Effectively speaking, all member states except Britain would be in the core.

Here, Ireland would have to determine for itself the timing and manner of its adherence to the various aspects of the *acquis communautaire*. But it would be understood by other member states that its ultimate goal was to do so. This scenario could permit Irish interests to be protected, although with greater difficulty than if it were at the core from the outset. For the first time since EEC membership, Ireland would have to consider derogations in order to adjust to common responsibilities while trading off against the costs arising from Britain's non-participation.

Belated Union

The third scenario is that predicted to be the most desirable for the future solidarity of the Union and may also be the most likely. It would consist of concentric circles with a group of the most willing and able comprising the *avant garde* of integration and with the others free to join later by mutual agreement. In this case Britain would continue the late-joiner syndrome, and for Ireland the dilemma would not be as acute as in the first two scenarios since Britain would be committed to eventual membership of all aspects of integration. The problem would be one of timing rather than of eventual goals.

Judgements would, of course, have to be made as to when Britain would join the various common policies, say in the case of the single currency. The costs and benefits of possible Irish responses would have to be estimated in each case and decisions made accordingly. But what is clear is that if this were to be the scenario that actually happens, an Irish decision to stay out with Britain during what proved to be an interim period would not have been in the interests of the Irish State, but would have unnecessarily damaged them.

THE GAMBLER

It is conceivable that the UK strategy might take a change of direction and decide to opt-in with each new initiative, but gamble on being able to change it later from the inside. To some extent, that has been the broad British strategy since joining the EEC; the EU budget is a case in point, although the Social Chapter revealed the limitations of this approach. In this scenario Ireland would continue more or less, as in the past, to protect its European interests by being at the centre of integration, managing its relations with Britain on a case-by-case basis. The determining characteristic of this scenario is that Britain and Ireland would be members of each initiative from the outset, but that Britain would try to alter the terms and conditions whenever it saw fit. As it would not be able to do so unilaterally, Irish interests would be protected to the extent that support from other member states could be secured. The CAP is a case in point. Britain as a gambler would be the cause of unpredictability within the broad integration process but, at least, the problem would be shared in common with all other member states. Tensions between Irish strategic objectives would be less than in the three previous scenarios.

THE LEADER

The most benign scenario for the Union as a whole would be a Britain fully committed to playing a leading role in shaping the future of Europe. Although it is the least likely, for the reasons advanced earlier, the prospect is so inherently attractive that other member states should persist in pursuing it as the desired end goal. This scenario would ensure balance between the large states, inject a plurality of values into the system which most would welcome, and ensure a robust cultural diversity which some believe could otherwise be lost. For Ireland, this would be the best of all worlds. British-

Irish relations could then be optimised and the benefits from EU membership maximised, providing large state/small state relations were not detrimentally affected through the emergence of a *directoire*.

IRELAND'S ROLE

In the light of these scenarios, it is in Ireland's interest and (in that of the Union as a whole) to foster those circumstances which could allow Britain to match the pace of its constitutional reform with its involvement in Europe. The point to be borne in mind is that the internal debate will dictate what may be possible in relations with Europe. All this suggests that the minimally acceptable scenario is that of a belated Union; anything less will pile up problems for all states, not least for Ireland.

In the last analysis, the pursuit of a strategy designed to keep Britain in the integration process, however uncomfortable the consequences, will require great sensitivity by other member states to Britain's constitutional conundrum. But the issues at stake in terms of political reform and societal renewal are not widely understood elsewhere and hence the requisite sympathy is often lacking; indeed impatience and exasperation are more evident than patience and forbearance — the BSE crisis is a case in point.

Throughout the IGC, particularly during the Presidency, Ireland can best secure its own interests and those of the Union, by acting where possible as mediator between the UK and the other member states or, perhaps, more accurately, as the privileged interpreter of two agendas which could easily prove contradictory rather than complementary. If Britain needs to understand Europe more accurately, there is a corresponding responsibility on Europe to learn about Britain. The temptation to go for 'an IGC of the Fourteen' should be avoided, preferably by coming to terms with the actualities of the debate within Britain about itself. For geographical and other reasons Ireland is *au fait* with these realities. The task must be to ensure that this becomes true of others.

There is an urgency about this prescription because throughout this study it has been concluded that the twin aims of Irish policy, peace in the island and prosperity within Europe, have created an interdependence with Britain which needs to be nourished and sustained. It is manifestly in Ireland's interests that this new interdependence should be self-reinforcing rather than mutually destructive. For that to happen, it is a precondition that Britain should remain close to the heart of Europe. The IGC will be the great test of whether this outcome can be secured.

◼ References and Further Reading

Albert, M. (1991), *Capitalism Contre Capitalisme*, Paris: Editions de Seuil.

Anderson, J. (1994), 'Problems of Inter-state Economic Integration', *Political Geography*, 13 (1), pp. 53–72.

Anderson, P. (1992), *English Questions*, London: Verso.

Ascherson, N. (1995 a), 'Dear Malcolm, it's time to ditch all those tired Foreign Office notions', *Independent on Sunday*, 9 July.

Ascherson, N. (1995 b), 'Someone should tell Rifkind that Europe is not a pick-and-mix counter', *Independent on Sunday*, 1 October.

Ascherson, N. (1996), 'When was Britain?', *Prospect*, 8 May, pp. 25–9.

Baker, T. (1993), 'Manufacturing Output and Employment by Market Area', *Quarterly Economic Report*, Dublin: Economic and Social Research Institute.

Bannon, S. (1996), 'EMU and Ireland's Sterling Trade', paper presented to the Statistical and Social Inquiry Society of Ireland, 28 March.

Barber, L. (1995), 'EU allies pin hopes for closer union on next UK leader', *Financial Times*, 6 February.

Barber, T. (1995), 'EU reform deal threatens Tory election hopes', *The Independent*, 1 September.

Barnett, A. (ed.) (1994), *Power and the Throne*, London: Vintage.

Barnett, C. (1995), *The Lost Victory, British Dreams, British Realities 1945–50*, London: Macmillan.

Barrington, T. (1987), 'Ireland: The Interplay of Territory and Function', in R. Rhodes and V. Wright (eds.), *Tensions in the Territorial Politics of Western Europe*, London: Frank Cass.

Beedham, B. (1996), 'Germany has a plan for Europe that goes too far too fast', *International Herald Tribune*, 1 January.

Bevins, A. (1996), 'Grandees issue grave warning on Europe', *The Independent*, 19 September.

Binyon, M. (1995), 'Erosion of goodwill feared in Whitehall', *The Times*, 15 March.

Black, I. (1995 a), 'Charting a new course for Britain in an uncertain world', *The Guardian*, 29 March.

Black, I. (1995 b), 'Major eyes distant markets for UK trade', *The Guardian*, 30 March.

Black, I. (1995 c), 'Rifkind to bat for Britain in UK', *The Guardian*, 7 July.

Black, J. (1994), *Convergence or Divergence? Britain and the Continent*, London: Macmillan.

Blair, T. (1994), address on EU policies, 6 July.

Blair, T. (1995 a), Brussels speech on EU policies, 10 January.

Blair, T. (1995 b), House of Commons speech on EU policies, 2 March.

Blair, T. (1995 c), address to Royal Institute of International Affairs, 5 April.

Blair, T. (1995 d), 'Britain in Europe: An Agenda for Reform', speech to the Friedrich-Ebert Stiftung, Bonn, 30 May.

Blair, T. (1996), speech in Bonn on EU policy, 18 June.

Blitz, J. (1996), 'Open stance urged for single currency', *Financial Times*, 17 September (result of Mori poll for European Movement on EMU).

Bogdanor, V. (1996 a), 'Sauce for goose', *The Guardian*, 31 January.

Bogdanor, V. (1996 b), *Politics and the Constitution*, Aldershot: Dartmouth.

Bradley, J. (1995), 'Exploring Economic Implications of the Northern Peace', paper presented at a symposium of the Statistical and Social Inquiry Society of Ireland on 'The Economic Implications of Peace in Ireland', 23 February.

Bradley, J. (1996), *An Island economy: Exploring long-term economic and social consequences of Peace and Reconciliation*, Dublin: Forum of Peace and Reconciliation.

Bradley, J. (1996 a), 'Economic Aspects of the Island of Ireland: Performance and Prospects', in Gillespie, P. (ed.), (1996 c).

Brittan, S. (1996), 'Comparisons are odious', *Financial Times*, 25 April.

Brock, G. (1996), 'Blair holds centre stage in Kohl's monetary union show', *The Times*, 17 June.

Brown, C. (1995), 'Cook claims pro-Europe youth vote', *The Independent*, 2 August.

Brown, K. (1995), 'Euro battle hides a remarkable consensus', *Financial Times*, 11 February.

Buller, J. (1995), 'Britain as an Awkward Partner: Reassessing Britain's Relations with the EU', *Politics: Surveys and Debates for Students of Politics*, 15, pp. 33–42.

Butler, M. (1994), 'A Europe fit for Britain', *The Times*, 8 September.

Butt, Philip A. (1992), 'British Pressure Groups and the European Community', in George (ed.) (1992), pp. 149–71.

Buxton, J. (1995), 'Ye will no' come back again', *Financial Times*, 11 February.

Cable, V. (1995 a), 'Europe and the US: the rift is growing wider', *The Independent*, 28 July.

Cable, V. (1995 b), 'Wake up Britain: Europe's not the world', paper to FCO/RIIA conference, 29 March, extracted in *The Independent*, 27 March.

Cadogan Group (1995), *Lost Accord: The 1995 Frameworks and the Search for a Settlement in Northern Ireland*, Belfast: Cadogan.

Cain, P. J. and A. G. Hopkins (1993), *British Imperialism: Innovation and Expansion 1688–1914*, London: Longman.

Cain, P. J. and A. G. Hopkins (1993), *British Imperialism: Crisis and Deconstruction, 1914–1990*, London: Longman

Cameron, F. (1995), 'The 1996 IGC: A Challenge for Europe', paper presented to the Fourth Biennial Conference of the European Community Studies Association (USA), Charleston, South Carolina, 12 May.

Cannadine, D. (1983), 'The British Monarchy and the "Invention of Tradition", c. 1820-1977' in Hobsbaum and Ranger (eds.), (1983).

Cannadine, D. (1990), *The Decline and Fall of the British Aristocracy*, New Haven: Yale.

Carnegy, H. (1996), 'Finns aim to be there when EMU takes off', *Financial Times*, 27 June.

Cassell, M. (1993), article in *Financial Times* supplement on Business Investment in Europe, 10 October.

CDU/CSU (1994), 'Reflections on European Policy', reprinted in *European Document Series* 6, Dublin: IEA, September.

Charmley, J. (1993), *Churchill: The End of Glory,* London: Hodder.

Chisholm, M. (1995), *Britain on the Edge of Europe,* London: Routledge.

Chown, J., G. Wood and M. Beber (1994), 'The Road To Monetary Union Revisited', *Current Controversies,* No. 8, Institute of Economic Affairs.

Clark, B. (1995), 'UK more sceptical on European defence', *Financial Times,* 16 March.

Cohen, R. (1994), *Frontiers of Identity, The British and the Others,* London: Longman.

Coker, C. (1992), 'Britain and the New World Order: The Special Relationship in the 1990s', *International Affairs,* 68 (3), pp. 407–21.

Colley, L. (1992), *Britons: Forging the Nation 1707–1837,* London: Pimlico.

Confederation of British Industry (1995 a), *Shaping the Future: A Europe that Works,* June.

Confederation of British Industry (1995 b), *Business in Europe* (results of MORI survey with British Chamber of Commerce), November.

Confederation of British Industry (1995 c), *European Monetary Union – Economic Brief,* November.

Confederation of British Industry (1996), *Building a Europe that works: An Agenda for the IGC,* June.

Connolly, B. (1995), *The Rotten Heart of Europe: The Dirty War for Europe's Money,* London: Faber.

Cook, R. (1995), speech to conference on 'Britain and Europe 1996', News Release, 30 Jan., London: Labour Party Campaigns and Communications Directorate.

Cowper-Coles, S. (1994), 'From Defence to Security: British Policy in Transition', *Survival,* 36 (1).

Cox, M. (1995), *US Foreign Policy after the Cold War: Superpower Without a Mission?,* London: RIIA.

Crafts, N.F.R. (1992), 'Institutions and Economic Growth: Recent British Experience in an International Context', *West European Politics,* 15 (4), October, pp. 16–38.

Crafts, N.F.R. (1996), 'Britain's Productivity Growth: Comparative Performance and Future Prospects', in Gillespie, P. (ed.), (1996 c).

Crafts, N.F.R. (1996 a), *Relative Economic Decline in Britain 1870-1995: A Quantitative Perspective,* London: Social Market Foundation.

Currid, N. (1995), 'Explaining "Anti-EC" Nationalism in Britain', paper presented to the UACES Research Conference, Birmingham, 18–19 September (available from UACES Secretariat, King's College, London, WC2R 2LS).

Curtis, M. (1995), *The Ambiguities of Power: British Foreign Policy since 1945,* London: Zed.

d'Ancona, M. (1994), 'Battle of Britain's future role', *The Times,* 9 May.

D'Arcy, M. and T. Dickson, (eds.) (1995), *Border Crossings: Developing Ireland's Island Economy,* Dublin: Gill and Macmillan.

Davidson, I. (1994 a), 'It's not on the menu', *Financial Times,* 18 May.

Davidson, I. (1994 b), ' "Hard core" dissent', *Financial Times,* 14 September.

Davidson, I. (1994 c), 'Blair's EU labours', *Financial Times,* 12 October.

Davidson, I. (1996), 'UK attitude problem', *Financial Times,* 26 June.

Davis, H. (1995), speech to Institute of Food Research, London, 9 February.

Davy Stockbrokers (1996), *The Outlook for EU Transfers to Ireland*, 11 March.

de Beer, P. (1996), 'Frondeuse Écosse', *Le Monde*, 17 May.

de Buitléir, D., Halpin, P. and McArdle, P. (1995), *EMU: Ireland's Strategic Options*, Dublin: Institute of European Affairs (unpublished paper)

Dell, E. (1995), *The Schuman Plan and the British Abdication of Leadership in Europe*, Oxford: Clarendon.

de La Serre, F. and H. Wallace (1995), *Les relations franco-brittaniques dans l'Europe de l'aprés-guerre froide*, Paris: CERI.

Denman, R. (1993), 'The decline of Britain in Europe', *International Herald Tribune*, 22 July.

Denman, R. (1995), 'Britain's complacent isolation could be ending soon', *International Herald Tribune*, 20 January.

Denman, R. (1996), *Missed Chances: Britain and Europe in the Twentieth Century*, London: Cassell.

Department of Finance (1996), *Economic Review and Outlook*, Dublin: Stationery Office.

DKM Economic Consultants (1993), 'Irish Exchange Rate Policy: The Significance of Economic Links with the UK', June.

Dodd, P. (1995), *The Battle Over Britain*, London: Demos.

Donaldson, J. (1995), 'Surprise at Trimble's election win highlights ignorance of unionism', *The Irish Times*, 13 September.

Downey, J. (1995), 'A Major Mess', *Business and Finance*, 2 February.

Drudy, P.J. (ed.) (1984), *Ireland and Britain Since 1922*, Cambridge: Cambridge University Press.

Dunn, J. (ed.) (1995), *Contemporary Crisis of the Nation State?*, London: Blackwell.

Eagleton, T. (1995), *Heathcliffe and the Great Hunger: Studies in Irish Culture*, London and New York: Verso.

Economic and Social Research Institute (1994), *Medium Term Review 1994–2000*, Dublin: Economic and Social Research Institute.

Economic and Social Research Institute (1996), *Economic Implications for Ireland of EMU*, Baker, T., J. FitzGerald and P. Honohan (eds.), Dublin: ESRI.

The Economist (1994), 'Labour's European Peace', 26 November, p. 42.

The Economist (1996), 'The tug for the flag', 29 June.

Eizenstat, S. (1995 a), address to EU–US conference of journalists, 21 October.

Eizenstat, S. (1995 b), 'Real steps toward a stronger US-EU partnership', *International Herald Tribune*, 8 December.

European Movement (1996), *Ireland in Europe, EMU and Security Policy – The Core Issues*, Dublin: European Movement.

Financial Times, (1995), editorial, 'The choice over Europe', 27 June.

Fanning, R. (1979), 'The United States and Irish participation in NATO: The Debate of 1950', *Irish Studies in International Affairs*, 1 (1), pp. 38–48.

Fanning, R. (1981-2), 'London and Belfast's response to the Declaration of the Republic of Ireland, 1948-49', *International Affairs*, 58 (1), pp. 95–114.

Fanning, R. (1983), *Independent Ireland*, Dublin: Helicon.

Ferguson, R. (1990), 'Locality and Political Traditions', in M. Crozier, (ed.), *Cultural Traditions in Northern Ireland*, Belfast: Institute of Irish Studies.

FitzGerald, G. (1990), John Mackintosh Memorial Lecture, Edinburgh University, 15 October.

FitzGerald, G. (1991), *All in a Life*, Dublin: Gill and Macmillan.

FitzGerald, G. (1993), 'Ireland in Europe – a Personal Experience', paper presented to Institute of European Affairs, Dublin, 27 May.

FitzGerald, G. (1994), 'Dangers in the great British EU débâcle', *The Irish Times*, 1 April.

FitzGerald, G. (1996), 'We need to discuss the EMU issue a lot more', *The Irish Times*, 3 August.

FitzGerald, G. (1996 a), 'The Irish Presidency and the British problem', *The Irish Times*, international report on EU Presidency, 2 July.

FitzGerald, G. (1996 b), 'The British Economy: Performance and Prospects', in Gillespie, P. (ed.), (1996 c).

FitzGerald, G. and P. Gillespie, (1996), 'Ireland's British Question', *Prospect*, 11 October, pp. 22–26.

FitzGerald, N. (1996), 'A European nightmare', *Financial Times*, 6 June.

Fitzpatrick Associates (1996), *EMU and the Irish Economy*, Dublin: IBEC, September.

Foreign and Commonwealth Office (1995), 'Memorandum on the United Kingdom Government's Approach to the Treatment of European Defence Issues at the 1996 Intergovernmental Conference'.

Foreign and Commonwealth Office (1996), *A Partnership of Nations: The British Approach to the European Union Intergovernmental Conference 1996*, London: HMSO, March.

Foster, R. (1993), *Paddy and Mr Punch: Connections in Irish History*, London: Allen Lane.

Frankenberger, K.-D. (1996), 'Britain in Europe: The View from Germany', in P. Gillespie, (ed.), (1996)

Freedland, J. (1996), article on Irish-American pressure, *The Guardian*, 23 February.

Friedman, A. (1996) 'EU heading for political crisis, Kohl aide says', *International Herald Tribune*, 5 February.

Gallagher, E. (1984), 'Anglo-Irish Relations in the European Community', *Irish Studies in International Affairs*, 2 (1), pp. 21–36.

Garel-Jones, T. (1993), 'The UK Presidency: An Inside View', *Journal of Common Market Studies*, 31, pp. 261-7.

Garton Ash, T. (1994), 'Britain? Where's Britain?', *The Independent*, 9 June.

Garton Ash, T. (1996), 'Back into Europe', *Prospect*, 9 June, pp. 24–9.

George, S. (ed.) (1989), 'Nationalism, Liberalism and the National Interest: Britain, France, and the European Community', *Strathclyde Papers on Government and Politics*, Glasgow: Department of Government, University of Strathclyde.

George, S. (ed.) (1992), *Britain and the European Community: The Politics of Semi-Detachment*, Oxford: Clarendon Press.

George, S. (1994 a), *An Awkward Partner: Britain in the European Community*, 2nd edn. Oxford: Oxford University Press.

George, S. (1994 b), 'Great Britain and the European Community', Annals, *AAPSS*, 531, January, pp. 44–55.

George, S. (1994 c), 'Cultural Diversity and European Integration: The British Political Parties', in Staffan Zetterholm (ed.), *National Cultures and European Integration: Exploratory Essays on Cultural Diversity and Common Policies*, Oxford: Berg, pp. 49–64.

George, S. (1995), 'Britain and the European Union after Maastricht', in P. Furlong and A. Cox (eds.), *The European Union at the Crossroads: Problems in Implementing the Single Market Project*, Boston, Lincs.: Earlsgate Press.

Gillespie, P. (1994 a), 'What ish my nation? Who knows?', *The Irish Times*, 2 April.

Gillespie, P. (1994 b), 'Neutrality, partition, Ireland and change', *The Irish Times*, 26 November.

Gillespie, P. (1995 a), 'Following interests that are eternal and perpetual', *The Irish Times*, 11 March.

Gillespie, P. (1995 b), 'Relationship in doubt as the Atlantic seems wider', *The Irish Times*, 4 November.

Gillespie, P. (1996 a), 'Kohl forges ahead with integration agenda', *The Irish Times*, 10 February.

Gillespie, P. (1996 b), 'Diversity in the Union', in B. Laffan (ed.), *Constitution-building in the European Union*, Dublin: Institute of European Affairs.

Gillespie, P. (ed.) (1996 c), *Britain's European Question: the Issues for Ireland. Seminar Papers*, Dublin: Institute of European Affairs.

Gilmour, I. (1992), *Dancing With Dogma: Britain under Thatcherism*, London: Simon and Schuster.

Guelke, A. (1996), 'The United States, Irish-Americans, and the Northern Ireland peace process,' *International Affairs*, 72 (3), July, pp. 521–536.

The Guardian (1995), series on the future of the monarchy, 7–11 January.

Harrison, B. (1996), *The Transformation of British Politics*, Oxford: Oxford University Press.

Heathcoat-Amory, D. (1994), 'The Next Step for Western European Union: A British View', *The World Today*, 50 (7), July.

Heathcoat-Amory, D. (1996), 'Why Europe has made me resign', *Daily Telegraph*, 23 July.

Heckler, M. (1995), *Internal Colonialism: The Celtic Fringe in British National Development, 1536–1966*, London: Routledge and Kegan Paul.

Helm, S. and J. Rentoul (1996), 'Germans undermine Major', *The Independent*, 24 June.

Heseltine, M. (1995), 'Britain must march behind Churchill into Europe', *The Sunday Times*, 5 February.

HMSO (1991), *Developments in the European Community, July–December 1990*, (Cmnd 1457) February.

Hoagland, J. (1995), 'Cold spell: Ulster and the Balkans come between Clinton and Major', *International Herald Tribune*, 16 March.

Hobsbaum, E. and T. Ranger (eds.) (1983), *The Invention of Tradition*, Cambridge: Cambridge University Press.

Hobsbaum, E. (1987), *The Age of Empire*, London: Weidenfeld and Nicholson.

Hodson, D. (1996), 'A crucial place at the table', *Financial Times*, 17 June.

Holmes, M. (1991), *Mrs Thatcher, Labour and the EEC*, The Bruges Group Occasional Paper 12, London: Bruges Group.

Hont, I. (1995), 'The Permanent Crisis of a Divided Mankind: "Contemporary Crisis of the Nation State" in Historical Perspective', in J. Dunn (ed.), (1995), pp. 166–231.

Hort, P. (1996), 'Zahlreiche Kompromisse und bemerenswerte Fortschritte', *Frankfurter Allgemeine Zeitung*, 8 August.

House of Commons (1995), *European Union: Preparations for the 1996 Inter-Governmental Conference*, Report of the Foreign Affairs Committee, London: HMSO, July.

House of Commons (1996), *The Inter-Governmental Conference Report*, Report of the Foreign Affairs Committee, London: HMSO, 14 August.

House of Lords (1995), *21st Report of the Select Committee on the European Communities*, 2 vol., London: HMSO, July and November.

Howard, M. (1994), 'The World According to Henry, From Metternich to Me', *Foreign Affairs*, 73 (3), May/June, pp. 132–140.

Howard, M. (1995), '1945–1995: Reflections on Half a Century of British Security Policy', *International Affairs*, 71 (4), pp. 705–15.

Howe, G. (1995), 'A better European policy for Britain', *Financial Times*, 30 January, p. 16.

Howe, G. (1996) , 'When it's right to resist', *Financial Times*, 8 August.

Howell, D. (1995 a), 'The shifting winds of British foreign policy', *The Wall Street Journal*, European edition, 2 February.

Howell, D. (1995 b), 'Britain abroad: no more Mr Nice Guy', *The Wall Street Journal*, European edition, 7–8 July.

Hurd, D. (1994 a), 'The future of the European Union', address to Institute of European Affairs seminar on Britain, 21 March, published in P. Gillespie (ed.) (1996 c).

Hurd, D. (1994 b), 'Developing the Common Foreign and Security Policy', *International Affairs*, 70 (3), July.

Hurd, D. (1994 c), 'Old foes but new friends', address to Franco-British Council, *The Times*, 28 October.

Hurd, D. (1995 a), speech in Stockholm, 14 February.

Hurd, D. (1995 b), speech in Berlin, 28 February.

Hurd, D. (1995 c), address to FCO/RIIA conference, 29 March.

Hurd, D. (1995 d), 'The Common Foreign and Security Policy: The Question of Majority Voting', *Die Suddeutsche Zeitung*, 17 June.

Hutton, W. (1994 a), *Britain and Northern Ireland: The State We're In – Failure and Opportunity*, Northern Ireland Economic Council, annual Sir Charles Carter Lecture, Report 114, November.

Hutton, W. (1994 b), *The State We're In*, London: Cape.

Hutton, W. (1995), 'Taxing question should be a matter of more not less', *The Guardian*, 3 July.

Hutton, W. (1995 a), 'Vacant site at the world's crossroads', *The Guardian*, 11 October.

Institute of Directors (1995), *A Single European Currency, Implications for the UK Economy*, London.

Institute of Directors (1996), *Social Europe, The Economic Implications of Current European Social Policy*, London.

Institute of European Affairs, (1993), *Maastricht Crisis of Confidence*, Dublin: IEA.

Institute of European Affairs (1995), *Intergovernmental Conference: Issues, Options, Implications*. Dublin: IEA.

The Independent, (1995), leading article, 'Britain's place on the map', 29 March.

The Independent (1996 a), 'For beef, Major and St George', opinion poll on Britain and Europe, 28 May.

The Independent, (1996 b), Editorial, 'Britain and Europe: A proposal', 3 June.

Irish Business and Employers Confederation (1995), *Ireland, The European Union and Economic Integration, A Business Perspective.* Dublin: IBEC.

Irish Farmers Association (1995), *IFA's position on the Single Currency/Economic and Monetary Union,* 12 December.

Irish Trade Statistics, 1988–1995.

Jack, I. (1995), 'In pursuit of Englishness', *Independent on Sunday,* 9 July.

Jacques, M. (1994), 'The erosion of the Establishment', *The Sunday Times,* 16 January.

Janning, J. (1996), 'A German Europe – a European Germany? On the debate over Germany's Foreign Policy', *International Affairs,* 72 (1), pp. 33–41.

Jenkins, S. (1995), *Accountable to None: The Tory Nationalisation of Britain,* London: Hamish Hamilton.

Johnson, B. (1996), 'Why he is still the best prime minister we've got', *The Daily Telegraph,* 1 May.

Kaletsky, A. (1996 a), 'How Labour would try to change the ways of business', *The Times,* 18 April.

Kaletsky, A. (1996 b), 'Economic consequences of the "War" against Europe' *The Times,* 23 May.

Kaletsky, A. (1996 c), 'Sterling could be overvalued locked in a single currency', *The Times,* 27 June.

Kearney, H. (1989), *The British Isles, A History of Four Nations,* Cambridge: Cambridge University Press.

Kearney, R. and R. Wilson (1994), 'Northern Ireland's Future as a European Region', *The Irish Review,* 15, Spring, pp. 51–69.

Keatinge, P. (1984), *A Singular Stance: Irish Neutrality in the 1980s,* Dublin: Institute of Public Administration.

Keatinge, P. (1995), *Towards a Safer Europe – Small State Security Policies and the European Union: Implications for Ireland,* Dublin: Institute of European Affairs.

Keatinge, P. (1996), *European Security: Ireland's Choices,* Dublin: Institute of European Affairs (forthcoming).

Kennedy, P. (1988), *The Rise and Fall of the Great Powers,* London: Unwin.

Keohane, R. and J. Nye, (1990), *Power and Interdependence,* 2nd ed. Boston: Little Brown.

Kiberd, D. (1995), *Inventing Ireland: The Literature of the Modern Nation,* London: Cape.

King, A. (1996), 'Britain lost beef war, say voters', *The Daily Telegraph,* 8 July.

King, A. and G. Jones, (1996), 'British mood turning against EU,' results of Gallup poll, 10 June.

Kissinger, H. (1995 a), address to FCO/RIIA conference, 29 March.

Kissinger, H. (1995 b), *Diplomacy,* London and New York: Simon and Schuster.

Kohl, H. (1996), speech at University of Leiden, 1 February.

Keohane, R. O. (ed.) (1986), *Neorealism and its Critics,* New York: Colombia University Press.

The Labour Party (1995), *The Future of the European Union,* September.

Lamers, K. (1994), 'Compelling case for monetary union', *Financial Times,* 11 November.

Lamers, K. (1996), 'Beyond the nation state – a German version of Europe', *The Times,* 27 April.

Lamont, N. (1996), 'Breaking down the Brussels barricades', *The Wall Street Journal,* 20 February.

Langellier, J.-P. (1995), 'Paris-Londres, les oeillades d'Albion', *Le Monde,* 8 February.

Langellier, J.-P. (1996), 'Britain in Europe: the View from France', in Gillespie, P. (ed.), (1996 c)

Lee, J. (1996), 'What Ireland should do if the EMU becomes an Albatross', *Sunday Tribune,* 11 February

Lemaître, P. (1995), 'Douze mois qui doivent changer l'Europe', *Le Monde,* 14 September.

Leys, C. (1995), 'A Radical Agenda for Britain', *New Left Review,* 212, July/August, pp. 3–13.

Liberal Democrat Party (1996), *Meeting the European Challenge,* London: LDP, March.

Lloyd, T.O. (1993), *Empire, Welfare State, Europe: English History 1906–1992,* Oxford: Oxford University Press.

Loughlin, J. (1995), *Ulster Unionism and British National Identity Since 1885,* London: Pinter.

Ludlow, P. (1993), 'The UK Presidency: A View from Brussels', *Journal of Common Market Studies,* 31, pp. 246–60.

Lyons, F.S.L. (1973), *Ireland Since the Famine,* London: Fontana.

McAleese, D. and M. Gallagher (1994), 'Ireland's Trade Dependence on the UK', *Irish Banking Review,* Spring.

MacIntyre, D. (1995), 'Blair turns back on regional assemblies', *Independent on Sunday,* 6 March.

MacShane, D. (1996), *Britain 1996 Europe,* London: European Policy Institute.

Major, J. (1993), 'Raise your eyes, there is a land beyond', *The Economist,* 25 September, pp. 23–7.

Major, J. (1994), William and Mary Lecture at Leiden University, 6 September.

Major, J. (1995), article in *The Daily Telegraph,* 18 December.

Marquand, D. (1994), 'Tories in a state on the state', *The Guardian,* 12 December.

Marquand, D. (1995), 'The State in Context: Travails of an Ancien Regime', in *The State of Britain,* Birmingham: ESRC, pp. 15–28.

Marr, A. (1994 a), '*Not a crisis* crisis, but big enough to change Britain', *The Independent,* 6 September.

Marr, A. (1994 b), 'Labour can win, or it can make history', *The Independent,* 15 December.

Marr, A. (1995 a), 'Why Europhobes get all the best headlines', *The Independent,* 31 January.

Marr, A. (1995 b), 'Can peace survive such sabotage?', *The Independent,* 2 February.

Marr, A. (1995 c), 'Make way for the globe-trotting trader', *The Independent,* 16 March.

Marr, A. (1995 d), 'Labour faces up to the English question', *The Independent,* 21 March.

Marr, A. (1995 e), 'The end of our decline? We shall see', *The Independent,* 30 March.

Marr, A. (1995 f), *Ruling Brittania,* London: Michael Joseph.

Marr, A. (1995 g), 'The secret that Blair and Major share', *The Independent*, 5 December.

Marr, A. (1996), 'A choice for Scotland, a risk for Blair', *The Independent*, 28 June.

Marsh, D. (1994), 'Germans and British hold similar view on European Union', *Financial Times*, 5 December.

Marsh, D. (1995), 'Kohl's loyal lieutenant', *Financial Times*, 21 March.

Marshall, A. (1995), 'Europe warms to Britain's defence scheme', *The Independent*, 21 March.

Mangan, O. (1996), 'EU transfers likely to be scaled back after 1999' *The Irish Times* international report on EU Presidency, 2 July.

McDowell, M. (1996), 'Realistic assessment punctures EMU hype', *The Sunday Tribune*, 4 August.

McRae, H. (1995 a), 'I've seen the future; it might work', *The Independent*, 3 August.

McRae, H. (1995 b), 'A seismic shift to the east', *Independent on Sunday*, 8 October.

Meier-Walser, R. (1994), 'Britain in Search of a Place "at the heart of Europe",' *Aussenpolitik*, 1, pp. 10–19.

Millar, F. (1995 a), 'John Major in fighting form, though Tory faultlines run deep', *The Irish Times*, 19 January.

Millar, F. (1995 b), 'Major plucked from brink by Unionists', *The Irish Times*, 20 January.

Millar, F. (1995 c), 'Focus on Blair's quest to make Labour electable', *The Irish Times*, 9 March.

Millar, F. (1995 d), interview with Tony Blair, *The Irish Times*, 4, 5 September.

Milward, A. (1994 edition), *The European Rescue of the Nation-State*, London: Routledge.

Milward, A. (1996), 'Euro-Money and the Left', *New Left Review*, 216, March/April.

Minford, P. (1996 a), 'The Conflict between British Economic Liberalism and Continental Statism? in Gillespie, P., (ed.) (1996 c).

Minford, P. (1996 b), 'Britain and Europe: the Balance Sheet', London: MCB University, for *European Business Review/New European*/Centre for European Studies, June.

Mitchell, J. (1996), *Strategies for Self-Government: The Campaign for a Scottish Parliament*, Edinburgh: Polygon.

Moravcsik, A. (1991), 'Negotiating the Single European Act: National Interests and Conventional Statecraft in the European Community', *International Organization* 45, pp 19-56.

Moreau Defargues, P. (1994), 'John Bull's divided love', *The Guardian*, 27 September.

Mortimer, E. (1996), 'The UK Dilemma', *Financial Times*, Report on Ireland, 24 June.

Moynihan, M. (ed.) (1980), *Speeches and Statements by Eamon de Valera 1917-73*, Dublin: Gill and Macmillan.

Nairn, T. (1994), *The Enchanted Glass: Britain and its Monarchy*, London: Vintage.

Nugent, N. (1992), 'British Public Opinion and the European Community', in George (ed.) (1992), pp. 172–201.

Nugent, N. (1994), *The Government and Politics of the European Union*, London: Macmillan.

O'Clery, C. (1996), *The Greening of the White House*, Dublin: Gill and Macmillan.

OECD (1995 a), *1995 Economic Outlook,* Paris: OECD.

OECD (1995 b), *Economic Surveys: United Kingdom 1995,* August, Paris: OECD.

OECD (1996), *Economic Surveys: United Kingdom 1996,* June, Paris: OECD.

O'Grady, J. (1996), 'An Irish policy born in the USA', *Foreign Affairs,* 75 (3) May–June, pp. 2–7.

Orwell, G. (1970), *The Collected Essays, Journalism and Letters, Vol. II: 'My Country Right or Left', 1940–43,* London: Penguin.

O'Toole, F. (1995), 'Defending the past is not an option for unionists', *The Irish Times,* 24 February.

O'Toole, F. (1996), 'End of Empire', *The Irish Times,* 8 June.

Palmer, J. 1996, 'Britain and the European Union: the Future', in Gillespie, P. (ed.) (1996 c)

Pfaff, W. (1995), 'Out on Europe's Fringe, a Struggle to Free Britain from its History', *International Herald Tribune,* 21 February.

Plaid Cymru (1995), *Wales in Europe - The Next Step,* Cardiff.

Plaid Cymru (1996), *The 1996/97 IGC - Plaid Cymru's Alternative White Paper for Wales in Europe,* Cardiff, 12 March.

Pocock, J.G.A. (1982), 'The Limits and Divisions of British History: in Search of an Unknown Subject,' *American Historical Review,* LXXXVii, pp. 311-36.

Porter, H. (1995), 'Churchill's children', *The Guardian,* 22 February.

Portillo, M. (1994), 'Poison of a New British Disease', *The Independent,* 16 January.

Portillo, M. (1995), '1996: substance and symbolism', WEU Assembly, 5 December.

Preston, P.W. (1994), *Europe, Democracy and the Dissolution of Britain: As Essay on the Issue of Europe in UK Public Discourse,* Aldershot: Dartmouth.

Quin, J. (1996), 'Britain in Europe: the View of the British Labour Party', in Gillespie, P. (ed.) (1996 c).

Quinlan, M. (1993), 'The Future of Nuclear Weapons: Policy for Western Possessors', *International Affairs,* 69 (3), July, pp. 485-496.

Radice, G. (ed.) (1996), *What Needs To change: New Visions for Britain,* London: Harper Collins.

Redwood, J. (1996 a), 'Saving Europe from itself', *The Times,* 29 March.

Redwood, J. (1996 b), 'How we can use beef to beat Kohl', *The Times,* 24 April.

Rees-Mogg, W. (1995), 'Now our independence hinges on the French', *The Times,* 6 March.

Riddell, P. (1994 a), 'Scepticism crosses the floor', *The Times,* 26 September.

Riddell, P. (1994 b), 'Perils of playing with reform', *The Times,* 10 October.

Riddell, P. (1995 a), 'Disgruntled voters see merit in idea of constitutional reform', *The Times,* 27 January.

Riddell, P. (1995 b), 'When push comes to shove', *The Times,* 20 February.

Rifkind, M. (1995 a), speech to the Belgian Institute of International Relations, Brussels, 30 January.

Rifkind, M. (1995 b), 'Securing the nation state', *The Times,* 31 January.

Rifkind, M. (1995 c), interview, *Financial Times,* 3 February.

Rifkind, M. (1995 d), speech on Britain and Europe, RIIA, 23 September.

Robbins, K. (1994 a), *The Eclipse of a Great Power: Modern Britain 1970–1992,* 2nd ed., London: Longman.

Robbins, K. (1994 b), 'Regions, nations and states: the United Kingdom and Europe', *The World Today,* November, pp. 218-221.

Rogaly, J. (1994), 'A dangerous battleground', *Financial Times,* 6 December.

Roll, E. (1995 a), 'Where and why did we go wrong?', *The Independent,* 13 March.

Roll, E. (1995 b), *Where Did We Go Wrong?,* London: Faber.

Rose, R. (1971), *Governing Without Consensus: An Irish Perspective,* London: Faber.

Rubenstein, W. D. (1993), *Capitalism, Culture and Decline in Britain 1750-1990,* London: Routledge.

Ryan, H. B. (1982), *The Vision of Anglo-America,* Cambridge: Cambridge University Press.

Sabin, Philip A. G. (1995), *British Strategic Priorities in the 1990s,* London.

Sabin, P. A. G., (1996), 'Britain in Europe: Defence and Security Aspects', in P. Gillespie (ed.), (1996 c).

Sampson, P. (1994), 'Ruthless world', *The Independent,* 16 November.

Samuel, R. (1989 a), 'In search of Britain', *New Statesman and Society,* 25 August.

Samuel, R. (1989 b), *Patriotism: The Making and Unmaking of British National Identity,* 3 vols., London and New York.

Schnapper, D. (1994), 'The Debate on Immigration and the Crisis of National Identity', *West European Politics,* 17 (2), April, pp. 127–139.

Scott, A., J. Peterson and D. Millar, (1994), 'Subsidiarity: A "Europe of the Regions" *v.* the British Constitution?', *Journal of Common Market Studies,* 32 (1), March, pp. 47–68.

Scott, D. (1994), *Ireland's Contribution to the European Union,* Dublin: Institute of European Affairs.

Scottish National Party, (1996 a), *European Policy,* Edinburgh: SNP, April.

Scottish National Party, (1996 b), *Best for Scotland, Independence in Europe,* Edinburgh: SNP, August.

Seitz, R. (1994), 'Britain belongs to Europe', *The Times,* 20 April.

Seyd, P. and P. Whiteley (1992), *Labour's Grass Roots: The Politics of Party Membership,* Oxford: Clarendon Press.

Seyd, P., P. Whiteley, and J. Richardson (1994), *True Blues: The Politics of Conservative Party Membership,* Oxford: Clarendon Press.

Sharp, Jane M.O. (ed.) (1996), *About Turn, Forward March with Europe,* London: Institute for Public Policy Research: Rivers Oram Press.

Shonfield, A. (1973), *Europe: Journey to an Unknown Destination,* Harmondsworth: Penguin.

Siedentop, L. (1995), 'Grim future for the UK's ancien regime', *Financial Times,* 13 January.

Simpson, A. (1995), 'A Cook's tour to nowhere', *The Guardian,* 3 August.

Smith, A. D. (1991), *National Identity,* London: Penguin.

Smith, A. D. (1992), 'National Identity and the Idea of European Unity', *International Affairs,* 68 (1), January, pp. 55-76.

Smith, D. (1995), 'The myth of falling competitiveness', *The Sunday Times,* 10 September.

Smith, G. (1992), 'Britain in the New Europe', *Foreign Affairs,* 71 (4), Fall, pp. 155–70.

Soley, C. (1995), 'Labour hopes for a united Ireland, but would accept NI agreement', *The Irish Times,* 21 September.

Spring, D. (1996), 'Britain in Europe: the View from Dublin, in P. Gillespie, (ed.), (1996 c).

Stephens, P. (1995 a), 'Wrapped in a bigger map', *Financial Times*, 24 March.

Stephens, P. (1995 b), 'Value-added sterling', *Financial Times*, 29 September.

Stephens, P. (1995 c), 'Seductive words', *Financial Times*, 2 February.

Stephens, P. (1996 a), *Politics and the Pound*. London: Macmillan.

Stephens, P. (1996 b), 'Put it to the vote', *Financial Times*, 14 June.

Stephens, P. (1996 c), 'Time to strike a deal', *Financial Times*, 21 June.

The Sun (1996), '20 ways of hitting back at Germany', 4 June.

Steele, J. (1994), series of three articles on Britain in Europe, *The Guardian*, 10–12 October.

Stephenson, J. (1993), 'Britain and Europe in the Later Twentieth Century: Identity, Sovereignty, Peculiarity?', in M. Fulbrook (1993), *National Histories and European History*, London: London University Press, pp. 230–54.

Strauss, E. (1952, new ed. 1994), *Irish Nationalism and British Democracy*, London: Greenwood Press.

Strong, R. (1996), *The Story of Britain*, London: Hutchinson.

Stürmer, M. (1995), 'An open relationship', *Financial Times*, 27 January.

Sutherland, V. (1995), speech to IBEC, 22 November.

Sutherland, V. (1996), address to Irish School of Ecumenics conference on 'Ethics and Foreign Policy', 8 February.

Taylor, C. (1995), interview with Maurice O'Connell, *The Irish Times*, 6 October.

Taylor, P. J. (1990), *Britain and the Cold War: 1945 as Geopolitical Transition*, London: Pinter.

Taylor, P. J. (1993 a), 'The meaning of the North: England's "foreign country" within?', *Political Geography*, 12 (2), March, pp. 136–55. Part of a debate in that issue on 'The break-up of England?'

Taylor, P. J. (1993 b), *Political Geography, World Economy, Nation-State and Locality*, 3rd edn., London: Longman.

Thatcher, M. (1988), 'Britain and Europe', Text of the speech delivered in Bruges by the Prime Minister on 20 September 1988, London: Conservative Political Centre.

The Times, (1995), editorial, 'Edge of Europe', 13 June.

Todd, J. (1995), 'Beyond the Community Conflict: Historic Compromise or Emancipatory Process?', *Irish Political Studies*, 10, pp. 161–178.

Trades Union Congress (1996), 'TUC Report on EMU', *Employment and Industrial Relations International*, February.

Traynor, I. (1995 a), 'US pressure nets Bosnian peace deal', *The Irish Times*, 16 October.

Traynor, I. (1995 b), 'Images of war fuel federal mission', *The Guardian*, 14 December.

Tully, J. (1995 a), 'The Crisis of Identification: the Case of Canada', in Dunn, J. (ed.), (1995), pp. 77–96,

Tully, J. (1995 b), *Strange Multiplicity: Constitutionalism in an Age of Diversity*, Cambridge: Cambridge University Press.

Vallely, P. (1996), 'With friends like this ...', *The Independent*, 29 April.

Wallace, H. (1995), 'L'approche brittanique de la CIG de 1996', *politique étrangère*, 61 (1), pp. 49–60.

Wallace, W. (1992), 'Redefining 'Britishness' – British foreign policy after the Cold War', *International Affairs,* 68 (3), July, pp. 423–42.

Wallace, W. (1994), *The Guardian,* 29 March.

Wallace, W. (1995 a), 'Rescue or Retreat? The Nation State in Western Europe, 1945–93', in J. Dunn, (ed.) 1995, pp. 52–76.

Wallace, W. (1995 b), 'German as Europe's leading power', *The World Today,* 51 (8–9), August–September, pp. 162–4.

Wallace, W. (1995 c), 'Fly the flag for a disunited kingdom', *The Guardian,* 5 September.

Walsh, B. (1993), *The Irish Pound and the ERM,* UCD Centre for Economic Research, May.

Watson, R. (1995), 'ECJ powers face reappraisal', *European Voice,* 2-8 November.

Witney, Nicholas K. J., (1994-95), 'British nuclear policy after the Cold War', *Survival,* 36 (4), Winter.

Willetts, D. (1996), *Blair's Gurus,* London: Centre for Policy Studies.

Young, J.W. (1993), *Britain and European Unity: 1945–1992,* London: Macmillan.

◼ APPENDIX

CONTENTS OF SEMINAR PAPERS VOLUME

Introduction
Paul Gillespie

1. The British Economy: Performance and Prospects
   Garret FitzGerald

2. Britain's Productivity Growth: Comparative Performance
   and Future Prospects
   Nicholas Crafts

3. The Conflict between British Economic Liberalism
   and Continental Statism
   Patrick Minford

4. Britain's Economic Policies and their European Dimension
   Christopher Huhne

5. The Challenge of Manufacturing Industry for the UK in
   a New Europe
   Mark H. J. Radcliffe

6. The European Union and the Irish Peace Process
   Paul Teague

7. Economic Aspects of the Island of Ireland: Performance
   and Prospects
   John Bradley

8. Northern Ireland and the Republic of Ireland: A Contrast
   at the Firm level
   Martin Rafferty

9. Northern Ireland in a European Context
   David Fell

INDEX

IEA PUBLICATIONS

Studies in European Union
Political Union
Editor: Patrick Keatinge
ISBN 1 874109 00 1, 200 pages, IR£12.95
Economic and Monetary Union
Editor: Rory O'Donnell
ISBN 1 874109 01 X, 148 pages, IR£12.95
Maastricht and Ireland: What the Treaty Means
Editor: Patrick Keatinge
ISBN 1 874109 03 6, 180 pages, IR£10.00
Social Europe: EC Social Policy and Ireland
Editor: Seamus Ó Cinnéide
ISBN 1 874109 06 0, 176 pages, IR£15.00
Constitution-building in the European Union
Editor: Brigid Laffan
ISBN 1 874109 21 4, 256 pages, IR£15.00
Britain's European Question: the Issues for Ireland
Editor: Paul Gillespie
ISBN 1 874109 22 2, 224 pages, IR£15.00
European Security: Ireland's Choices
Patrick Keatinge
ISBN 1 874109 24 9, 224 pages, IR£15.00 (forthcoming)

Implications for Ireland
Political Union
Paul Gillespie and Rodney Rice
ISBN 1 874109 02 8, 60 pages, IR£5.00
EMU and Irish Fiscal Policy
Donal de Buitléir and Don Thornhill
ISBN 1 874109 05 2, 74 pages, IR£7.50
Ireland and the IGC
Dermot Scott
ISBN 1 874109 19 2, 64 pages, IR£3.95

Understanding Europe
Eastern Exchanges
Interchange of Education, Training and Professional Formation between Ireland and Czechoslovakia, Hungary and Poland.
Miriam Hederman O'Brien
ISBN 1 874109 04 4, 48 pages, IR£5.00
Managing the Finances of the EU: the Role of the European Court of Auditors
Barry Desmond
ISBN 1 874109 35 7, 80 pages, IR£7.50 (forthcoming)

Occasional Papers
No. 1   **Irish Public Opinion on Neutrality and European Union**
         Michael Marsh IR£4.00
No.2   **The Economic Consequences of Maastricht**
         Paul Tansey IR£5.00
No. 3   **Subsidiarity: Its Application in Practice**
         Ciaran F. Walker IR£5.00
No. 4   **Ireland's Contribution to the European Union**
         Dermot Scott ISBN 1-874109-08-7, 48 pages, IR£7.50
No. 5   **Knowledge of the European Union in Irish Public Opinion: Sources and Implications**
         Richard Sinnott   ISBN 1-874109-09-5, 48 pages, IR£7.50

No. 6   **Citizenship of the European Union**
Niamh Hyland, Claire Loftus, Anthony Whelan
ISBN 1-874109-13-3, 64 pages, IR£7.50

No. 7   **The Role of the Commission and Qualified Majority Voting**
John Temple Lang and Eamonn Gallagher
ISBN 1-874109-14-1, 48 pages, IR£7.50

Final Reports
Maastricht: Crisis of Confidence
Paul Gillespie • *Brendan Halligan* • *Philip Halpin* • *Patrick Keatinge* • *Brigid Laffan,*
IR£4.00

What Price CAP? Issues and Challenges Facing Agricultural and Rural Policy in the European Union
Editor: Brendan Kearney ISBN 1 874109 15 X, IR£30.00

The 1996 Intergovernmental Conference: Issues, Options, Implications
ISBN 1-874109-18-4, 288 pages, IR£30.00

Interim Reports
Europe – Community and Continent: the enlargement of the European Union and its relationships with its continental neighbours
Tony Brown, 250 pages, IR£12.50

Towards a Safer Europe – Small State Security Policies and the European Union: Implications for Ireland
Editor: Patrick Keatinge ISBN 1-874109-10-9, 160 pages, IR£30.00

Summary of Interim Reports
Europe Community and Continent
Tony Brown ISBN 1-874109-10-9, 48 pages, IR£4.00

Towards a Safer Europe
Editor: Patrick Keatinge ISBN 1-874109-11-7, 56 pages, IR£7.50

Seminar Papers
Recent Changes in Multilateral Security
Foreword: Patrick Keatinge
Facsimile pages, IR£10.00

Britain's European Question: the Issues for Ireland – Seminar Papers
Editor: Paul Gillespie
ISBN 1-874109-23-0, 176 pages, IR£20.00 (forthcoming)

Seminar Reports
Austria our New Partner
Tony Brown (Rapporteur) ISBN 1-874109-15-X, 44 pages, IR£7.50

Sweden in the European Union
Tony Brown (Rapporteur) ISBN 1-874109-17-6, 48 pages, IR£7.50

Finland in the European Union
Tony Brown (Rapporteur) ISBN 1-874109-16-8, 48 pages, IR£7.50

Norway and the European Union
Tony Brown (Rapporteur) ISBN 1-874109-20-6, 48 pages, IR£7.50

Published on behalf of the European Commission Representation in Ireland
European Social Policy – Options for the Union
David Gardner (Rapporteur): Free distribution

Contemporary/Historic Documents Archive
European Document Series
Editor Tony Brown c. 64 pages an issue, 297 x 210 mm ISSN 0791-8097
Annual subscription (4 issues) IR£40.00
Annual subscription to members IR£25.00, Individual issues IR£15.00
Back issues available – current issue No. 14 summer 1996

Newsletter for Members
IEA NEWS
Editor: Dermot Scott
Quarterly
Current issue No. 14, summer 1996